Data Warehousing with Informix: Best Practices

To see a complete list of Informix Press Titles, point to
http://www.prenhall.com/~informix

Data Warehousing with Informix: Best Practices

Edited by
Angela Sanchez

Prentice Hall PTR
Upper Saddle River, New Jersey 07458
http://www.phptr.com

Editorial/Production Supervision: Kathleen M. Caren
Acquisitions Editor: Mark L. Taub
Editorial Assistant: Tara Ruggiero
Buyer: Alexis Heydt
Cover Design: Anthony Gemmellaro
Cover Design Direction: Jerry Votta
Art Director: Gail Cocker-Bogusz
Series Design: Claudia Durrell Design
Marketing Manager: Dan Rush

© 1998 Informix Press
Published by Prentice-Hall, Inc.
A Simon & Schuster Company
Upper Saddle River, NJ 07458

Informix Press
Informix Software, Inc.
4100 Bohannon Drive
Menlo Park, CA 94025

The following are worldwide trademarks of Informix Software, Inc., or its subsidiaries, registered in the United States of America as indicated by ®, and in numerous other countries worldwide:
INFORMIX®, Informix DataBlade® Module, Informix Dynamic Scalable Architecture™, Informix Illustra™ Server, InformixLink®, INFORMIX-4GL, INFORMIX-4GL Compiled, INFORMIX®-CLI, INFORMIX®-Connect, INFORMIX®-ESQL/C, INFORMIX®-MetaCube™, INFORMIX®-Mobile, INFORMIX®-NET, INFORMIX®-NewEra™, INFORMIX®-NewEra™ Viewpoint™, INFORMIX®-NewEra™ Viewpoint™ Pro, INFORMIX®-OnLine, INFORMIX®-OnLine Dynamic Server™, INFORMIX®-OnLine Workgroup Server, INFORMIX®-OnLine Workstation, INFORMIX®-SE, INFORMIX®-SQL, INFORMIX-Superview™, INFORMIX®-Universal Server All product names mentioned herein are the trademarks of their respective owners.

The publisher offers discounts on this book when ordered in bulk quantities.
For more information, contact
Corporate Sales Department,
Prentice Hall PTR
One Lake Street
Upper Saddle River, NJ 07458
Phone: 800-382-3419; FAX: 201-236-7141
E-mail (Internet): corpsales@prenhall.com

ISBN 0-13-079622-0

Prentice-Hall International (UK) Limited, *London*
Prentice-Hall of Australia Pty. Limited, *Sydney*
Prentice-Hall Canada Inc., *Toronto*
Prentice-Hall Hispanoamericana, S.A., *Mexico*
Prentice-Hall of India Private Limited, *New Delhi*
Prentice-Hall of Japan, Inc., *Tokyo*
Simon & Schuster Asia Pte. Ltd., *Singapore*
Editora Prentice-Hall do Brasil, Ltda., *Rio de Janeiro*

Contents

PART 2 • DESIGN AND IMPLEMENTATION FOR DECISION SUPPORT   27

Chapter 6 Designing an OLAP Data Mart on Relational Databases

Chapter 12 The Backup and Recovery of
Very Large Databases
by Daniel A. Wood

Chapter 13 A Manager's Guide to Informix Database Protection

Chapter 14 Determining Available dbspaces

PART 4 • THE FUTURE OF DATA WAREHOUSING   273

Chapter 15 A Platform for the Universal Warehouse

Foreword

1997 will be noted as the year data warehousing "crossed the chasm," becoming a standard business practice in industries such as retail, telecommunications, and financial services. Data warehousing is rapidly gaining momentum in other industries as well, including hospitality, health care, manufacturing, transportation, and government.

Just how much momentum? International Data Corporation (IDC) reported compelling statistics: Over 20 percent of organizations are using data warehouses, and over 30 percent or more are either implementing or evaluating the building of data warehouse implementations.[1] There's no doubt that these numbers will continue to rise—the promise of competitive advantage for those who implement the technology will mandate data warehousing as a key strategic weapon.

Whether you are a data warehousing novice or veteran, this book has something for you. The advice, experiences, and lessons learned from some of the industry's most well known early adopters, authorities, and vendors are contained in this volume.

"Part One: The Decision Support Community" illustrates the roles of the key constituencies surrounding a data warehouse— end users, application developers, and warehouse administrators. Each participant in a data warehouse project must eventually learn the new skills described in this section. It is our experience that the most successful data warehouse implementations are those that foster a strong sense of community and teamwork, qualities that are essential in overcoming the barriers created by traditional organizational structures.

[1]IDC, Technology Integration Panel Study, 1997.

In many ways, building a data warehouse is less a classic computer science IT problem and more a challenge of coordination. "Part Two: Design and Implementation for Decision Support" defines a complete data warehouse architecture. This section starts with a bird's-eye view of decision support, then moves on to specific components of a data warehouse, including data modeling, data integration, OLAP data marts, and data mining.

"Part Three: Hardware, Storage, and Backup Issues in a Data Warehouse" provides guidelines and insight on choosing the right physical hardware architectures for the data warehouse, including the computers and disk systems. This section also includes insight on massively parallel computers, symmetric multiprocessors, and clusters, with examples of hardware architectures from Digital Equipment Corporation, IBM Corporation, and the Hewlett-Packard Company, all of which complement Informix's products. An excellent example of MCI's real-world warehouse implementation is also provided.

The book concludes with "Part Four: The Future of Data Warehousing," with the spotlight on Informix's database technology vision, including a case study on the use of object-relational technology. Informix intends to capitalize on this architectural lead in data warehousing, which in turn can translate into competitive and strategic advantages for your organization into the 21st century.

We hope you enjoy the book.

Tony Rodoni
General Manager, Data Warehousing
Informix Software, Inc.

The Decision Support Community

The DSS Community: Tourists, Explorers, and Farmers

by William H. Inmon

Introduction

The world of decision support systems (DSS) is filled with contradictions. Response time is wildly different from one transaction to the next in the world of the DSS. In a typical scenario, one end user sits in an executive office and another end user sits in a back office cubicle. One end user accesses data once a quarter, while the other end user accesses data ten times a day. The list of differences goes on and on. There is extreme diversity among the audience accessing the DSS and in the ways in which the DSS is used.

Data warehouse administrators (DWA) must first understand the community of DSS users before they can manage the wide diversity of the DSS environment. Understanding the constituents of the DSS community and their individual perspectives clarifies the many contradictions found in the DSS environment. Moreover, if the DWA does not understand how to cope with the many contradictions found in the world of DSS, the DWA will be unable to effectively manage the DSS environment.

The DSS Community

There are many different ways to characterize the DSS community. One way is to characterize end users as either "power users" or pre-canned query users. It is most instructive, however, to categorize the DSS community in terms of the use of DSS capabilities. With this approach, three general categories can describe the users of DSS processing, as follows:

- Tourists;
- Explorers; and
- Farmers.

Regarding DSS utilization, each category employs a vastly different perspective and set of expectations.

Tourists

Tourists are DSS users who cover much ground. Tourists seldom look at the same thing twice and look at very little in depth. Tourists cover a large breadth of territory. The access pattern of tourists is quite spontaneous and sporadic. Attempting to predict tourist access patterns and habits is almost impossible.

The Internet is a favorite tool of the tourist—although the tourist makes use of metadata when it is presented properly. Libraries, directories, and table of contents are the places in which the tourist feels comfortable. The tourist is a good person to assign to the task of performing basic research which canvasses an entire field or looks across a lengthy vista. Figure 1-1 depicts a tourist.

Tourist

Figure 1-1 *Tourists form one branch of the DSS community.*

Explorers

Explorers are end users who want to know one particular part of a company very well. The explorer studies and examines one particular part of the DSS environment in minute detail. Conversely, the tourist covers much breadth of material but is seldom involved in much detailed exploration, whereas the explorer covers very little breadth and yet analyzes one area in great depth. The primary difference between the tourist and the explorer is that the explorer is interested in depth and the tourist is interested in breadth. The explorer looks to detail as the basic unit of interest. Usually, the explorer works with many details.

The explorer is concerned with a very low level of detail; the explorer looks for previously hidden or unknown relationships and facts. The explorer requires not only details, but a significant amount of history as well. Explorers perform their analyses spontaneously and heuristically, and, typically, such analyses incorporate large amounts of data.

Occasionally, explorers make significant discoveries. The explorer requires a wide variety of information types to analyze, as well as a vast bulk of information. The explorer operates in a random, non-repetitive fashion, with little predictability in the way that the work is accomplished. The explorer makes heavy use of metadata when it is available and looks at the many relationship possibilities that are possible among different types of data. The response time that the explorer expects is widely variant. Some explorations take very long amounts of time—24 hours or more. Other explorations require only an hour or so. Figure 1-2 depicts explorers.

Explorer

Figure 1-2 Explorers form another facet of the DSS community.

Farmers

Farmers are DSS analysts who know exactly what they want. Farmers employ a repetitive pattern of activity and often perform the same activity many times, albeit on different occurrences of data. Farmers know exactly where to look and consequently do not need to analyze huge amounts of data. They can operate on either detailed or summary data. Farmers pay little attention to metadata and even less attention to the Internet. They operate on small amounts of data and require quick response times. A five- to ten-minute response time is the range that the farmer expects. Although farmers regularly make small informational discoveries, they are the backbone of the DSS environment. On a day-in-and-day-out basis, the DSS environment can be justified on the basis of the farmers' needs alone. Figure 1-3 depicts farmers in the DSS environment.

Together, tourists, explorers, and farmers make up the DSS community. Taken as a whole, these subcommunities form a powerful force for decision making. However, the approaches to analysis and the way that different objectives are accomplished are quite different from one DSS subcommunity to another. There are many salient differences among the different subcommunities of DSS processing.

Figure 1-3 *Farmers are the third constituency of the DSS community.*

Development Life Cycles

The differences between the different subcommunities of DSS processing are most evident in the development life cycles that each DSS subcommunity employs.

The tourist, by definition, does not have a regular life cycle for system development. The best that can be said about the tourist's development life cycle is that many varied types of data are rambled over occasionally. Thus, no systematic effort supports the system development intended for the tourist.

Conversely, there is a development life cycle that occurs for farmers. The life cycle can best be described as the classic system development life cycle (SDLC). Figure 1-4 portrays the SDLC.

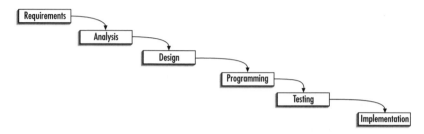

Figure 1-4 The classic SDLC—a "waterfall" methodology.

The SDLC is the life cycle commonly discussed in literature; it is otherwise known as the "waterfall development life cycle." The SDLC begins with requirements and ends with an implemented system. Farmers employ the SDLC because they know their needs *before* processing begins and they repeatedly perform the same activity. Therefore, the SDLC meets the needs of the DSS farmer quite nicely.

The opposite of the SDLC, or the linear waterfall life cycle of the farmer, is the circular development life cycle (CLDS). The CLDS is the life cycle that best fits the explorer. The CLDS begins with implemented data and ends with an understanding of the requirements for processing. Figure 1-5 illustrates a simple version of the CLDS.

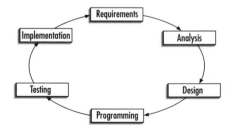

Figure 1-5 The CLDS—an approach to development that is iterative and exploratory.

The CLDS is essentially a circular life cycle where iteration and exploration are the norm. There is no guarantee that anything productive will come out of the development accomplished under the CLDS. In many cases, there are no productive results. Yet in some cases, unexpected results appear which are quite useful. Due to the circular exploratory nature of the CLDS, it meets the needs of the explorer subcommunity.

Interestingly enough, despite the differences in the development life cycles for the farmer and the explorer, there is an important intersection of development between the explorer and the farmer subcommunities. Upon making a significant informational discovery, the explorer asks the question, "How do I obtain that same information on a regular basis?" When the explorer discovers the requirement, the explorer turns into a farmer. Figure 1-6 shows this intersection of interest between the farmer and the explorer.

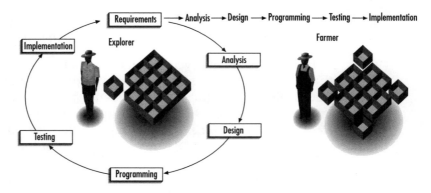

Figure 1-6 *The intersection of interest between the explorer and farmer.*

Figure 1-6 illustrates that the two development life cycles intersect upon the successful discovery of information and the desire to turn that information into a regular part of the business. The circular discovery life cycle turns into a regular information factory. It is at this point that the interests of the farmer and the explorer merge.

Database Design

But life cycle development differences are not the only differences between tourists, explorers, and farmers. Another major difference between the DSS subcommunities centers on the data design that is appropriate to the different subcommunities. Figure 1-7 indicates that quite different data design techniques are appropriate to the different DSS subcommunities.

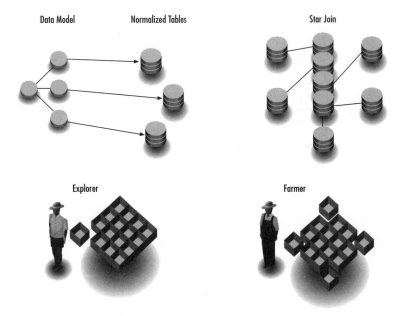

Figure 1-7 *Different kinds of data structures are applicable to different subcommunities.*

The normalization of data is the database design technique best suited to explorers. When data is normalized, the data is nonredundant and arranged so that each unit of data depends only on itself for its existence. Data normalization favors no one path of access. Instead, the dynamic linkage of data must be performed so that two or more units of data can be connected. Since there is no preconceived notion of a favored path or an arrangement of data with normalization and because the data can be linked dynamically, normalization fits the needs of the explorer.

Another type of data structure found in the DSS environment is that of the star join structure, wherein the organization of data depends on the volume of data and the anticipated use of data. Some units of data have many more occurrences than other units of data. Because of the volume of data, these voluminous structures must be prejoined for ease of use and so that they do not require on-line dynamic joins. In addition to consideration of the volume of data, there is also the issue of the expected use of data. When there is a regular pattern of data usage, the pattern can be anticipated by prejoining of the data so that it is simple to use. In addition, the data being rejoined will look like the data the end user is accustomed to handling. Since star joins rely on a foundation of known utilization, they form a sound foundation for the data processing required by farmers.

The star join structure differs from the normalization structure. However, both apply equally well to different parts of the DSS environment.

Different Data Warehouses

Database design is not the only difference between data for the different DSS subcommunities. The data warehouses themselves are quite different. Figure 1-8 illustrates the differences in the kinds of data warehouses that apply to explorers and farmers.

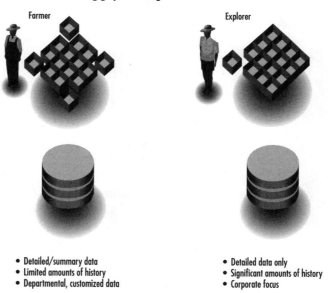

Farmer

Explorer

- Detailed/summary data
- Limited amounts of history
- Departmental, customized data

- Detailed data only
- Significant amounts of history
- Corporate focus

Figure 1-8 Different kinds of data warehouses apply to different subcommunities.

The data warehouse that applies to the explorer is one which is very detailed. The explorer's data warehouse reflects a robust amount of history as well as the corporate point of view. The explorer's data warehouse is well integrated, with its contents carefully divided into subject areas.

The data warehouse that applies to the farmer is vastly different. The farmer's data warehouse contains both detailed and summary data. A limited amount of history is to be found in such a data warehouse. If the farmer represents a department, it is likely that the data warehouse contains data that is customized to meet the needs of the department, rather than the entire corporation. In some cases, the farmer's data warehouse can be called a data mart.

Infrastructure

Another important aspect of data warehousing—and one which makes a big difference to the various subcommunities of DSS users—is that of the infrastructure. Explorers make heavy use of one part of the infrastructure, tourists another, and farmers yet another. The relevance and the importance of the various aspects of the infrastructure to the different DSS subcommunities is seen in Figure 1-9.

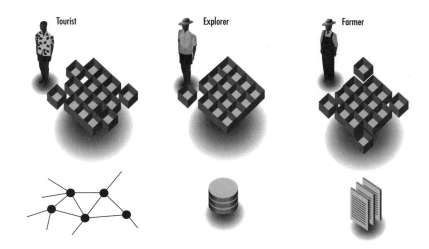

Figure 1-9 Different subcommunities are different parts of the DSS infrastructure.

Tourists make frequent use of the Internet and tools to cover a great breadth of ground. The explorer makes heavy use of the metadata infrastructure. Explorers use metadata—when it is available—to locate the most productive places in which to search for meaningful relationships among data. Farmers make use of data that is housed in the data warehouse. Stated differently, farmers make little or no use of the Internet, tourists make little or no use of the data in the warehouse, and explorers make limited use of all of the facilities found in the world of data marts.

Tools

The different parts of the infrastructure have relevance to the DSS subcommunities. Moreover, the tools of access and analysis also have great relevance. Figure 1-10 displays some of the tools of access and analysis.

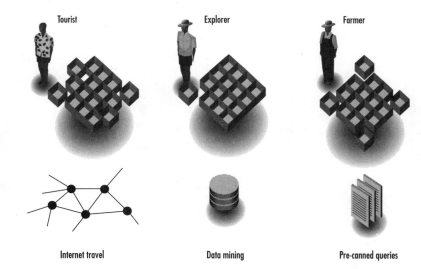

Figure 1-10 *The kinds of activities performed by the different subcommunities differ.*

The tourist is interested in tools which scan data in an unstructured manner. The explorer is interested in data mining tools, and the farmer is interested in preestablished queries.

The Cycle of DSS Users

At any one time, a DSS user is either a tourist, an explorer, or a farmer. Yet, at any given time, the DSS analyst can change roles and act as a tourist, explorer, or farmer. Figure 1-11 illustrates the normal cycle in which a DSS analyst participates.

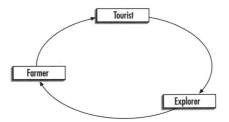

Figure 1-11 Over a lifetime, a DSS analyst can be a tourist, explorer, or farmer. The cycle through which the DSS analyst passes is circular.

Figure 1-11 indicates the progression of the DSS analyst from tourist to explorer to farmer. While it is possible for an analyst to go from one state to another in an order other than the one suggested, it is not typical. For example, it is possible for an analyst to go from farmer to explorer, or from tourist to farmer. However, such a transition requires special circumstances, which are not readily observable. Of course, it is entirely possible for an analyst to stay in the same state forever. The transition suggested in Figure 1-11 is not mandatory and may not apply to many DSS analysts.

The Organization Chart

There is a curious relationship of the notion of tourists, explorers, and farmers to the organization chart. This relationship is suggested in Figure 1-12.

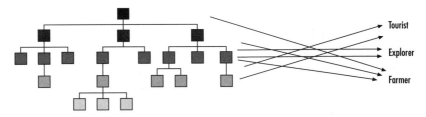

Figure 1-12 Tourists, farmers, and explorers can originate from any part of the organization.

Figure 1-12 suggests that there is no correlation of the level of management to the type of DSS analysis which is performed. Tourists, explorers, and farmers originate from any level of management. There simply is no pattern governing where these subcommunities are located in the organization structure.

Summary

There are different types of DSS analysts. The three most discernible types are tourists, explorers, and farmers. There are distinguishable differences between the different DSS subcommunities. Some of these differences focus on the following factors:

• The development life cycle;
• The database design;
• The type of data warehouse itself;
• The usage of the infrastructure;
• The tools for access and analysis; and so forth.

About the Author

William (Bill) H. Inmon, the father of the data warehouse concept, has written 32 books on data management, data warehouse, design review, and the management of data processing. Of these books, 21 are book club selections with publishers such as Prentice-Hall, John Wiley, and QED. Translations have been produced in Russian, German, French, Korean, Japanese, and Chinese.

Bill has written over 250 articles in trade journals such as Datamation, ComputerWorld, and DataBase Programming/Design. Currently, Bill is a columnist with Data Management Review.

Bill founded and took public a Silicon Valley company, Prism Solutions, which automates the process of building data warehouses in standard database technologies—such as Informix—by integrating and transforming data from older database technologies, such as IMS, VSAM, IDMS, and ADABAS, into a data warehouse. Bill

Inmon's latest venture, Pine Cone Systems (a Colorado company), is the leader in building data warehouse administration software to manage the data warehouse, DSS environment.

About Pine Cone Systems

Pine Cone Systems builds software for managing and administering the data warehouse. The initial products that Pine Cone brings to the marketplace include an activity monitor, which reports what data is and is not used in the warehouse; a data monitor, which reports what growth is experienced and what bad data has entered the data warehouse; a charge-back manager, which allows the end user to see what resources are consumed on a departmental basis; and a refreshment tracker, which allows the end user to see when and how much data was entered into the data warehouse. Pine Cone Systems is a Colorado-based company founded by William H. Inmon.

Managing the Data Warehouse: The Advent of the Data Warehouse Administrator

by William H. Inmon

As the business of data warehousing grows from the concept stage to a full-fledged discipline, two observations arise. First, data warehouses usually deliver the full potential pledged at their inception. In many cases, data warehouses deliver benefits beyond the original expectations. Second, for all its success, data warehousing is expensive and complex, especially in the case of a large data warehouse.

Managing the Data Warehouse Environment

These observations lead organizations to the realization that the data warehouse—or decision-support system (DSS)—environment requires management. Moreover, it is important to note that systems management for data warehousing differs from systems management for the operational systems environment. Over time, an infrastructure for the management of operational systems typically includes:

• Database administration;
• Capacity planning;

- Data administration;
- Systems support; and
- Network administration.

Most organizations believe that their existing systems support infrastructure can serve the needs of the DSS environment. Indeed, for some systems management activities, the existing systems support infrastructure suffices. However, for a variety of important reasons, there is a need for a different kind of support staff: Data Warehouse Administrators (DWA).

Operational and Informational Differences

The DSS environment requires a completely different skill set and approach from the skill set required for operational systems management. What is important in the management of the operational environment is often unimportant or irrelevant to the DSS environment. Consider transaction processing. Transaction processing is the backbone of operational processing. Response time, system availability, and adequate capacity are all factors central to the success of the operational environment. Thus, the focus of systems management is on the care and tending of transactions.

While transactions certainly run in the DSS environment, the transactions in the operational environment are of an entirely different nature. The range of DSS transactions varies in size—from the small to the massive. The DSS transaction is rarely used to update the database; its primary task is to query data.

At times, the DSS environment handles numerous analytical and informational activities, while at other times the DSS environment is lightly loaded. Most DSS transactions are performed for analytical, informational purposes; thus, response time is an interesting measurement but is not a critical factor in systems management.

When it comes to transactions, then, support is completely different for operational and DSS systems. Another important difference between the two environments focuses on the volume of data. The operational systems administrator must account for large amounts of data. But, the operational system administrator does not face the large data volumes that are handled by the DWA. Up to two orders of magnitude separate the amount of data found in the DSS environment versus the data found in the operational environment.

Furthermore, the operational systems administrator can often predict the volume of future data and the rate of data growth over time.

The DWA, however, deals with massively more data volume than the operational systems administrator. The rate of growth in the DSS environment is far different from that experienced in the operational systems environment. The DWA witnesses and must manage the explosive and unpredictable growth of the DSS environment's data volume.

Due to these fundamental differences, the role of traditional operational systems administration does not measure up to the demands of DSS processing.

The Role of the DWA

Several important functions concern the DWA:

- Managing the volume of data in the DSS environment;
- Keeping the costs of data warehousing down to acceptable levels;
- Creating and managing a technical infrastructure that meets an organization's informational processing needs;
- Fostering an organizational and political environment where data warehouses can thrive; and
- Creating a proper systems architecture for DSS processing.

This chapter explores each of these functions.

Managing Volumes of Data

The volumes of data associated with data warehousing are measured in gigabytes and terabytes. This level of storage is one to two orders of magnitude greater than that experienced in most operational environments. The explosive growth of data experienced in the DSS environment stems from the following factors:

- Data warehousing recognizes the worth of historical data and encourages the orderly and organized saving of historical data;
- Data warehousing recognizes the value of both summarized and detailed data;

- Data warehousing recognizes the need for storing both obscure and well-traveled types of data, since the DSS analyst may desire to look at all kinds of relationships; and
- Data warehousing recognizes the need for the autonomy of processing at the departmental level—in the form of data marts.

For these reasons, massive volumes of data are the norm for the DSS environment.

One of the burning issues relevant to the massive growth of data is dormant data. As the volume of data grows in the data warehouse, there is a decrease in the actual percentage of data used. Figure 2-1 illustrates this phenomenon.

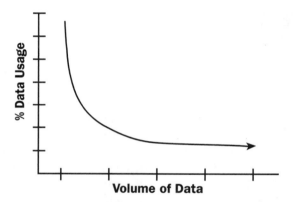

Figure 2-1 *The percentage of data used will decrease as the volume of data grows.*

Figure 2-1 shows that after the advent of the data warehouse, the end-user community uses most of the available data. However, as time passes and the volume of data grows, there is a decrease in the percentage of data which is used. Ironically, as the data warehouse matures and as volumes of data are added, less data is used (expressed as a percentage of the data warehouse which is accessed).

Dormant data costs a lot, for two reasons. Dormant data interferes with efficient access to useful data, and it also wastes valuable storage capacity. The cost of wasted storage can be measured by both the cost of storage itself and the cost of the ongoing maintenance and management of the storage once it is acquired. One of the most important jobs of the DWA is to find and remove dormant data from the DSS environment.

Regarding the management of large volumes of data, another challenging issue is to select the proper platform for data volume management. Both the hardware and database management system (DBMS) platforms must be selected wisely, to provide the technical foundation which is necessary in managing large amounts of data.

Keeping Costs Down

Hand in hand with the management of data in the DSS environment is the issue of budget management. Budgets tend to grow to the point where the amount of expenditures made on behalf of the data warehouse is often surprising. One of the reasons for the "creeping budget" phenomenon is that many DSS expenditures are paid for by individual departments—finance, marketing, sales, etc.—in the form of expenditures for data marts, end-user access, and analysis tools. The creeping budget phenomenon makes it difficult for an organization to take a collective look at how much money is spent on data warehousing. The inevitable day arrives when someone looks across all departments and discovers that the collective amount of money spent on data warehousing is more than a trivial amount.

In addition, there is another reason for the creeping budget phenomenon. At first glance, the DSS environment seems easy to implement. Users and programmers often underestimate the challenges of data warehousing. With scant preparation and forethought, some users and programmers dive into data warehouse development. Brief thought is given to the architecture, the issues of integration and transformation, or the massive amounts of data which are entailed. These programmers and users soon awaken to find themselves in an uncomfortable position. They can no longer go forward with the infrastructure as built, and it is quite expensive to start over and build the data warehouse right the second time around. Unfortunately, more money is thrown at the problem in the hopes that additional resources will somehow bring about improvements.

The major categories of expenditure which the DWA must manage are one-time capital expenses and ongoing expenses.

The one-time capital expenses include:

- The cost of the hardware platform, including disk storage;
- The cost of the underlying DBMS;
- The cost of end-users' access and analysis tools;
- The cost of integration and transformation; and
- The cost of establishing the metadata infrastructure.

The ongoing expenses include:

- The cost of refreshing the data warehouse;
- The cost of maintaining the integration and transformation programs;
- The cost of maintaining the metadata infrastructure; and
- The cost of processing end-user queries.

Creating and Managing the Technical Infrastructure

Perhaps the most important strategic decision of the DWA is to select and manage the technical foundation for the DSS environment. The technical foundation consists of the hardware platform and the underlying DBMS. The choice of the technical environment is complex since many facets complicate the decision. Important issues of the platform selection process are reflected in the following questions:

- Can the technical foundation support the volume of data required for the long term?
- Is the technical foundation so expensive that it prevents the initial development of the DSS environment?
- Can the technical foundation support the process of discovery for end users?
- Can the technical foundation be monitored and tuned as data and processing conditions change in the future?
- Can the technical foundation support diverse DSS processing?
- Can the technical foundation support the transmission of various datatypes into and out of the data warehouse?

Regarding the technical platform, the DWA plays both selector and caretaker roles, since the DWA must make the technical foundation work. Therefore, the DWA has a vested interest in choosing the technical foundation carefully.

Fostering an Organizational Environment

While the technical aspects of the DWA's role are important, they represent only one dimension. Another key aspect of the DWA's responsibilities is to foster an organizational and political environment where the data warehouse can succeed. In some regards, this responsibility is the most important task of the DWA.

One political responsibility of the DWA involves management feedback. It is incumbent on the DWA to speak directly with management about the successes and failures of the data warehouse. When there is no direct communication between the DWA and management, serious problems result. Data warehousing costs are too high and the data warehouse's ultimate success is too important to risk a weak linkage between the DWA and management. The DWA must compete for resources. As successes occur, an organization's management team must be apprised, so that management can see the fruits of their efforts and investment. Therefore, an important organizational responsibility of the DWA is to ensure that communications between the DWA and management are open, healthy, and constant.

In addition, the DWA must pay attention to the organizational and political landscape, since data warehousing projects often involve many different departments within an organization. In the past, the information systems (IS) organization had a reputation of hiring individuals who buried themselves in the bowels of technology. Many IS professionals began their careers in the open air and emerged 25 years later at retirement. During their employment, only human resources kept track of the IS professionals employed by the organization. Such a pattern of low visibility is not acceptable for the DWA. With the data warehouse, the DWA is involved with the marketing, sales, finance, and accounting departments, to name a few. The very essence of the DWA is that of influence and visibility across many different organizational units, and this is not accomplished with low-visibility individuals.

A third reason for the political and organizational dimension of the DWA is due to the conflict and competition which can occur among the different data warehouse users, as it relates to data marts. Data marts are a normal and useful part of the DSS environment. However, data marts must be positioned properly within the architecture of the data warehouse. If data marts are not structured properly, they defeat the purpose of having a data warehouse in the first place. In essence, data marts are departmental structures. As such, departments express a great deal of autonomy regarding their own data marts. The DWA has an important role to play in balancing the need for the architectural integrity of the data warehouse and end users' feelings of autonomy toward the data mart.

One of the primary issues is that of the department which desires to build the data mart directly from the operational environment. The DWA needs to point out to responsible management that bypassing current detailed data positions the data mart incorrectly. Building the data marts directly from the operational environment is one of the worst mistakes a company can make.

Creating a Proper Architecture

Perhaps the most important long-term role of the DWA is to understand what is meant by a "proper" data warehouse and the DSS architecture and to transfer that vision to the organization. The DWA must understand that—for all the advantages of the data warehouse—if the environment is not structured properly in an architectural sense, the organization will not reap the full benefits of the data warehouse.

The architectural issues that challenge the DWA include the following:

- Identifying the relation of current detailed data and data marts;
- Determining the level of detail to be stored;
- Creating profile records in the right circumstance;
- Archiving data effectively;
- Managing summary data;
- Creating and managing the metadata infrastructure;
- Integrating and transforming data, without incurring enormous resource costs; and
- Managing the DSS environment after its initial rollout.

Summary

The recognition of the DWA as a new and important organizational entity comes with the maturity of the DSS environment. The world of data warehousing is sufficiently alien to the world of operational processing, such that the existing systems support functions do not allow data warehouses to thrive and grow. The DWA's responsibilities include the following:

- Managing huge volumes of data;
- Keeping the costs of data warehousing down to acceptable levels;
- Creating and managing the technical infrastructure required to support the data warehouse;
- Fostering an organizational and technical environment where data warehouses can thrive; and
- Understanding and establishing an architectural infrastructure suitable for data warehousing.

About the Author

Bill Inmon, the father of the data warehouse concept, has written 32 books on data management, data warehouse, design review, and the management of data processing. Twenty-one of the books have been book club selections with publishers such as Prentice-Hall, John Wiley, and QED. Translations have been produced in Russian, German, French, Korean, Japanese, and Chinese.

Bill has written over 250 articles in trade journals such as Datamation, ComputerWorld, DataBase Programming/Design. Currently, Bill is a columnist with Data Management Review.

Bill founded and took public a Silicon Valley company, Prism Solutions, which automates the process of building data warehouses in standard database technologies—such as Informix—by integrating and transforming data from older database technologies, such as IMS, VSAM, IDMS, and ADABAS, into a data warehouse. Bill Inmon's latest venture, Pine Cone Systems (a Colorado company), is the leader in building data warehouse administration software for managing the data warehouse, DSS environment.

About Pine Cone Systems

Pine Cone Systems builds software for managing and administering the data warehouse. The initial products that Pine Cone brings to the marketplace include an activity monitor, which reports what data is and is not used in the warehouse; a data monitor, which reports what growth is experienced and what bad data has entered the data warehouse; a charge-back manager, which allows the end user to see what resources are consumed on a departmental basis; and a refreshment tracker, which allows the end user to see when and how much data was entered into the data warehouse. Pine Cone Systems is a Colorado-based company founded by William H. Inmon.

Design and Implementation for Decision Support

Using a Rational Approach to Build Your Data Warehouse

by Dale Mietla and Marvin Miller

Introduction

Data warehousing is enjoying success as a method to analyze business trends and improve the competitiveness of the sponsoring organization. It is also rapidly becoming a necessity, as more companies begin data warehouse projects.

Data warehousing has spawned an entirely new set of acronyms, buzzwords, design concepts, and measurements. System configurations, usage patterns, and the methods of work performed by end users in data warehousing differ radically from those of operational systems. These differences have resulted in a dizzying array of choices in systems, software, and services. Most of these choices overlap to some degree, which further complicates arriving at a clear picture of data warehousing or, specifically, determining what data warehousing means to an organization.

In the race to implement a data warehouse, most companies miss the obvious point of selecting the best products and services to meet their needs. In the attempt to gain a competitive advantage, they focus on selecting the latest, the fastest, or the largest products.

The use of a rational process to define the business problem and solve it is often overlooked or ignored.

Nonetheless, data warehousing requires a well-designed process workflow to select the correct technology and organize the development work so that the finished product is a valuable tool for managing business. This is due to the scale of most data warehouse projects and the range of technology available today.

This article organizes the various technology choices available for data warehousing and addresses the need for a process to implement the data warehouse application. This article contains a concise roadmap that illustrates the relationships of software and hardware products and service providers. The roadmap is a set of tasks that explain the interaction of the technology choices in the building of a data warehouse.

Key Components

Following are the key components of data warehousing.

Data Warehouse Products

The purpose of the data warehouse system is to analyze corporate data. The knowledge gained from the analyses is used to guide organizations. This intent is fundamentally different from operational systems, whose purpose is to keep organizations running each day.

The difference of these two functions is illustrated by their acronyms. Operational systems are referred to as online transaction processing (OLTP) systems, and data warehouse systems are sometimes referred to as online analytical processing (OLAP) systems. Each system has different usage characteristics and generally requires different hardware and software configurations in order to achieve maximum performance.

In general, the data warehouse system is tuned for a smaller community of users who generate a small number of transactions. Because the data in the database is analyzed, it is rarely updated during transactions; instead, the data is repeatedly read and combined in different ways. The transactions, however, are very large and sometimes require scanning entire tables.

Operational systems, on the other hand, are tuned for a large community of users, with a high volume of relatively simple transactions. Since transactions update the individual records in the database, data is always current. As such, the database is organized to quickly retrieve individual data items and to update only the pieces of information that change.

One way to understand the products which compose a data warehouse system is to follow the flow of data from operational systems to the data warehouse system. A successful data warehouse system must be stocked with data from operational systems. The data in the data warehouse system usually contains a deeper history than the data in operational systems. Often, three to five years' worth of data is stored in the data warehouse. The data must be accurate, without duplications or inconsistencies. The selected data must be moved to the data warehouse system and stored in a database management system.

Current database technology for data warehousing offers a variety of choices, from multidimensional database management systems (MDBMS) to relational database management systems (RDBMS), such as Informix Dynamic Server. Due to recent advances, MDBMS support vast amounts of data, provide rapid data retrieval, and offer various combinations of data; refer to Figure 3-1.

Building the Data Warehouse

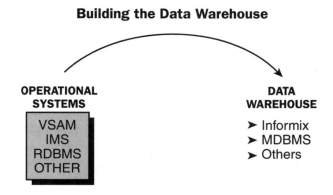

Figure 3-1 *Building the data warehouse from data in operational systems.*

The actual movement of data from operational systems to the data warehouse is accomplished by a group of software tools that bridge the gap between the older data access methods—including

VSAM, IMS, and others—and transport the data into the RDBMS and MDBMS of the '90s. Software tools execute a series of steps to select, match, filter, cleanse, and copy selected operational data into the data warehouse; refer to Figure 3-2.

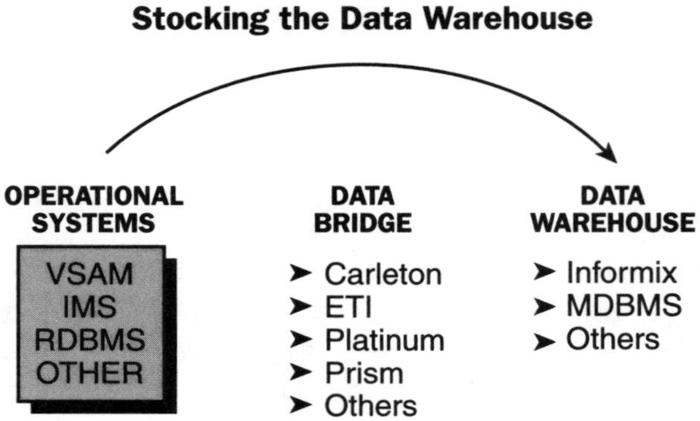

Stocking the Data Warehouse

OPERATIONAL SYSTEMS	DATA BRIDGE	DATA WAREHOUSE
VSAM IMS RDBMS OTHER	➤ Carleton ➤ ETI ➤ Platinum ➤ Prism ➤ Others	➤ Informix ➤ MDBMS ➤ Others

Figure 3-2 *Stocking the data warehouse via data-bridging software tools.*

Portions of the operational data can be duplicated since the data is stored in several sources. Data sources grow over time as new OLTP applications are developed. This overlap can present itself as similar names for data items (CUST, CUST_NAME, etc.), or as partially overlapping fields (PART_NUMBER, ASSEMBLY, SUB_ASSEMBLY, etc.).

Note that the data-bridging software products require a method to keep track of data items, so that the items are correctly combined in the data warehouse system. This requirement can be met by use of a data dictionary, or *metadata*.

Metadata acts as a traffic cop for data that enters the data warehouse. Metadata tracks changes to field names, enters timestamps that indicate when data sets were loaded into the data warehouse, and tracks versions of both the operational and data warehouse field names.

The next group of products in the roadmap are the viewing tools. Since the analytical function is so critical to the success of the data warehouse project, a large number of these tools are available. These tools:

1. Generate sophisticated queries of the data warehouse system; and
2. Present the results of queries in a variety of graphical formats.

The viewing tools are the primary contact that end users have with the data warehouse; thus, the tools must be flexible and easy to understand. They must also provide a variety of choices to generate the query, present the results, and keep track of the flow of the ana-lytical session. These qualities are necessary because most analytical sessions are based on an *ad hoc* approach, where the outcome, and even the process of arriving at the outcome, are unknown.

Most data warehouse queries answer a specific set of questions that relate to an organization. For example, a retail store chain analyzes market baskets, shelf-space allocation, or the effectiveness of targeted marketing programs. A healthcare provider is interested in fraud detection, the efficiency of various reimbursement plans, or usage tracking for various medications.

Some analyses are saved for repeated use. These analyses can be thought of as data warehouse applications for end users. Note that these applications are not written (compiled, debugged, etc.) by traditional management information systems (MIS) departments but are built by end users to answer repetitive questions, such as: "What are the latest sales trends as of today?" or "What is the effectiveness of my largest suppliers?"

The viewing tools must also use metadata, so that the data items are used consistently and the results can be matched to existing operational data. These points are illustrated in Figure 3-3.

The previous points address the requirements of data warehouse software products. Once these requirements are met, the roadmap is

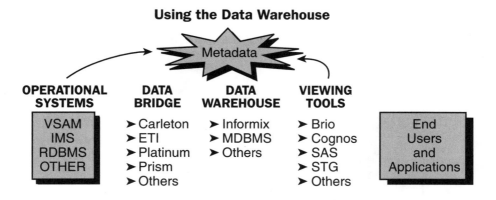

Using the Data Warehouse

Figure 3-3 Metadata provides consistancy and matches results to existing operational data.

complete from a software perspective. However, it is equally important that the hardware system supports the extreme demands of data warehouse environments. Due to the vast volumes of data stored in a data warehouse, traditional 32-bit computers have limitations that reduce the size, performance, and scalability required for data warehouse projects.

Specifically, 32-bit systems are limited to files and file systems that are 2 GB or less in maximum size. This means that data must be partitioned or segmented into smaller groups so that the 32-bit system can handle it. This limitation results in huge operational problems for backup, recovery, design, and maintenance, especially when data warehouse projects frequently approach 1 TB in size.

The next step in computer architecture is 64-bit computing. Systems, such as the Digital Equipment Corporation (Digital) AlphaServer family, are fully 64-bit capable and run fully adapted 64-bit applications, like Informix Dynamic Server. With such systems, there are essentially no constraints for growth, usage, or design. In addition, 64-bit applications have the added benefit of outperforming their 32-bit predecessors because of the economies of scale provided in 64-bit architectures (see Figure 3-4).

Hardware systems provide the foundation for a data warehouse, supporting rapid growth as data is added to the data warehouse and handling increasingly complex queries from a growing user community. It is important to select a hardware platform—such as 64-bit systems—that supports future growth. Otherwise, more users, smarter users, and data can cause traditional 32-bit systems to collapse, provide extremely slow performance, or limit analyses to sizes which they can accommodate.

Supporting the Data Warehouse

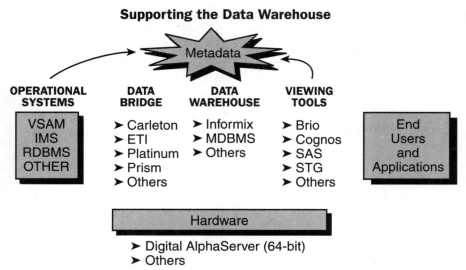

Figure 3-4 *64-bit hardware meets the changing needs of the data warehouse.*

Data Warehouse Services

The previous section described the products required to build the data warehouse. The final portion of the data warehouse roadmap focuses on the services required to build the data warehouse. Most data warehouse installations require additional outside assistance to build a total solution.

Outside consulting services are usually required for several reasons:

1. Data warehouse projects are large efforts which usually take several months or longer to design, create, and maintain.
2. The projects require a wide variety of skills, from database design to data modeling, to user viewing tools.
3. The existing MIS staff is often overburdened with application development and the management of the operational systems.
4. Data warehouse expertise is rare and seldom part of an organization's existing MIS departmental skill set.

Typically, a systems integrator supports, manages, and delivers a data warehouse project. In fact, most MIS departments have worked on other projects with systems integrators. Most data warehouse needs can be met by the larger systems integrator—provided that the integrator has experience with data warehouse systems; refer to Figure 3-5.

Servicing the Data Warehouse

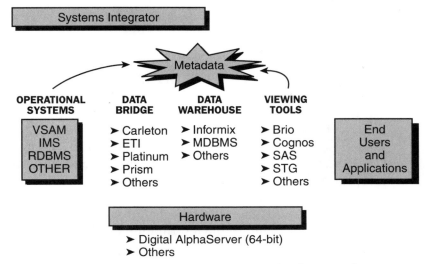

Figure 3-5 *The systems integrator services the data warehouse.*

However, an additional service provider—extremely useful for most data warehouse projects—is the independent data warehouse consultant. Independent data warehouse consultants have carved out a valuable niche for themselves over the past two years. They actually provide the "grease" to keep the entire project running smoothly. The added value of independent consultants is that they can address the needs of end users in the *language* of end users, instead of in the language of computer technology.

Data warehouse projects are often built to allow end users to analyze business issues efficiently. When the analysis is complete, the new knowledge is put into practice to improve the functioning of an organization. Therefore, end users become implementers.

There are different perspectives of the data warehouse component roadmap, depending on who views it:

- End users view the roadmap as starting at the right-hand side of the page. They see the viewing tools primarily and, possibly, some portions of the database engine.
- MIS departments and system integrators view the roadmap as starting at the left-hand side of the page. They see the operational systems, the data-bridging software (due to its impact to the operational systems), and, probably, the database engine.

The point is that the two views do not naturally have any common ground for discussion, design, development, or testing. The two views begin from different perspectives and end with different goals.

Successful data warehouse projects require a focus on the solution by both MIS and end users at each stage. The independent consultants can bridge this gap and create the common ground where solution sharing can occur. These consultants are trained to listen to end users, develop a set of requirements that are business based (not technology based), and translate end-user requirements into traditional MIS requirements.

Please note the completed roadmap in Figure 3-6.

The completed roadmap offers the reader a chance to organize the technology options into categories that explain their function, purpose, and relationship to one another. Products and services are two fundamental requirements of any data warehouse project.

The next section presents the process for analyzing, designing, and implementing the information technology components of the data warehouse roadmap.

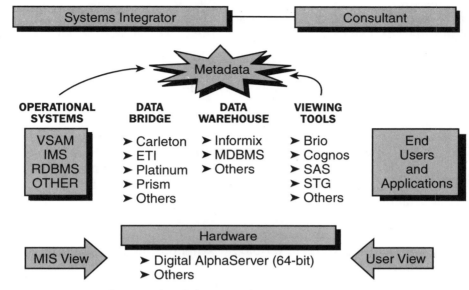

The Complete Data Warehouse Roadmap

Figure 3-6 *The completed data warehouse roadmap.*

Data Warehousing Process

We are in the initial stages of data warehousing maturity. Marketplace excitement and hype, preoccupation with solutions and technologies, and many project failures characterize this stage. Various publications provide articles about star schemas, bitmapped indexing, OLAP, and VLDB. A recent industry publication conducted a survey to determine who has the largest database. Survey respondents bragged, and everyone focused on the wrong set of issues. Unfortunately, and maybe unknowingly, the "bigger is better" premise earned undue credibility.

To further understand the "state of the art" in data warehousing today, it is helpful to inquire how many data warehousing teams ask the following questions:

1. What business information keeps the company in business today? What business information can put the company out of business tomorrow?
2. What business information should always be a click of an icon away?
3. What business conditions, inside and outside the enterprise, drive the need for business information?

4. What are the business objectives, strategies, and problems that must be addressed? Which ones are the most important?
5. What types of insight, understanding, and learning are needed?
6. What are the elements of information that fulfill these needs?

This line of questioning focuses the project team on the business problem of enabling shared enterprise knowledge, which leads to increased business performance. Yet, the previous set of questions is conspicuously absent from the dialogue of many data warehouse project teams. This is a significant problem, since the issue of where value is added remains to be discussed. This vacuum is usually filled by discussion about data mining, parallel architectures, and the movement of data into the warehouse.

It is time to move from the excitement about data warehouse technology to an understanding of the real business and technical issues which are central to data warehousing. It is also time to move from "trial and error" projects to development efforts that address the engineering complexities inherent in building a data warehouse. A well-defined data warehousing process can help organizations make the transition to a higher level of maturity and more predictable results.

What Is a Process?

First of all, a process is not a methodology. A methodology is a *theoretical* set of concepts and practices for producing a specified result—in this case, a functional data warehouse. In other words, properly applying the theory defined by methodologists to a project results in the desired outcome. Methodology "binderware" continues to adorn shelves, as ready evidence to the QA audit team that a methodology exists.

A process, on the other hand, is an *applied* set of concepts and practices for producing a specified result. This is a subtle but important distinction. A process is the product of real projects, not a product of methodologists' theories. Acquired knowledge contains the combined best practices of project teams for producing a solution. Processes commonly exist in an automated form and are an integral part of the project team's infrastructure for the delivery of a solution.

A well-defined data warehousing process helps project teams to:

- Understand the critical business and technical issues of data warehousing;
- Create project outcomes and evaluate their quality;
- Apply a process workflow (tasks) and a set of techniques for developing a data warehouse solution;
- Understand the roles and responsibilities of team members; and
- Determine the project schedule and level of effort.

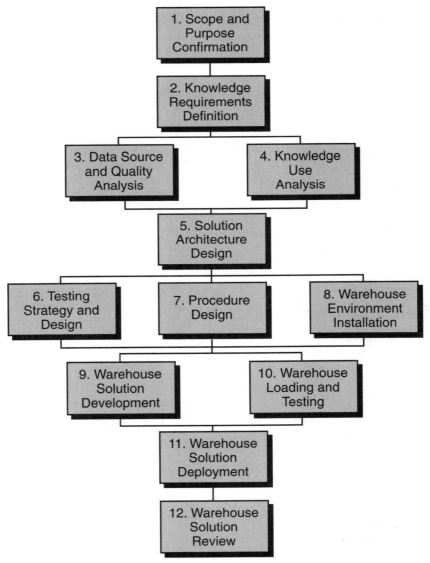

Figure 3-7 NewTHINK's 12 stages of data warehousing.

A process that provides guidelines, pitfalls, strategies, hints, examples, lessons learned, and other types of practical tips is considerably more useful to project teams than a detailed "cookbook" task structure that encourages blind adherence. A good process energizes the creativity and thinking of the project team, instead of stifling it.

Once an organization has accepted the need for a data warehousing process, the next key challenge is to define and evaluate a process. The two most common approaches are "acquire and adapt," or "build your own." In either case, the process consumer must take full control and ownership of the data warehousing process to pave the way for its acceptance and use.

The 12 stages of data warehousing (Figure 3-7) are provided to assist organizations in defining or evaluating a process. These stages are the "essential blocks of development activities" that must be present in a data warehousing process to completely address the business and technical issues involved in developing a data warehouse. The stages define a high-level framework or an architecture of a process but cannot be applied without additional details.

Figure 3-7 illustrates a process workflow of data warehousing, showing each stage and its primary dependencies to other stages. The diagram does not explicitly depict sequence.

The following sections provide a description of each stage and some of the key issues addressed by each (the issue lists are not exhaustive).

Project Startup

Scope and Purpose Confirmation

Explicitly defining project boundaries from a business and technical perspective provides positioning (context) and allows a project to move into high gear. Project team members and key stakeholders must have a shared vision of the project and its results. The central issues to be addressed include:

- Does the project add business value? What constitutes success?
- What forms the basis for competition in the marketplace of the future?
- Does the project address the key business drivers? Which are most important?

- What part of business operations is affected? Which processes, subjects, locations, and organizations are impacted?
- Who are the key stakeholders, and what are their expectations?
- Who are the consumers and producers of knowledge? What types of knowledge do they require?
- What technology standards are in place which constrain the project?
- What are the funding, schedule, and resource constraints?
- What is the relationship between the project and other data warehousing solutions or projects?

Knowledge Analysis

Knowledge Requirements Definition

Information is understanding the events of the past. Knowledge, on the other hand, is insight which enables the prediction and creation of events in the future. The focus of data warehousing must be on the development of knowledge, and not just the reporting of information.

In this stage, the project team works with business customers to define the knowledge requirements for the data warehousing solution. Dialogue takes place in a natural business language, with many visualizations to help team members and business customers feel confident that their requirements are understood. The central issues to be addressed include:

- What are the business objectives, strategies, and problems that require measurement and analysis? What opportunities and challenges drive the need for knowledge?
- What types of insight, understanding, and learning are needed? Which are historical versus predictive in nature? Who needs this knowledge? Where is this knowledge needed, and how often?
- What are the elements of information that lead to insight, understanding, and learning? Where can these elements be acquired?
- What are the business rules that govern the elements of information?
- What types of analytical methods are used to develop knowledge?

- How are the results of these analytical methods visualized?
- How is information about knowledge requirements represented as metadata?

Note that star schema versus relational schema is not an issue here. These are storage structures which must be considered in the solution architecture. The knowledge models created in this stage are intended for a business audience.

Data Source and Quality Analysis

As the knowledge requirements are defined, the project team must map the requirements to the discrete elements of internal and external data sources. In many cases, the mapping is to data fields in existing OLTP systems. The team must also address one of the most difficult problems in data warehousing: how to handle "dirty" data. The central issues to be addressed include the following:

- What are the potential internal and external sources of information? What discrete facts (data) must be leveraged from these sources?
- Which sources are closest to the point of data entry?
- How often are the sources updated? How volatile and current are the sources?
- What business rules constrain each discrete fact of data? Which business rules are inconsistent with the business rules in the knowledge model?
- Are the business rules applied uniformly to the data sources? What percentage of the data is "dirty"?
- Which sources satisfy the knowledge requirements?
- How is information about the selected sources represented as metadata?

Knowledge Use Analysis

As the knowledge requirements are defined, the project team must also understand the usage metrics (for example, size, volume, frequency) for the requirements. Scalability is an important issue in data warehousing. The metrics on knowledge usage, which relate to scalability, must be visible and understood early. The central issues to be addressed include the following:

- What is the estimated size of each element of information?
- How many instances are contained in each information set?
- What analytical operations are performed? Which sets of information are involved? How often are the operations performed?
- How often is each information set refreshed with new data from internal or external sources? What are the sizes of the source data sets?
- How often are instances removed from each information set? What are the criteria for removal?
- How are statistics on information usage represented as metadata?

Solution Design

Solution Architecture Design

The project team—using its understanding of the knowledge requirements, usage, and data sources—designs the data warehousing solution. The solution architecture is a specification containing four of the key components of data warehouse solutions, presented earlier in this article (that is, data bridge, data warehouse, viewing tools, hardware). The central issues to be addressed include the following:

- What existing standards and infrastructure (that is, hardware, software, network) constrain the solution? How does the project team leverage the existing infrastructure to shorten the development time cycle?
- What data warehousing tools (in current use) must be considered?
- What classes of business customers must the solution support and where are the business customers? What levels of security must be provided?
- What viewing tools (for example, query, reporting, analytical, visualization) must be provided?
- How is access to metadata provided to business customers? How is metadata kept consistent with data in the warehouse?
- What is the data architecture of the solution? What storage struc-

tures (for example, star schema, relational schema) and indexing methods must be used? How is the data summarized, partitioned, and distributed?

- What is the application architecture of the solution? What programs and logic are needed to extract, transform, cleanse, and load the operational data? How is the application logic partitioned and distributed?
- What is the technology architecture of the solution? What hardware, systems software, and networks must be used to support the solution? How is the technology distributed to support the data and application architectures?

Testing Strategy and Design

As the solution architecture is defined, the project team must develop strategies, procedures, and data to test the data warehousing solution. The four key components of the solution should be addressed in the test strategy and design. However, the data-bridging component is likely to require the most testing. The central issues to be addressed include the following:

- What is the potential business impact to the enterprise (for example, the decisions made, or actions taken) from the use of the data warehouse? What degree of testing rigor must be applied?
- What degree of data correctness must exist? How is data correctness proven?
- How are data-bridging programs tested? How is the correctness of the extraction, transformation, cleansing, and loading logic proven?
- How are viewing tools tested? How is the correctness of the tools' results and visualizations proven?
- In what sequence are components tested? What procedures and test data are used?
- Who will perform the testing? How are test results reported and evaluated?
- What tests must be completed successfully prior to system acceptance?

Procedure Design

As the design of the solution architecture unfolds, the project team must also focus on the procedures required to operate and administer the data warehouse. The design of automated and/or manual procedures must provide availability, security, performance, and storage management. The central issues to be addressed include the following:

- What are the procedures for backup and recovery?
- What are the procedures for data refresh and archival?
- What are the procedures for monitoring and tuning data warehouse performance?
- What are the procedures for data warehouse security?
- What are the procedures for extending and scaling data storage?

Data Warehouse Environment Installation

Before the development of the data warehouse solution begins, the hardware, system software, and network must be installed and/or made available to the project team. Each infrastructure component must be thoroughly tested and certified. Testing and certification of the environment can save the implementation team time in isolating problems during the development of the solution.

Solution Implementation

Warehouse Solution Development

The project team builds the data warehousing solution according to the specifications of the solution architecture and design procedures. The project team should expect to spend most of its effort on the data-bridging component of the solution architecture.

Warehouse Loading and Testing

As the project team assembles the components of the data warehousing solution, an independent testing team must prove the correctness of the solution. The testing strategy and design should guide the testing team as they construct test data, test the data-bridging components, load the data warehouse, and test the viewing tool components. Business customers should test the viewing tool components and conduct the final acceptance test before the deployment of the data warehouse solution.

Data Warehouse Solution Deployment

After its accceptance, the accepted data warehouse solution is installed, tested, and made available at the targeted sites. The extraction and load processes bring the data warehouse to a production status. At this stage, end users and the operations staff receive documentation. Training helps end users to understand the solution's potential and to become comfortable with the functionality of the viewing tools.

Project Wrap-Up

Warehouse Solution Review

After deploying the solution, the project team archives important project documentation and data and conducts a final meeting to discuss the project process and results. The central issues to be addressed during the discussion include the following:

- Is the solution complete and correct? How satisfied were business customers with the solution?
- What portion of the original scope was "thrown overboard" and must be incorporated into a future project? What improvements must be made to the current solution?
- How well did the development process work? What improvements must be made to the workflow and techniques?
- How well did the project team work together? What improvements must be made to the roles, responsibilities, and allocation of workloads?
- How well did the development tools work? What workarounds or utilities must be implemented to increase usability or functionality?

Iterative Application of the Process

It is a well-known fact that implementing a data warehouse is an iterative process. Consequently, the previous process must be performed iteratively under the control of a process that determines the sequence and scope of each project, as illustrated in Figure 3-8. Data warehousing scope and iteration management is an ongoing process and employs estimating and release management techniques to implement the data warehouse vision through a series of process iterations. Other ongoing processes, such as configuration management, change control, process and project management,

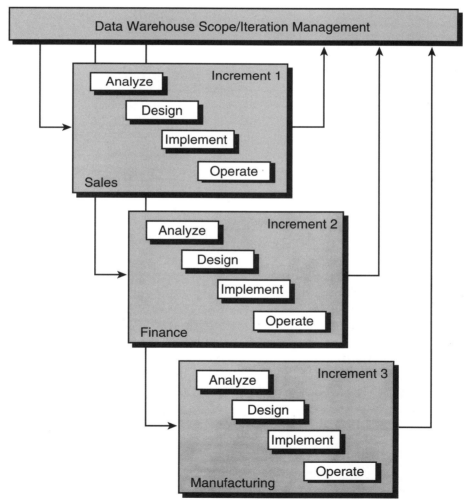

Figure 3-8 A data warehouse process iteration.

and architecture management, must also interface with each iteration of the data warehouse process.

Concurrent Engineering Shortens Cycle Time

To shorten the time cycle, the data warehousing project team should be a multidisciplined team of managers, business customers, analysts, solution architects, and implementers. A concurrent engineering team is a key ingredient in shortening the implementation cycle. For example, the involvement of solution architects during the analysis of knowledge requirements allows for the discussion of solution tradeoffs early in the project cycle. Before considerable resources are consumed, unfeasible or expensive options can be discarded. Also, solution architects can begin positioning the solution architecture earlier in the project. Likewise, the involvement of business customers and analysts during the design and implementation phases can speed up the resolution of issues related to requirements. In addition, business customers and analysts can be invaluable resources during testing.

Keys to Project Success

Before implementing a data warehousing process in an organization, keep the following keys for success in mind:

- **Use the process as a guide, not a cookbook.** A *process* is a framework, or generalization, to guide project teams from problem to solution. A data warehousing process must be customized by each project team to address the specific needs and constraints of their project. A process is not a replacement for thinking and innovation.
- **Keep the scope manageable.** An enterprisewide data warehousing project may sound appealing but can quickly become a sinkhole—collapsing from the weight of its own complexity. Think "big picture," and act in small, quick steps. It is fine to have an enterprisewide vision. However, use solid release management techniques to implement the vision step by step.
- **Set expectations up front between management, users, and developers.** Developing a shared vision between key stakeholders at the beginning of the project is critical to project success. An

honest and open discussion about the business problem, and the cost and capability of available solutions can help to set the right expectations.

- **Create an environment for experimentation and learning.** More learning must take place before mature data warehousing processes are practiced in most organizations. It is best to give the project team great latitude and support during the first few iterations of a new process. Use consultants with proven experiences that are consistent with the project scope to guide the team and to facilitate technology transfer. At the end of each iteration, capture the team's learning in the data warehousing process so that subsequent teams benefit.

Conclusion

Data warehousing can be a valuable analytical tool and competitive weapon. It can also be a large waste of time, resources, and money. The difference between these two outcomes is beginning the data warehouse project with a set of clearly focused goals and following a rational approach in the building of the data warehouse.

The goals of the project and the data warehouse component roadmap described in this article allow an organization to select the technology best suited to its needs. A coordinated project plan—including the process of definition, analysis, design, and deployment involving MIS staff and key end users—helps to ensure a successful data warehouse implementation, on time and within budget.

About the Authors

Dale Mietla is the director of consulting services for NewTHINK, Inc., where he helps clients visualize the knowledge requirements that define the data warehouse, and the architectures and processes that deliver the data warehouse. He has over 17 years of experience with an emphasis in the areas of enterprise architecture, business and information modeling, application design, and development processes and technologies. Dale can be contacted at: dmietla@newthink.com.

Marvin Miller is a senior consultant for Digital Equipment Corporation, where he works closely with data warehouse companies and customers on large-scale data warehousing opportunities. He has over 20 years of experience in the computer industry, including large-scale system design, performance benchmarks, and application migrations. Marvin can be contacted at: marvin.miller@ohf.mts.dec.com.

About NewTHINK, Inc.

NewTHINK, Inc., is a rapidly growing international consultancy organization, providing clients with industry-leading solutions using data warehousing technologies. NewTHINK's team of experienced data warehousing professionals brings focus and clarity to the key issues of architecture, process, modeling enterprise knowledge, and the role of the Internet.

About Digital Equipment Corporation

Digital Equipment Corporation is the leading worldwide supplier of 64-bit networked computer systems, software, and services. The AlphaServer family includes a complete range of systems—from workgroup to server—based on the same 64-bit RISC technology. Digital pioneered and leads the industry in interactive, distributed, and multi-vendor computing. An international company—more than half of Digital's business comes from outside the United States—Digital develops and manufactures products and provides customer services in the Americas, Europe, Asia, and the Pacific Rim.

Starting the Data Warehouse from a Data Model

by Larry Heinrich

What Are Template Data Models?

A data model is a graphical representation of the data for a specific area of interest. That area of interest may be as broad as all the integrated data requirements of an entire business organization, such as an "Enterprise Data Model," or as focused as a single business area or application. Frequently, a data model represents a functional business area (CUSTOMER, MARKETING, SALES, MANUFACTURING, etc.) or a business area that is to be analyzed or automated (LEAD TRACKING, PROBLEM REPORTING, WARRANTIES, etc.).

The function of the data model is to clearly convey data and its relationships, attributes, definitions, and the business rules that govern the data. Data models are the accepted way of representing and designing databases.

The data models for a company in a specific industry tend not to change greatly over time, unless the company changes the fundamental manner in which it conducts business. The way that data is used, and all associated processes, can vary greatly even between organizations in the same industry. However, the data required by companies within the same industry tends to be similar. Then, it is possible to assume that data models have basic stability within the organization, while process models are relatively unstable and undergoing constant change. This common functional data is the basic premise that allows "template" data models for an industry to be applied to the individual companies which operate in that industry.

Template data models are prebuilt, fully functional data models for a specific industry that closely approximate the results achieved if the models are built from scratch.

Template data models can be built for every conceivable data modeling requirement, including the following types of applications:

- Enterprise systems;
- Data warehouses;
- Business area applications;
- Decision support systems (DSS) and data marts; and
- Dimensional systems.

Template data models of the highest standards have common characteristics:

- They are constructed for a specific industry or industry segment; and
- They are clear, unambiguous, detailed, and fully attributed.

Template data models are based upon detailed industry analysis that enables fully attributed models to be developed. This attention to detail accelerates the planning, analysis, and design phases and renders the use of template data models of real value. Each entity should closely approximate a table that a design architect (DA) uses to design an application, and that a database administrator (DBA) uses to build that application. Without identification of the columns that comprise a table, the work has just begun.

Each entity and attribute must be completely defined in industry terminology, including appropriate examples. It is not unusual for a suite of industry template data models to be supported by 5,000 to 7,000 pages of bound documentation. In addition, every relationship must be named in a template data model.

The data model should tell the story of the subject area of interest as the relationships between entities are read. Note the following example:

"... CELLULAR TELEPHONE operates under one RATE PLAN consisting of..."

Data models must also be presented in large-format graphic representation, since few individuals read stacks of reports. If the model is to be used, it must be presented in large-format graphics.

Template data models must be completely integrated. This is the function of a strong computer assisted software engineering (CASE) tool that is capable of supporting the development, integration, and synchronization of models.

For example, as the definition of CUSTOMER is modified, it can be propagated immediately to all related models by linked schemas within the CASE tool environment. The selection of the right CASE tool simplifies this process. Selecting the wrong CASE tool, however, results in needless, labor-intensive activities.

Why Use Template Data Models?

The typical information systems (IS) project consists of long planning, analysis, design, and implementation phases that incorporate a host of hardware, software, and staffing activities. The most challenging, expensive, and difficult phases to predict are the planning, analysis, and project design stages. In fact, 60 percent of data warehouse implementations fail in these phases, and not in the hardware or software selection process. It is here that the decisions are made as to which data is important, how the data will be structured, and how the data is ultimately represented in the data warehouse, DSS, and data marts.

There is no way to shorten the 12 to 18 months of planning, analysis, and design. Nor is there a way to predict what will result, or if the organization will ultimately obtain a return on the investment (ROI), unless a set of detailed, industry-specific template data models is used to bootstrap these activities. Template data models provide a close approximation of what can be achieved at a small fraction of the cost during that lengthy period. Their value must be immediately apparent upon inspection. Template data models are not a "plan to plan," the starting point for some deliverable in the future. They are the deliverable that is intended to jump-start and dramatically shorten the planning, analysis, and design phases. It takes a few hours to determine their value. Those few hours can save the project months of work and millions of dollars in costs. Template data models are flexible. They are designed to be modified, extended, and integrated with other data models.

Applied Data Research Management (ADRM) often presents an example of an Enterprise Data Model, which is approximately 16-feet long (paperwise), and incorporates 350 tables and 2,500 columns, with 1,000 pages of documentation. It's a compelling argument to tell senior management, "You will never have less than what you see before you. You can accurately predict project, resource, and staffing costs by analyzing the areas of the models that need to be extended. Furthermore, it can be installed and available in one hour." Contrast this to an expensive, disruptive information engineering effort, which is frequently controlled by a third party, whose results will not be readily apparent for many months.

Template data models can be used immediately for the following purposes:

- Building new data models;
- Establishing a DA function;
- Estimating resource requirements;
- Analyzing gaps;
- Transferring industry knowledge;
- Planning projects;
- Quantifying ROI;
- Defining standards; and
- Training and educating staff.

Template data models provide a clear, predictable view of the future, without the wait for implementation.

The Cost of Entry

In the search for template data models, it is often surprising that there are few to choose from, and the level of detail can vary considerably. Why is this? To build good template data models requires the following unique skills:

- Broad industry experience at each level;
- Senior data modeling expertise;
- Extensive DBA expertise since, ultimately, the goal is to build systems and not data models; and
- The ability to blend the efforts of data modelers, data archi-

tects, and DBAs to construct data models that meet a broad range of requirements and expectations.

This combination of skills, expertise, and long development cycles makes template data models unique. It also makes them extremely valuable.

What Types of Industries Are Supported?

ADRM develops industry data models and packages them as a "Data Environment" for that industry. Each Data Environment consists of an Enterprise Data Model, a multilevel Data Warehouse Model, and 20 to 23 Business Area Models appropriately named, such as the "Semiconductor Data Environment." ADRM supplies 18 different industry Data Environments to companies throughout the world, including the following categories:

- Banking;
- Brokerage;
- Financial Services;
- Food and Beverage;
- High Technology;
- Insurance—"Annuity";
- Insurance—"Health and Disability";
- Insurance—"Life";
- Insurance—"Property and Casualty";
- Landline;
- Mutual Funds;
- Pharmaceutical;
- Products, Goods, and Services;
- Retail;
- Semiconductor;
- Software;
- Staffing; and
- Wireless.

These models are frequently combined or integrated with other models to meet the unique requirements of specific industries. For example, the banking industry is addressed by a single Banking Data Environment. However, it is frequently combined with the

Insurance, Mutual Funds, and Brokerage Data Environments to provide a comprehensive data model that describes everything a bank accomplishes in the current operating environment. The data models are developed from a common core of building blocks so that they can be rapidly integrated and still provide consistent definitions of Customer, Channel, Geography, and other common data structures.

Everything Begins with the Enterprise Data Model

Regardless of what is being built—data warehouse, DSS/data marts, applications—it must be put into a larger context if it is to be successfully integrated with other systems. That larger data context is the "Enterprise Data Model."

The Enterprise Data Model (Figure 4-1) sets the stage by identifying all the data within the purview of a typical operating company in that industry—Customer Types, Channels, Beneficiaries, Life Insurance Products, Rate Plans, Business Ratios, SIC Categories, and so on.

Template Enterprise Data Models for specific industries are based upon an in-depth analysis of that industry's common functions, business areas, terminology, data relationships, definitions, examples, and business rules.

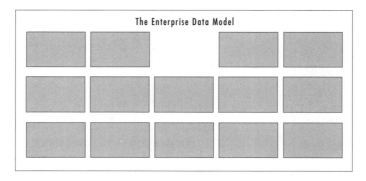

Figure 4-1 *The Enterprise Data Model.*

The Enterprise Data Model is the primary data tool for strategic planning—communicating data requirements throughout the organization, implementing integrated systems, and organizing data in the data warehouse, DSS/data marts, and applications.

The Enterprise Data Model graphically depicts entities by subject area, keys, attributes, relationships, and cardinalities. A typical Enterprise Data Modeling effort requires 6 to 12 months of effort with associated development, staffing, and training costs. A detailed Enterprise Data Model may be of sufficient detail to reduce this timeframe to 3 to 4 weeks. The business organization is able to launch its data modeling efforts immediately and leverage the entire project accordingly.

In some cases, it is desirable to achieve a more modest objective than the building of enterprisewide systems. The benefits to be derived from Enterprise Data Models are still impressive. Important questions to consider include the following:

- What is the larger context of an organization's efforts?
- Where are the points of data integration between functional areas?
- How can data be defined consistently between business areas?
- What are the applicable definitions, examples, and business rules?

Most organizations never regret having a complete, fully defined Enterprise Data Model to work from.

Beyond building systems, the Enterprise Data Model is an ideal tool for educating new staff and describing in relatively simple terms how a complex business works. It's also a good place to document the processes which occur within the organization. Important questions to consider include the following:

- Who built the system?
- How much did the system cost?
- What was the project architecture, and where are the files?
- Who studied CUSTOMER, and where are the results?
- Which third parties were involved and how, when, and where?

The Enterprise Data Model can provide a point of integration for the entire company if it is easy to understand, concise, well-presented graphically, supported by definitions and project information. It is a powerful tool for understanding the business and for planning to make it more efficient and effective.

Business Areas Are the Building Blocks for the Data Warehouse

Developing the data warehouse does not start with its development as the focus of analysis. It begins with the analysis of the business areas that contribute data to the data warehouse and receive information from the data warehouse. Business Area Data Models describe the lower levels of detailed data that are appropriate to building applications and DSS/data marts for a specific part of the business.

Each Business Area Model is constructed from a core of entities taken from subject areas within the Enterprise Data Model. This ensures that Business Area Models will be based on common entities and will have common keys, attributes, and definitions through the data architecture. This approach also supports the consistent integration of existing data models and the development of new data models.

Business Area Models contain the greatest level of detail and represent the lowest level of data granularity in the data model hierarchy. As new information is learned about business areas, the information is added to the corresponding Business Area Model. That information may also be incorporated into the Enterprise Data Model, Data Warehouse Model, or application data models. Using Business Area Models as a basis for analysis and design provides a solid foundation of industry-specific knowledge that accelerates planning and development.

To understand the interrelated requirements of the data warehouse requires an understanding of a host of seemingly unrelated data. For example, note the following inquiries:

- How do Bookings, Billings, Backlog, Cancellations, and Returns relate to Customers, Markets, Products, and Products Types for a specific period?
- What is the relationship of cellular telephone churn to customer demographics and rate plan?
- What legal entity relationships exist in the customer base beyond the obvious Customer purchasing relationships?

The ability to report this information flexibly depends upon the ability of data architects to plan and develop systems that consistently define, load, and maintain that data.

Examples of Business Area Data Models include the following:

- Bookings, Billings, and Backlog;
- Channel;
- Commissions;
- Contract;
- Customer;
- Customer Sales;
- Employee;
- Financial;
- Forecast;
- Geography;
- Inventory;
- Market;
- Marketing Event;
- Order;
- Pricing;
- Problem Reporting;
- Prospective Customer;
- Shop Floor Control/Manufacturing;
- Standard Terms and Conditions; and
- Training and Education.

Individual models can be easily combined or integrated to create other models.

For example, a "Customer Care" (Figure 4-2, page 60) prototype data model can be quickly built from seven to eight individual Business Area Models in a few hours.

Using Template Data Models to Build the Data Warehouse and Data Marts

Once the Enterprise Data Model and Business Area Model components are in place, it is possible to introduce the template Data Warehouse Models. The Data Warehouse Model represents the integrated decision support and information-reporting requirements of the business. The data warehouse is the center of the decision support and reporting data architecture—the ultimate source of clean, consistent data for the entire organization. The data warehouse may be surrounded by any number of functional DSSs, or data

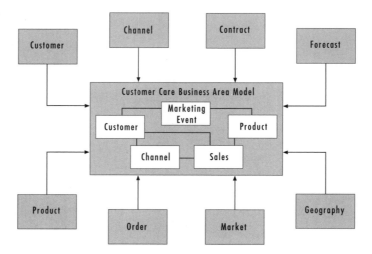

Figure 4-2 *The Customer Care Business Area Model.*

marts, serving the associated functional business areas. As data moves from the data warehouse to local DSS or data marts, control of the data is turned over to local administrators. The data warehouse remains the consistent source of reliable data.

The Data Warehouse Model is constructed directly from the same-industry Enterprise Data Model, which is the high-level data blueprint describing the organization's integrated information requirements. This approach ensures that the collective information requirements of the enterprise are represented in the Data Warehouse Model. Each subject area in the Enterprise Data Model has a corresponding Data Warehouse Model component.

ADRM implements the Data Warehouse Model in two distinct functional levels:

- Level 1—Decision Support System (DSS) data; and
- Level 2—Summarized data.

The Level 1—DSS data model describes data at the lowest level of detail appropriate for detailed analysis and decision making:

- Orders from a specific customer for a period of time;
- Quantity sales for a specific channel for a period of time; and
- Sales revenue from the sales of a specific product via a channel for a period of time.

The Level 2—Summary model depicts summarized data based upon the data which is defined in the Level 1—DSS model. This is the level of data that senior management uses to base their decisions:

- Total sales revenues from all orders for a period from all customers;
- Total new versus rebuy orders for a period from all customers;
- Total quantity sales from all channels for a period of time;
- Total sales revenues from sales of a specific product for a period of time;
- Total sales revenues from sales of a specific product line for a period of time;
- Total sales revenues from sales of all products for a period of time; and
- Period debt to equity ratio.

It might seem difficult to develop a template Data Warehouse Model for a company. However, in practice, it is an exercise primarily in decision making and secondarily in model building. Note the following decision-support inquiries:

- What are our customer types?
- What are our markets and market segments?
- How will our geographies be defined?
- How will we define product families and product lines?

A building-block approach can be applied to constructing the data warehouse.

In Figure 4-3 (page 62), the following steps are illustrated:

1. The Enterprise Data Model sets the stage.
2. The Business Area Models develop the detail from the Enterprise Data Model.
3. The Data Warehouse Models are first-cut, "good practice" data models that contain a view of what a well-rounded data warehouse might contain.
4. Detail data from the Business Area Models is added to the warehouse data model in a series of building-block steps.
5. Legacy data is considered and integrated into the Data Warehouse Model as needed.

The data warehouse is built from existing template data model

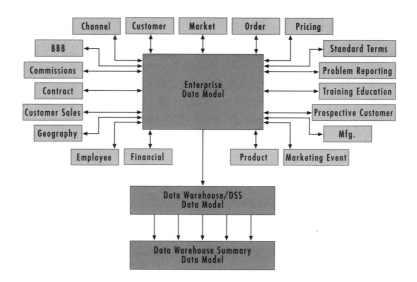

Figure 4-3 *Attaining the Data Warehouse Summary Data Model.*

components that represent the way the business intends to do business, which are then modified to meet the realities of legacy data and existing applications. The process is greatly accelerated when it utilizes standard industry data building blocks that can readily be modified, extended, or integrated to meet specific data requirements.

Each of these models is modified and contributes data to related models. Because the models are broken up into functional building blocks, progress can be made in many areas without a wait for any single decision to be made. Product data can be designed without the wait for the final customer data structures. Channel values can be defined later, while the foreign key relationships are defined immediately. Progress can be made in many areas with the confidence that the final results will fit together.

The level of detail in the Business Area Models is consistent with that of the DSS/data marts. This consistency makes it relatively easy to develop DSS/data marts that dovetail with the data warehouse. It also simplifies the promotion of data structures from the Business Area Models to the Data Warehouse Mode, or related Business Area Models.

A good example is inventory. The ADRM industry Enterprise Data Models do not describe inventory in detail because the models would become too dense. That detail is carried in the Inventory Business Area Model. However, if inventory data is of enough significance to the business organization, it can easily be integrated at any level of detail from the Inventory Business Area Model into the Data Warehouse Model (see Figure 4-4).

What would have been a significant analytic exercise can be dramatically accelerated by starting with detailed, good baseline models that can be quickly modified to meet specific requirements. The focus of the effort becomes a decision-making and not model-building process.

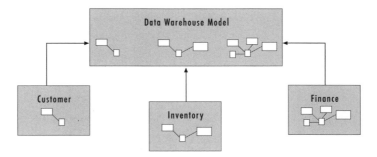

Figure 4-4 *The Data Warehouse Model.*

Comparing the Costs

A complete suite of industry-specific data models—Enterprise, Data Warehouse, Business Area, Dimension, and DSS/Data Marts—can cost from $100,000 to $200,000.

A typical information engineering project is measured in many millions of dollars. A target return on cost of models should be a minimum of 20:1. A project should easily see $1 to $2 million dollars in benefits by the introduction of the template data models. Even if the template data models are used as an advanced starting point from which to focus the project, they will have repaid their value many times over.

What cannot be quantified are the intangibles such as:

• Directing resources upon focused objectives immediately;
• Reduced disruption to the organization;
• The ability to clearly convey and describe the objectives at a detailed level; and
• Identifying clear roles and objectives for participants.

It is always wise to consider the use of template data models.

Guidelines for Using Template Data Models

Following are guidelines for the use of template data models:

1. Clearly define data objectives.
   - Are template data models appropriate for the data objectives?
   - Is the level of detail appropriate?
   - How much additional work is required?
   - Is the terminology consistent with that of the organization?
   - Does the staff see the value immediately?
2. Always develop an Enterprise Data Model either as a primary activity or as an adjunct ongoing activity.
3. Use template data models as a tool to simplify IS tasks, educate staff, and help to better understand what can be achieved.
4. Don't consider template data models as turn-key solutions. Understand their strengths and weaknesses relative to the data objectives. They are another tool to be utilized to address specific objectives.
5. Look for a conservative return of 20:1 on the price of template data models.
6. Strive to simplify the data required by the organization at every opportunity to dramatically streamline IS systems with corresponding savings. It also renders the integration of systems easier and enables the staff to understand the workings of the company and contribute to a broad range of activities.
7. Use true experts to extend and develop the template data models. Assigning someone to CUSTOMER with little experience in that subject area will not yield improvements. Consider assigning a data modeler and an acknowledged expert to address the most critical areas of the project.

   Hire the best people available. Quality people produce quality results. Interview candidates in depth. They should demonstrate how they would tackle problems and present a clear picture of the ultimate results to be achieved. You are planning systems for your business. Make sure that the results will be acceptable to your business community.
8. Never assume that you can't do a good job yourself. If you have the time and resources, your staff are the best people to build your data models. Why? Commitment. You will live with the results. It is your company that you are changing for the future. No one else can possibly have that same level of commitment and ownership that is so critical to success.

9. Don't be afraid to succeed. Do not agonize over making decisions. Make good, solid decisions. If it is reasonable, well thought, and consistent with how you intend to do business, consider it done. Move on to the next challenge. Common sense is an underestimated business skill.

   If you make a mistake, fix it. It is only natural to learn new things as the project and your skills evolve. If you have made a serious error in defining PRODUCT, correct it now.

10. Enjoy the process. It is a fascinating, rare opportunity to look to the future and change the way a company operates. Enjoy the camaraderie that develops as you work with the best and brightest people in the company, and celebrate your accomplishments at every opportunity.

The Right Tools Make the Job Easier

While building data models is the central focus, the CASE tool that enables and support these activities is essential. CASE is used to build, modify, integrate, and maintain data models. Each CASE tool takes a different approach to business problems.

ADRM has been fortunate to have worked with Computer Systems Advisors (CSA), the Informix CASE tool provider and partner, for over 10 years. CSA CASE tools are well known for the following unique characteristics:

- Intuitive user interface;
- Ability to propagate changes between multiple levels of models and individual models, while controlling each parameter;
- Strong graphical support;
- Multilanguage support;
- Multiplatform support (PC, Macintosh®, and UNIX); and
- Outstanding design and leading theory turned into practice.

Summary

To benefit from good data technology, a business must make the commitment to make their data useful. Only then can they apply a broad spectrum of tools and technologies consistently across the business. Template data models provide a data platform for designing new data and integrating legacy data at an accelerated pace with reduced overall costs.

The 60 percent failure rate in the building of data warehouses is a function of planning, analysis, and design—and not due to the hardware or software selection process. Success can be attained when a company's best efforts are applied to this most likely point of failure. Template data models are one of the few tools that can be applied at once to produce immediate results at nominal costs. The cost to investigate template data models is usually a few hours of investigation. The results may change the way an organization accomplishes business far into the future.

About the Author

Larry Heinrich is president of Applied Data Resource Management, and has served as a data modeler and industry consultant for over 20 years. He can be contacted directly via phone at 415 383 3759.

About Allied Data Resource Management

Applied Data Resource Management (ADRM), an Informix Solutions partner, provides Enterprise, Data Warehouse, Business Area, DSS/Data Mart, and Dimensional data models for 18 industries to clients throughout the world. ADRM is located at 902 Vernal Avenue, Mill Valley, California, 94941. For more information, contact ADRM via phone at 415 451 7060, email at adrm@ix.netcom.com, or the Web at http://www.adrm.com.

Integrating Data to Populate the Data Warehouse

by Patricia Klauer and Vidette Poe

Introduction

Imagine yourself as the director of the marketing organization for a retail bank. You would like to have a better understanding of the relationships between the demographics of your customers and the kinds of financial products they tend to use. Such knowledge will help to focus advertising campaigns to the specific households that represent certain age groups and income levels that return a higher value per dollar spent in your advertising budget. You believe it would help to have a data warehouse to collect account information from systems throughout the bank that provide operational support for the various products and services offered by the bank. You also think that additional information from an external vendor who specializes in gathering demographic statistics can be used to categorize and sort the account information already available on customers. With this in mind, you explore the idea of building a data warehouse that will provide this information to your department.

Understanding the Business Purpose of the Data Warehouse

Business users usually know what information they want from a data warehouse. However, they may not always ascertain if the available data will actually provide the needed information. For example, the marketing group may want to compile all data collected by transaction systems that support teller activity, loans, credit cards, ATM, real estate, and investment accounts on a daily basis. The systems that collect this data were primarily, if not solely, designed to conduct a transaction specific to the operation of that particular business function. The information that the marketing department is interested in determining about a customer is likely to be very different from what is necessary to process a transaction and perform the proper accounting to manage a savings or checking account.

However, if that data (transaction amount, transaction type, account type, account number, transaction location, etc.) is collected and sorted according to geographical region, age group, or income level, suddenly it is no longer disparate bits of data but a profile of information that allows the marketing director to obtain a report, graph, or even a three-dimensional landscape representation of account activity for current customers within definable ranges or dimensions. This is an example of the metamorphosis from data to information.

Defining Data versus Information

Now we are in a position to differentiate between data and information. Often, we hear these words used interchangeably, but they are quite distinct in their meaning and this difference is why we build data warehouses. The term "data" implies a collection of discrete elements, such as a file. Data is collected and stored in a data structure that is designed for use by a computer system that supports a specific process. Operational systems process data to support the daily business activities of the organization.

When data is merged, aggregated, derived, sorted, structured, and displayed, it becomes "information." This is why we build data warehouses—to provide a staging area for collecting, integrating, and storing data, so that we can perform actions with the data, actions which enrich and enhance the value of the data and which literally transform the data into information (Figure 5-1).

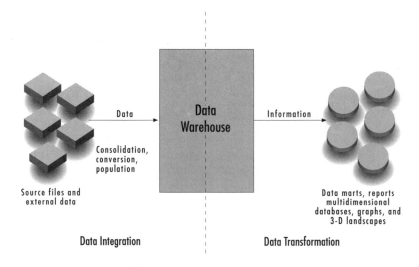

Figure 5-1 *Data integration versus data transformation.*

The Data Integration Process

Think of the data integration process as the "preprocessing" of data to standardize names and values, resolve discrepancies in the representation of the data, merge common values, resolve "equivalent" values of data from the disparate sources that represent approximately the same business facts, and establish various access paths by identifying primary, alternate, and nonunique keys. These benefits are the added values that the integrated data warehouse provides as a staging area for data ready to be transformed into information. The data integration process performs the work up front to ensure that the business user can compare "apples to apples" and not be tempted or forced to compare "apples" to "eggplant," or "apples" to "fruit."

The steps required to integrate data will be repeated whether they are to perform the initial development of the target data warehouse, add new sources to an existing target data warehouse, or to distribute data from the warehouse to business users, and whether they use query tools or import the data into other corporate systems. In fact, the data integration process is the "product" even more so than the data warehouse itself. In other words, the process is the deliverable.

It is impossible to integrate data without a "point of view." Data is created from the point of view of its usage in the source operational system. The data warehouse will have a point of view different from that of the source data since it is built for a specific business purpose that is not currently supported by other systems in the organization. The business objectives for building the data warehouse give it its point of view.

If the data warehouse is to support a particular business area within the organization, the point of view is simplified, and the integration process proceeds more quickly. We may have to maintain a neutral point of view, if the business purpose of the data warehouse is to provide integration for anyone in the organization who wants to collect data for any kind of business analysis. In this case, we are required to wear many hats and obtain as many points of view as possible about the source data to provide a flexible data structure that is powerful enough to serve the requests of a variety of business areas. However, this approach is far more difficult and prone to failure because of non-specific business objectives. In either case, we need to understand the point of view taken by the data warehouse and realize that a successful data warehouse implementation derives its point of view from the benefits the business sponsors expect to realize by building it.

Data Architecture

Data architecture is the underlying framework of the data warehouse. You must establish it early in the project and based on the business objectives, constraints, and priorities of the organization. The questions answered while determining the data architecture will drive the process for sourcing, integrating, storing, and accessing data from the data warehouse. The data model of the data warehouse will also be derived on the basis of the data architecture and the business user's access requirements. The data architecture and data modeling efforts will drive the physical database design of the data warehouse. Once the data warehouse architecture is defined, the data integration process—which consolidates and converts the content of the source data into the target data warehouse—can be performed over and over again as new sources are identified.

Data Architecture Tip

One of the most important things to remember when establishing the data architecture is that it must be designed to support change. Change is the only constant in the development and management of a data warehouse. Establish architecture, procedures, methods, and tools to manage change. During the design phase, it is difficult to project yourself into the future and imagine an environment as volatile as a production data warehouse, so it is important to obtain guidance from someone who is experienced in managing a production data warehouse at the project's beginning. Nothing in the repertoire of systems development can prepare you for the scale of volatility that is the norm in a successful production data warehouse environment.

Metadata

Metadata is data about data. Metadata is found in the documentation that describes source systems. For example, metadata describing the data element "transaction type" can include the following:

- name (tran-type);
- definition (the particular kind of transaction recorded, such as "deposit," "debit," "transfer," etc.);
- datatype and length (char(5));
- allowable values (01 = debit, 02=credit, 03=transfer); and
- key identifier (primary key or foreign key).

Metadata is used to analyze the source files that are selected to populate the target data warehouse. It is also produced at every point of the data's journey through the data integration process. Therefore, as an important by-product of the data integration process, it is essential for many people's work.

- Managers of a production data warehouse rely heavily on the collection and storage of metadata for an understanding of the content of the source, the necessary conversion steps, and how data is finally described in the data warehouse or target system;

- Business users who want to understand the data warehouse's content need metadata, in particular, the definitions and business rules that describe the calculations for derived data;
- Developers use metadata to help them develop the programs, queries, controls, and procedure to manage and manipulate the warehouse data;
- Managers need metadata to create reports and graphs in front-end data access tools, as well as in the management of enterprisewide data and report changes for the end user; and
- Change management relies on metadata to facilitate their admin-

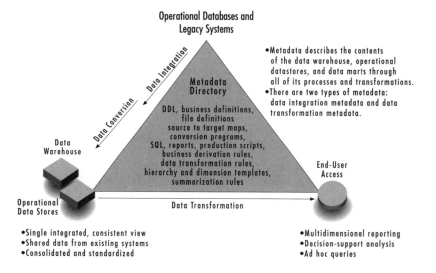

Figure 5-2 *Metadata.*

istration of all related objects that are impacted by a change request (e.g., data model, conversion programs, load jobs, DDL, etc.) in the warehouse.

Data Integration Phases

The data integration process can be used for any migration project where data from source files must be populated into a new integrated database. The data integration process consists of the following phases:

- **Data Sourcing** focuses on the meaning of the data by identifying the source files and fields that support the business objectives and requirements of the target system. The deliverable is the correct source files and fields that fulfill the business objective of the target system (data warehouse).

- **Data Consolidation** focuses on the data's structure by consolidating the sources into a single integrated target structure, whether it is the initial model or the addition of new sources into an existing model. The deliverable is an integrated data model or the physical database design.
- **Data Conversion** focuses on the content of the data by specifying how to alter the source data to fit into the integrated target data structure. The deliverable is the conversion specifications used by programmers to load the source data into the target database.
- **Data Population** represents the necessary steps to physically load the source data into the integrated target data structure. The deliverable is the conversion programs which are run to load source data into the target database.

Data Sourcing

The first step in data integration is making sure you have the "right" data. Understanding what the business user expects to gain from building the data warehouse is critical to determining if the data sources selected to populate the warehouse will render the expected benefits. Sourcing data is where the analysis process begins. A good warehouse data analyst must be part analyst, part modeler, and part sleuth. It is important not to take for granted that the identified sources will deliver the expected benefit. The analyst must perform some initial analysis (and sleuthing) to obtain a fundamental understanding of the source data. This study enables the analyst to determine if the data source is complete enough so that, when integrated, it provides the expected business value.

Often, you already know the internal systems from which you intend to source. You may have tried alternative methods to access data to produce the desired reports and have failed to achieve the anticipated results. You may not know if other sources are more appropriate to your objectives or if external data available from information services can augment what is collected by internal systems, thus extending the business value of desired data. It is essential to invest time up front to determine what data is available internally, what formats and platforms it is delivered on, and whether the data will contribute to the business value of the data warehouse.

A thorough inventory of the available sources allows you to prioritize and scope the initial load of the data warehouse and guarantees a better chance for success. Review the user interface being designed to access the data. Understand how the user wants to use the data. What is the specific business problem the user wants to solve? The cost and time it takes to analyze, integrate, convert, and populate a data warehouse can be considerable. Making sure that the initial population of the data warehouse renders business value depends on taking a thorough inventory of the available sources.

Data Consolidation Steps

Data consolidation is a data modeling activity. It is the process of analyzing and combining data from disparate sources or systems into a single, integrated data structure. You consolidate data by identifying data that is common across the various source files, investigating the business rules that govern the usage of data, and determining the new integrated data model that represents an accurate consolidation of the source data. Data is consolidated during the initial modeling of the data warehouse and each time that a new source is added.

Following are steps for performing the data consolidation process:

- Analyze source data documentation;
- Flatten out data into logical records;
- Perform domain analysis;
- Determine primary keys; and
- Determine foreign keys.

The deliverable is an integrated data model or physical data warehouse database design.

Analyze Source Data Documentation

Even though the source data documentation may be dubious, you must review and refer to it throughout the analysis process. It provides the first blush of knowledge about the source data. Assess the quality of the documentation by examining the contents for completeness, depth, accessibility, currency, and consistency.

- Completeness—Every field in the files is documented;
- Depth—Detailed information is available;
- Accessibility—Ease of access to documentation is maintained; (electronic versus hardcopy);
- Currency—Up-to-date information is available; and
- Consistency—Multiple references of the same fields, or synonyms, are consistently described.

Following are examples of metadata which, depending on the thoroughness of the documentation, represent the information that can be obtained from the source data:

- System overview description;
- File name and the description of its use or purpose; and
- Data element (or attribute), name, description, datatype, length, range of values, valid values (if the element has a finite domain of values, such as "State Code"), value definitions, position in the file (depending on the file format), null rule, default value (the value inserted when there is no specific data to populate the field), whether it is a primary key (or an alternate key, foreign key, nonunique key), and the control information necessary to understand the file formats.

Source Data Documentation Tip

Assessing the quality of the documentation is important not only for performing the data analysis process but also for estimating the time to analyze, integrate, and convert the source data. The analysis phase is classically the most time-consuming part of the entire project, and the guidelines for producing accurate estimates are important for project management in general, as well as for managing the expectations of business sponsors. The quality of the source documentation has a direct impact on project timelines and the productivity of the data analysts in this phase.

Flatten Out the Data Into Logical Records

After obtaining the documentation, one of the first things to determine is the file format of the data. Initially, the analysis process must focus on the format of the source data. For instance, the process to accomplish this—if the data is from an IMS database—is to link "segments." If the data is converted from an IDMS database, "walk the set" from parent to child records, and link the records into logical record types. Often, data is formatted into a file called a "flat file." This is sequential files that are padded with control characters, or fields, to include multiple logical records of information in one file. Flat files are a convenient way to store different logical file types together in the same physical file when space is at a premium.

A logical record is a grouping of related information which has a key or identifier. For example, customer information may have a customer identifier followed by name, address, age, employment history, credit history, rental history, etc., grouped in one file. Upon examination, it is possible to discover that a person has a name, age, and current address but may have held many jobs that can be identified by dates of employment. In this case, the main record can be the customer record, followed by a second record type that provides employer name, address, phone number, position, years employed, start date, etc.

Job history information can be stored in a second record type. Because a customer may have held many jobs, there are likely to be multiple job history records for each customer record. To associate the job history with the correct customer information, a control field indicates which job history records accompanied specific customer records. It is usually structured so that the different record types of related information follow each customer record. In addition, a control field indicates the new customer record and the next related record types, and so on for all customer records in the file. Once this information is flattened out, the flat file may end up representing as many as 20 logical files.

Data provided by external data providers for demographic or financial information, or data stored in an internal COBOL table using an "occurs clause," is often formatted in flat files. Referring to the documentation that comes with the external vendor data or reading the COBOL copybook and related system documentation is the only way to determine how the data is structured, and also requires understanding the way in which the file was constructed.

During this phase of analysis, commission a program that references the control data and allows you to separate out the source data correctly into separate files for accurate analysis. Failure to do this makes analysis impossible because each field in the sequential file has multiple, unrelated values associated with it. In other words, data is meaningless if it is solely dumped into another file or table, without file processing to separate the data out. This "flattening out" process converts the data into the first normal form—*every field represents only one business fact*. Note that you must perform this step to convert the data so that it can populate the warehouse, whether or not data-driven analysis is performed.

The control information, such as record type, provided by the data provider is used to understand how the data is formatted. Control information is data that is significant to the conversion process of the data but is not significant to the business content populated into the warehouse. Data analysts who are responsible for writing the conversion specifications for the data should take care not to inadvertently proliferate this system data into the warehouse.

Logical Record Tip

Although it may seem faster and more direct, taking a strictly metadata-driven approach to analysis engenders the risk of discovering unexpected "surprises" at load time, such as the discovery that the field that was supposed to be the primary key isn't unique or sometimes has a null value. Flatten the files early in the analysis process and perform the analysis on the logical groupings of information to understand the business rules embedded in the data. Once the source data is thoroughly understood, write the conversion specifications to populate the warehouse.

Perform Domain Analysis

After the data is processed into logical records, begin analyzing the data itself. The first area of analysis focuses on the content of each attribute in the source file. This aspect is referred to as domain analysis because, by definition, each attribute contains characteristic information that participates in a specific domain.

The domain of an attribute describes the content of the data and is defined by the datatype (character, alphanumeric, integer, etc.), the length of the attribute, the expected range of values associated with the attribute based on a minimum and maximum (if defined), the default value of the populated attribute (if no specific value is supplied for the field, such as a "blank," a "0," or a phrase such as "not known"). Some attributes have a finite set of allowed values, for example, "gender" has the two values "male" or "female." Another characteristic of an attribute which defines its domain is its associated "null" rule. The attribute may be defined as a mandatory field in the record, wherein the null rule will be "NOT NULL," meaning that it must have a value. Otherwise, the rule is "NULLS ALLOWED."

The analysis of each attribute's domain, compared to the metadata or to the documentation provided about the source data, reveals how "clean" the data is. As mentioned earlier, errors have most likely crept into the data, and it is difficult to discover the errors without a thorough analysis process. If discrepancies are discovered between the actual data and the metadata, the data analyst must inform the business sponsor and the data steward (the individual responsible for the accuracy of the source data). The discrepancies may be actual errors or undocumented features or changes in the source file. Such errors must be identified, documented, and taken into consideration during the data integration process to ensure data quality in the data warehouse.

The first step in domain analysis is to determine whether the domain information actually matches the documented information on the data. Even if there are no apparent errors, the meaning of the data can begin to "drift." Domain analysis of the actual data can potentially reveal additional values in the actual data that are not documented in an allowed value set. The usage may have changed to add values that were never documented, and it is critical to determine what they mean so they can be converted correctly in the warehouse.

It is also significant, although less critical, to discover if the documented values are not present at all in the data set. There could be many reasons for their absence. For instance, the sample of data may not be sufficient to cover all cases. For example, regional sales data—with a sample from only one region—will not have the values that represent the other regions. Another reason may be that the documented value is infrequently used because it depends on a business rule that applies only at specific times of the year or under special processing.

The datatype, length, and null value rules are other areas that are significant in understanding whether the differences are within the range of the documented information. If the actual data conflicts with the documented information, determine whether there was an undocumented change or whether the processing system where the data originated does not enforce these rules, allowing errors to creep in. Understanding the true nature of the data to be integrated and converted is essential to writing accurate conversion specifications to populate the data warehouse. For example, if a null rule is not enforced, then there is a risk that a key field may have a null value—which can fail in the load process.

Representative Data Tip

It is important to obtain a representative set of data for analysis. If the data is a small sample size, there may not be enough data to determine a true picture of the data characteristics. If the source data is a daily transaction file, the data may be different on the first or last day of the month, depending on the patterns of activity in the particular industry. Hence, there may not be representative quarter-end or year-end data unless you specifically request samples that reflect the data to be analyzed.

Determine the Primary Keys

Once you have performed domain analysis, consider each file's certain unique fields with distinct values as candidates for the primary key or identifier of the file information. In the domain analysis process, determine whether the documented primary key is, in fact, unique. If not, then determine if an error exists in the sample data or if an additional field must be concatenated with that primary key to make it unique—often a date field serves this purpose, and sometimes a record type or system-generated control field can establish uniqueness. Thus, the data analyst should carefully analyze the data for business content and logical identifiers, instead of proliferating system data into the warehouse because it was used by the source system to enforce uniqueness.

Candidate keys provide a way to uniquely identify a record. To convert data into a data warehouse, use a field that carries actual business-relevant information into the warehouse instead of using system-generated identifiers. System-generated identifiers proliferate in operational systems, especially OLTP systems, to promote speed of processing and data management, especially when users are heavily involved in update and insert activity. The architecture of the data warehouse is different from typical OLTP systems because it is primarily designed for the bulk loading and unloading of data and read-only access, which generally precludes the necessity for a system-generated key. Another reason to avoid system-generated keys is that often the access paths required for many data warehouse queries are supplied by simply hitting the index, since the key information is the only business content required. This approach speeds up rather than slows down a query because the database does not need to perform the second lookup for the actual data, as would be necessary if the key was generated by the system.

An exception to this occurs when the key is representative of a field that is identified as a synonym or analog to other identifiers of source files from different systems. Most likely the key is targeted for integration with these files in the warehouse and may need to be treated differently than a typical primary key. Even if these keys are clearly synonyms in a business context, because of the different formats from the different source systems, you should create a single system-generated warehouse key as an identifier to cross-reference all source file identifiers. This step may add an extra join or lookup but promotes the integration of data from multiple systems to provide a cross-organizational view of information.

When determining the primary keys, another significant analysis task is to look for additional logical groupings of data embedded in a logical record. These groupings are known as the *second normal form*. To return to the customer example, recognize that there are several attributes in the logical record devoted to describing address information. Customers can have many addresses associated with their file. You may have to break out address information into a separate record and identify a primary key that uniquely identifies the address as belonging to a particular customer, and, perhaps, you may have to create another field that describes the use of that address, such as "home," "mailing," or "office." Understanding the additional groupings of data embedded in a logical record is consequential to analyzing the source data and determining the target data warehouse model or writing the conversion specifications to populate an existing model.

If the target model has address information that is separate from the customer information, then the specifications must be very clear to transform the correct address from the source to the data warehouse's data structure. In the example presented in Table 5-1, the conversion specifications must be written so it is clear that, when loading the data from the source file, the appropriate source address is loaded into the target table with the corresponding address type.

The program must be written to read the "Home Address" and populate the Customer ID associated with it, then populate the "Address Type" with the value representing "home," before moving each field into the data warehouse table. The program then processes the source record for every address type populated—in this case, three times to populate home, mailing, and office address information.

Table 5-1 Converting source to target data structure.

Source Customer File	Data Warehouse Customer Address Table
Customer ID	Customer ID
Customer Name	Address Type
Customer Home Street Address	Street Address
Customer Home City	City
Customer Home State	State
Customer Home Country	Country
Customer Home Postal Code	Postal Code
Customer Mailing Street Address	
Customer Mailing City	
Customer Mailing State	
Customer Mailing Country	
Customer Mailing Postal Code	
Customer Office Street Address	
Customer Office City	
Customer Office State	
Customer Office Country	
Customer Office Postal Code	

Data Analyst Skill Set Tip

Experienced data analysts know how to identify groupings of attributes that are embedded in source files and how to model data so that it is clear and unambiguous in meaning, even if the analysts are not familiar with the particular business or industry modeled. They can perform a significant amount of analyses and discovery on source files—especially with the availability of the actual data to analyze—before requiring the assistance of a business knowledge expert. An experienced data analyst knows when to call in business users to answer questions and resolve discrepancies in the information discovered in the analysis process. It is extremely important to the success of the data warehouse project to recognize that a data analyst with experience in the data integration process is a must. This role is fundamental to the speed, accuracy, and integrity of the final product. It pays to invest in the tools, expertise, time, and training for the right personnel to perform the data integration process.

Identify Foreign Keys

After analysis of the individual fields for the domain information and determination of the logical records and primary keys, identify the interrelationships between logical files. Ideally, each attribute within a set of logical records from a single source is represented only once in the logical record with other attributes of like business meaning. For example, the "Customer Home State" is unlikely to be repeated in more than one logical record from a single source system, except if the attribute is a "foreign key." As mentioned earlier, one of the tasks in identifying overlapping data is determining if attributes in different records are synonyms—data elements that have common business meaning even though the names are different. The domain analysis performed on each attribute earlier in the process greatly assists in determining if there are synonyms between attributes in different files by presenting a subset of attributes which have overlapping domain values.

The process of discovering synonyms across files is critical to the integration process—it establishes connections between logical records. The example at the beginning of this section discussed a customer record that may have a separate set of job history following it. The Customer ID in the Customer record and the Customer ID in the Job History record can be synonyms, and associating them demonstrates the logical connection between the two records. The Customer ID in the Job History record is called a foreign key because it represents the same field as the Primary Key in the Customer record, and it is the way in which relational databases "point" to the related information. This process is called "referencing by value." The value for Customer ID in the Customer record matches the value for Customer ID in the Job History record; thus, it is clear that the job history attributes describe the customer who is identified by that Customer ID. The processing that accesses the data described in this matter is called a "join." You must identify the synonyms across files to correctly represent the related data so that you can design the data model accurately and write conversion specifications to populate the warehouse to reflect the logical relationships of the source data. Foreign keys are the most common synonyms found in the analysis process.

When you identify foreign keys, you must clearly understand the business meaning of the overlapping domain information. For example, the social security number in the Customer record is likely to refer to the customer's social security number. There may be another logical record from the same source system that provides a social security number that can be identified as a synonym, since it is an alternative way in which the source system identified the customer. This could be the case, and it is certainly a logical assumption; however, it may also represent a different business fact, such as the social security number of the customer's beneficiary or next of kin. This is an example of uncovering homonyms—two attributes with the same name which represent different business facts.

This phase of analysis is extremely critical because it is typically the point when overlapping data within a single source system is identified. The business rules implicit in the data relationships are uncovered through a thorough understanding of the true business meaning of the data. Data with the same name that means different things, or *homonyms*, such as our social security number example, and *analogs* (data elements that have equivalent values) are usually uncovered at this phase if they were not identified earlier. At this phase of the analysis process, the data analyst needs to draw assistance liberally from the business knowledge experts.

Synonyming Tip

After the analysis is complete for each source systems, repeat the synonyming process across all source files to be loaded into the data warehouse. This is the stage at which you finally identify the potential overlapping fields and the points of integration that have not been uncovered already. The involvement of the business knowledge experts is essential at this phase of the analysis process, when the business context and shades of meaning must be clearly understood. This final step in the analysis directly feeds the conversion process of mapping the source data into the target data warehouse model.

Data Analysis Needed for Data Consolidation

After identifying the data sources to be consolidated, you begin the analysis process to determine the business meaning of the data. By uncovering the underlying business rules inherent in the usage of data in the source systems, you can identify the overlapping data between the different source files. The usage of data in the operational system is what gives the data its business meaning. The data patterns that exist in the operating systems are the footprints of the business rules that govern its usage.

Understanding the business rules helps you to identify common subject areas; to correctly distinguish between synonyms, homonyms, and analogs; and to identify the primary and alternate keys existing in the data. The way you discover the meaning of the data depends on the structure and culture of the organization and on the tools and timeframe available to perform the analysis. Another factor that contributes to the data analysis approach centers on whether the data model for the warehouse has been built. If the data analysis process is expected to result in a data model to be used in building the data warehouse, the approach is different than if the analysis process focuses on fitting a source file into an existing data warehouse.

Identifying Overlapping Data: Subject Area Analysis

Subject areas represent collections of data elements and files that are related to each other and, by definition, to a certain topic or area of concern within the organization. The most common subject areas chosen for data integration are customer, account, transaction, event, product, organizational unit, person, and location. These subject areas are typically the underpinnings of a data warehouse, and most of the data captured and stored describes or supports these primary areas.

Determining the correct subject areas for a data warehouse is the art of identifying the overlapping areas of data within the source files which are selected to populate the data warehouse. Usually, there are specific attributes that often point to subject areas, such as Customer ID, Account ID, Org Code, Product ID, etc. During the data consolidation phase, the data modeler/analyst's job is to discover the set of overlapping data in the source files that constitute a subject area and to determine how to render an integrated yet meaningful data structure of different subject areas of data to support the business objective of the data warehouse.

Identifying Overlapping Data: Synonyms, Homonyms, and Analogs

Data consolidation involves an analysis of the interrelationships between the source files that have been selected to provide the source of data to the warehouse. The data modeler/analyst is challenged to identify the overlapping data from the various source files by determining the data elements with common business meaning—even though the names are different (synonyms). Note the following example of a synonym: in one file, a data element identifies that a product may be called "PROD-NUM," while in another file, the data element identifies a product called "Product-ID." The data elements represent the same business fact in each file.

Additionally, it is just as important to distinguish the data elements across different sources that may have the same name, but represent different business facts (homonyms). An example of a homonym is as follows: in one file is a data element called "PROD-CODE," and in another file the exact same name PROD-CODE occurs. However, careful analysis reveals that the meaning of PROD-CODE in the first file represents a unique numeric identifier for a specific product, whereas PROD-CODE in the second file represents a value that is not unique and that describes a type of product.

The real challenge is identifying the data elements in the sources that have equivalent values (analogs). Identifying and resolving the equivalent meanings between analogs for the purpose of integration does not imply that the data elements are incorrect in the context of their original operational systems. Be careful to distinguish this critical point from data scrubbing, which is performed when errors are discovered in the source data. Analogous data often appears to be a synonym but in the overlapping data elements has shades of different meanings that are significant to a business understanding of the data. If these differences and similarities are not identified and understood in the modeling and analysis process, the source data will not be integrated correctly. We cannot emphasize enough that this is where you should spend the lion's share of effort—understanding how to design the data warehouse to achieve data integration.

Following is an example of an analog: In one file, a data element called "product-type" describes the various groupings of products, such as "checking and savings," "homeowner loans," and "retirement fund management." Another file has a similar data element called "PROD-TYPE," which includes values such as "business checking," "small business loan," "secured credit card savings," etc. Upon first inspection, these data elements seem like synonyms. However, further analysis reveals that the first data element, "product-type," represents groupings of services, whereas the data element from the other source file, "PROD-TYPE," represents specific product offerings. The information represented by these two data elements carries some overlapping values, and the business meaning is related, but the data elements do not represent the exact same business fact and thus cannot be considered as synonyms. Finding, understanding, and consolidating these subtle differences in meaning is what renders analyzing analogs both critical and time consuming.

The failure to understand the importance of correctly identifying synonyms, homonyms, and especially analogs in the source files can result in one or two unfortunate scenarios. Failing to identify these overlapping data elements results in populating the data warehouse with disparate data that fails to provide true integration points across files, which in turn results in the propagation of the existing vertical view of the data, adding little additional value to the warehouse. If you fail to distinguish the differences between synonyms, homonyms, and analogs, you end up creating even more confusion by integrating data that is actually different, although similar in meaning, without resolving the differences in the conversion process. This second scenario is more detrimental because it results in a falsely cohesive view of the data that delivers the wrong information. Instead of adding value by building a data warehouse, what actually happens is the reverse. The data warehousing effort succeeds in rendering the source data less meaningful than in its original state.

An integrated data warehouse model is designed to support the common data elements of the source files. Those shared data elements are converted into a neutral format to derive "horizontal" business value by making data available to queries that cross organizational and system boundaries. The rest of the data is populated into the model at the level of depth and breadth necessary to support the queries that provide business users with the information required to make business decisions.

Analyzing Data to Integrate It into an Existing Data Warehouse

Understanding the source system data and the integration points between the source files selected to populate the warehouse is the objective of the analysis process—whether to model a warehouse for the first time or to populate data to an existing warehouse on an ongoing basis. However, once there is a "fixed target"—an existing data warehouse that is already populated with data—the challenge is to integrate new source files with the existing database design.

Data modelers and analysts must make exacting distinctions between the shades of meaning in data elements when analyzing data for integration into an existing warehouse. The requirements for adding the new source files may diverge from the original objective of the data warehouse, and the expectations to be gained from the addition of the new data may be a point of view that diverges from the initial design of the warehouse. If divergence is the case, you must manage the expectations of the business users who request new data—regardless of the usability of the data for their purposes. However, everyone benefits from attention paid to these distinctions, because the quality and veracity of the data and, ultimately, the usability and success of the data warehouse depend on it.

Data Analysis Tip

When developing the initial model of a data warehouse, keep in mind that whatever you implement is destined to change. If the first data warehouse implementation is successful, there will be requests for more data. The certainty of this cannot be overemphasized. Realize that the analysis and modeling which must be performed should be accomplished from the viewpoint of potential change. This phase is not the only time that source data will be analyzed and integrated; it will be endlessly analyzed and integrated. The first population of the warehouse will be the easiest in some ways because there is a finite set of source files which, hopefully, has been correctly assessed as the "right" data to support the identified business objectives to populate the warehouse. Every subsequent change in the data warehouse will require the analysis and modeling of data for consolidation purposes.

Understanding Business Rules and Nuances of Meaning

To better understand business rules and nuances of meaning, let's examine a familiar example found in the banking industry. The data warehouse has the original point of view: collecting all information about account activity or transactions across all departments in the bank. Then, the data warehouse analyzes the data for patterns and trends in the use of products and services. This is a product- or sales-driven point of view. Incidentally, this is probably the most common business objective for building data warehouses in all industries and market segments. Since this data warehouse successfully fulfilled the need to understand product and sales activity, the marketing organization wants to take the next step and populate the warehouse with customer information so that they can discover the product penetration specific to customer demographics, enabling them to target specific customer segments for new products and services.

This goal prompts the marketing organization to initiate a request to add new sources to the warehouse with customer information that integrates with the existing warehouse data that describes account, product, and transaction history. The marketing organization is actually requesting a new point of view of the data in the warehouse. Now, it is the job of the data analyst to understand if the source files identified for integration into the data warehouse can successfully provide the marketing organization with this new point of view.

Unfortunately for the marketing organization, the majority of banks and financial institutions do not have sufficient information to identify a customer specifically. Financial institutions are account driven, and an account may have many account names associated with it. The use of the account can vary, based on the needs of the person(s) who opened it or are named on it. In attempting to determine a true customer, the data analyst can sometimes decide that the business rule will be as follows: "The first name on the account will be considered to be the primary user of the account, and that person will be identified as the customer." However, there is no way to determine the identity of the primary user of the account, regardless of the ability to collect and analyze all account activity. This information is not available in the bank's account-driven source systems.

When data is populated into the warehouse, using the example business rule, there is a danger that the marketing organization can assume a false sense of confidence in the information gathered from the warehouse—unless the organization is clearly informed of the decision to use this business rule and understands the implications. Even if a different business rule, such as "every name on the account will be considered a customer," is adopted to gain a more accurate view of customer, there is still a false representation of information regarding account activity. Again, consider your own accounts as an example. There are many cases where someone is named on an account of yours or you are named on someone else's account and neither of you ever experiences any direct activity associated with that account, such as acting as trustees, guarantors, fiduciaries, etc.

If the marketing organization is aware of or, even better, selects the business rule to be used to populate the warehouse with customer data, the data analyst must be sure that the marketing people are aware of the differences between a customer and someone who is named on an account. This is a good example of an analog, or data which has equivalent meaning.

In another example, imagine the following situation: An automobile loan department institutes a business process that associates a customer identifier, separate from an account number, for every person who opens an account for a car loan. This process clearly identifies the customer as the person buying or making the payments on the car loan, as opposed to a person named on the account who was a guarantor or lien holder. When reviewing the data from the automobile loan department system and comparing the data to the customer information that comes from credit cards, demand deposit (checking and savings) accounts, and other departments in the banks, the analyst must understand how to integrate the Customer-ID with customer information from other areas.

Since there is an Account-ID in every source file which can be clearly identified as a synonym, Customer-ID cannot be associated with Account-ID. The analogous or equivalent data elements are Customer-ID and a combination of Account-ID, and accountholder-name or Account-ID and first-accountholder-name. The analogous data elements represent approximately the same business fact, but differences in the shades of meaning between the two are significant. A business decision must be made by the business sponsor who understands the differences in meaning between the analogous data elements, grasps the implications of integrating Customer-ID with the Account-ID and accountholder-name, and agrees to populate the data warehouse with these data elements integrated as Customer-ID.

The thoroughness of the analysis performed to integrate the data and document the decisions directly affects the evolution of the data warehouse. Failure to perform a thorough analysis eventually results in murky data, and the quality and usability of the data warehouse degrades with every new source file added. Conversely, if the analysis and integration of data is scrupulously performed and documented, the data warehouse evolves into a repository of valuable corporate information. The judicious care in integrating data and the various points of view that are invariably imposed on the data warehouse will provide a synergistic source of corporate knowledge and an invaluable tool for decision making.

Business Rule Tip

Data analysts must understand and accept the responsibility to clearly and unambiguously document business rules. Doing so helps business users understand how to correctly interpret the contents of their queries. These business rules are examples of metadata. It is equally important for the data analysts who integrate other source data into the warehouse to understand the business rules that prompted the initial decisions for the integration between the data elements that currently exist in the warehouse. Knowledge of business rules ensures that future decisions are based on a clear understanding of the data's meaning.

Data-Driver Analysis

Since we haven't been consistent in our proliferation of data structures to support operational systems over the years, it is necessary to take particular care in analyzing the business rules embedded in the data, which are the footprint of the processing that occurs. This, the delicate art of alchemy, is the hallmark of experienced data analysts. To rely solely on source system documentation, or *metadata*, is folly. Even if documentation was written when a system is first built, it is rarely kept up to date as changes are made.

Anyone who programs or supports production applications knows how often bug fixes are documented. When a system goes down in the middle of the night and the user is screaming because the batch job that records and resolves all account activity for the previous day is halted, any short cut taken to simply get it up and running again is justified. It is a rare occurrence that the bleary-eyed programmer who received a call in the wee hours is inspired, or expected and encouraged, to stay and document the exact actions taken and the changes enacted after the system has been corrected successfully. Even if the programmer(s) were conscientious enough to thoroughly document what occurred and the actions taken, it is likely that such information remained in a log somewhere and never found its way into the standard system documentation handed out upon request. This is why we emphasize the importance of maintaining metadata in the data warehouse environment. You cannot keep up with the requests for changes and additions to the data warehouse without accurate up-to-date metadata.

Given the reality of the operational emergencies that affect most systems, it is prudent to use the actual data, in addition to the documentation provided about the data, as a basis for analysis. This practice is called data-driven analysis. The biggest problem with data-driven analysis is that, without tools, it is difficult to perform a thorough job because there is so much data. How can all that data be analyzed to discover anomalies which contradict the documentation? Upon performing a thorough, systematic analysis of actual data, you begin to realize the quantity of metadata generated and can then use your analytical skills to take a different approach. At such time, you may request that the source systems' developers find time to provide detailed explanations. Otherwise, look to the system documentation and use the "cross your fingers" technique when it comes time to load the data warehouse.

We discuss the steps for analysis by using a data-driven approach—assuming we are in a perfect world and the necessary tools are available. We outline and describe how to perform the analysis to consolidate and convert data from source files into the target data warehouse data structure. Perform these steps, with a few additions or exceptions, if your objective is to analyze the data so that the initial data model can be designed for the data warehouse, or when making additions to an existing, populated warehouse.

Expect the analysis phase of the data integration process to be the longest—very few tools are available to assist data analysts in the formidable task of working through the data to uncover the undocumented business rules embedded in the source files. Additionally, very few people possess the skill set, expertise, patience, and sheer fortitude required to pursue subtle shades of meaning between attributes, understand the points of view implicit in the structure of the data, and communicate clearly the business implications of proliferating errors and assumptions into a new database environment.

Data-Driven Analysis Tip

The need to perform a thorough analysis and the dearth of adequate tools to aid in that effort leaves you in a difficult situation. The criticality of analyzing the data to correctly consolidate and convert it is essential to the success of the data warehouse. However, the tools available to perform this analysis accurately, even adequately, are almost nonexistent. One tool which supports data-driven analysis is DBStar's Migration Architect and Migration Control Client™. This powerful tool uses actual data to perform all the analysis tasks necessary to correctly model, consolidate, and convert data to populate the data warehouse.

Data Conversion

It is rare to find an organization that consistently represents the same business fact across all operational systems. Many companies have as many as 40 different customer files, product hierarchies, and organizational hierarchies within their organizations, depending on which department is interviewed or which system is sourced from. For these and other reasons, data must undergo a conversion process to fit into the target integrated data structure.

After you have designed the new, integrated data model, you must convert the source data to populate the new model. Now, data conversion must be performed for each data element that is to populate the new target data structures. Data analysts for each field of every source file that populates the warehouse perform the conversion. The data conversion instructions are the program specifications used to write the conversion programs that load the data into the data warehouse.

Producing conversion specifications involves mapping the source attributes, values, and default values to the data warehouse model. The instructions for mapping the fields from source files to the target data warehouse are based on the insight resulting from the analysis in the consolidation phase. At this point, the data analyst writes the conversion specifications, and programmers write the programs to process the source data and to load the data warehouse's database. If the analysis phase is performed thoroughly, this next phase can proceed quickly and smoothly. However, if the analysts and programmers are bogged down with numerous questions, clarifications, and rework on the conversion specifications and programs, the project manager must determine the reason for the delay—perhaps because of insufficient time or inexperienced data analysts—to obviate the problems in the future.

Data conversion focuses on the data's content by specifying how to alter the source data to fit into the integrated target data structure. The steps of the data conversion process include the following:

• Map the source file attributes to the data warehouse's physical data structure;
• Map the source attributes' allowable values to a target value;
• Specify default values; and
• Write conversion specifications.

Map Source File Attributes to the Data Warehouse's Physical Data Structure

After all source fields are analyzed and understood, they are mapped against the target data warehouse model. In some cases, mapping involves only a straightforward move from one field to another. Often, however, the mapping requires more complex processing to accurately convert the source data to fit into the warehouse structure, because of the significant difference in the data structures (refer to the example of customer addresses). The source-to-target maps represent newly created metadata about the information in the warehouse that describes the specific business rules implemented in the data warehouse. These maps are extremely valuable and must be maintained in a metadata repository for access by future analysts and developers—as well as business users of the warehouse—to understand the nature of the information as consolidated and converted from the source system or external file into the data warehouse.

Map Source Attributes' Allowable Values to Target Value

At the same time that the attributes are mapped to the target warehouse model, the attributes with a finite set of allowable values must be specifically identified so that the individual source file values can be correctly mapped to the target warehouse value. Usually, this identification process generates a cross-reference table that processes the data as it is loaded into the warehouse.

Specify Default Values

Part of the conversion specifications, in addition to the attribute and allowed value mappings, includes documenting the rules to handle default values. During the domain analysis step in the analysis phase, the default values for the source file data are uncovered. This information is used to explicitly specify how to handle blanks, zeros, or values not available or known as processed in the source files and to translate them to the equivalent default values, as defined and standardized for the data warehouse.

Conversion Specifications

Conversion specifications are the deliverable of the data conversion phase of the data integration process. The conversion specifications are the rules for populating the data warehouse tables and columns from the source data attributes. As a significant and persistent deliverable of the data integration process, there should be a review and sign-off by the key members of the data warehouse development team and the business sponsor. After sign-off and assignment to the programmers to write the programs, maintain the conversion specifications under a change management system.

Data Population

The following steps summarize the remaining steps of the data integration process which must be followed to physically load data into the data warehouse. These steps are universally well understood, since they are typically performed, regardless of whether the target system is a data warehouse or any system that requires data migration. Experienced developers are generally available to perform these tasks because the tasks represent standard activities that are performed daily in every data center. The only difference in the data warehouse environment is that these steps are performed repeatedly for change requests to add or modify sources that populate the data warehouse.

Data population represents the steps that must be performed to physically load the source data into the integrated target data structure. The deliverable is the conversion programs that load the source data into the target database. Following are the steps for data population:

- Write conversion programs;
- Conduct testing;
- Determine exception processing;
- Collect statistics;
- Conduct Q.A.; and
- Perform stress testing.

Write Conversion Programs

After the conversion specifications are signed off, developers write the programs (or generate programs based on tool usage) that load the target data warehouse. After the programs are completed, they must be signed off and put into change management under the same version number as the associated conversion specifications against which they were written.

Test the Conversion

After unit testing is completed, perform system testing by running the conversion programs that will load data into the data warehouse test environment. Make available the test plans and tools that review the data as it is populated and that determine if the business rules were written correctly. At this phase, expect to discover the typical errors and the exceptions to be wary of in the load process. The errors which occur may require that conversion specifications be rewritten or may reveal "dirty data" that requires feedback to the person in the operational system area who is responsible for maintaining the source file.

Determine Exception Processing

When, for any reason, a record cannot be processed, the contents of the record are written to an exception file with control information that describes the file the record came from and the associated reason for the exception, as well as a date and timestamp. Review this file as soon as possible and research the information to determine the reason for the failure to process. This effort can result in modifications in the conversion specification or the conversion program, or the failure can be the result of an error in constructing the file at the source. You must identify the reason, trace it, and resolve the issue to support the ongoing delivery of data into and from the data warehouse.

Analyze the potential reasons for exceptions and develop an exception strategy. This strategy could specify when, under certain exception conditions, to write out an error message to an exception log and continue loading. In some cases, the exception error may affect a field which prohibits the continuation of the load process, that is, if the field is used to perform a calculation, or if there is an attempt to load a null value in a primary key, which can require the program to abort the load and generate an exception report.

Collect Statistics

Generate log files to gather statistics regarding the load. For example, note how many records are processed and record start and end times.

Conduct Quality Assurance

Use the conversion specifications as a basis to determine the accuracy of the data that populates the data warehouse. Review the exception file and repeat the necessary steps in the data integration process as needed.

Perform Stress Test

Test the data load processing against the maximum volumes that are expected to simulate the performance requirements, and highlight any specific tuning that needs to be performed to refine the data load strategy. Determine the accurate processing estimates for the batch window. Write the scripts to automate and schedule job processing.

Summary

Data integration is the process of consolidating and converting data from disparate source systems, thus providing a consistent view of data throughout the organization. It is the cornerstone of any successful data warehouse implementation. Addressing the issues, problems, and challenges involved in the data integration process will substantially enhance and enrich the value of the content of the data warehouse.

About the Authors

Patricia Klauer, a co-founder of Manage Data, Inc., has developed strategies to support the use, distribution, and management of data for enterprisewide applications for the last ten years. She specializes in assisting large organizations in designing the infrastructure, architecture, organizational structure, and procedures to support Information Services specializing in enterprise management and strategic integration of data.

Patricia has designed integrated databases and data warehouses for a variety of strategic OLTP and DSS applications, including Risk Management, Market Analysis, Financial Instrument, and Client Relationship Management Systems.

Vidette Poe (warehs@aol.com) is a senior consultant with InER-G

Solutions, Ltd., and president of Strategic Business Solutions, Inc. Vidette's specialty is developing enterprisewide data architectures and strategies for decision support systems, hands-on management of project teams through data warehouse development and implementation, and setting up infrastructures to support data-focused, decision-support environments. She has experience in developing data warehouses, operational data stores, and related business strategies for the retail, financial, manufacturing, pharmaceutical, and agricultural industries.

Vidette is the author of the first edition of "Building a Data Warehouse for Decision Support," published by Prentice Hall in 1996. In September 1997, the second edition of the book, co-authored with Patricia Klauer and Stephen Brobst, became available. The new edition includes three new chapters and four data warehouse case studies.

About Manage Data, Inc.

Manage Data, Inc., provides software and strategic consulting for Internet and enterprisewide management, distribution, access, and the storage of data. For more information, please send email to pklauer@aol.com.

About InER-G Solutions, Ltd.

InER-G Solutions, Ltd. was founded in 1994 to provide business intelligence and decision-enabling solutions to assist clients in gaining competitive advantage through the leveraging of information assets. InER-G's focus and experience in data intelligence includes numerous high-profile and sucessful data warehouse planning, prototyping, and development projects.

The expertise and experience of InER-G Solutions' staff of highly recognized experts is captured in InER-G Cycle™, a proprietary data warehouse-centered methodology, which is driven through a knowledge-based tool called InER-G Cycle Tool (ICT). Additionally, InER-G publishes the *Inside Decisions Journal*, providing companies with business intelligence and related information. For more information, call 303 759 0217 or send email to warehs@aol.com.

Designing an OLAP Data Mart on Relational Databases

by Jonathan Kraft

Introduction

As markets become increasingly competitive, the ability to react quickly and decisively to market trends is more critical than ever. The volume and complexity of information available to corporations can be overwhelming. Companies that organize and analyze this barrage of data most effectively gain a tremendous competitive advantage. For this reason, data warehousing is emerging as a key component of corporate strategy.

Data warehousing is the process of integrating enterprisewide corporate data into a single repository from which end users can run reports and perform ad hoc data analysis. Since enormous quantities of information are available to companies, data warehouses often grow to be very large. As a result, one of the most significant challenges of implementing a data warehouse is ensuring high performance.

Classic Entity-Relationship Modeling and Decision Support

Decision support software (DSS) enables complex data analysis. Data models designed to support data warehouses require optimization strategies to handle the challenges of DSS.

One of the many reasons that traditional entity-relationship (ER) models fail in the context of decision support is poor performance. Standard, highly normalized data models are designed to provide extremely efficient data access for large numbers of transactions involving very few records. Decision support systems tend to have relatively few concurrent transactions—each accessing very large numbers of records. This is what differentiates on-line analytical processing (OLAP) or decision support systems from on-line transaction processing (OLTP) systems. Such a difference presents serious implications for the data warehouse designer. Table 6-1 shows the differences between decision support functions and OLTP functions.

Table 6-1: A comparison of the functionality of decision support and operational systems.

Items or Functions	Operational Systems	Decision Support Systems
Data content	Current values	Archival data, summarized data, and calculated data
Organization of data	Application-by-application	Subject areas across enterprise
Nature of data	Dynamic	Static until refreshed
Data structure format	Complex; suitable for operational computation	Simple; suitable for business analysis
Access probability	High	Moderate to low
Data update	Updated on a field-by-field basis	Accessed and manipulated; no direct update
Usage	Highly-structured, repetitive processing	Highly unstructured, analytical processing
Response time	Sub-second to 2-3 seconds	Seconds to minutes

Since data processing in OLTP systems is highly structured, complex data models work well. Transactions generally involve only one or two tables at a time and often deal with only a single record. This means that complex table relationships do not interfere with performance. In contrast, DSS processing can involve accessing hundreds of thousands of rows at a time. In such cases, complex joins can seriously compromise performance.

A second reason that typical entity-relationship models fail in the context of decision support is that they tend to be very complex and difficult to navigate; see Figure 6-1. In OLTP systems, this is never an

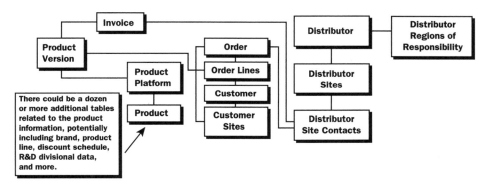

Figure 6-1 A sample ER diagram. The diagram represents a partial schema for storing transactional sales data. Actual ER models are significantly more complex.

issue. Usage and access paths in an OLTP environment are well known, and applications can be hardcoded to use particular data structures. In DSS, usage is unstructured; users often decide what data to analyze moments before it is requested. Users who must give more thought on how to access data—rather than on what data to view—often find decision support environments inadequate.

Proprietary Multidimensional Databases

Vendors of the proprietary "multidimensional" databases have emerged as a response to problems with classic ER modeling and DSS. "Dimensions" represent ways of looking at information. A multidimensional database is organized according to these dimensions. For example, an analyst might want to view sales data either by geography, time, or product—three typical dimensions used to organize data. Vendors of multi-dimensional databases argue that their software presents a view of corporate data that closely matches the way users intuitively think of their business. They contrast this view with the traditional RDBMS "rows and columns" view, which is decidedly more difficult to navigate. These vendors also claim that their mid-sized proprietary databases achieve better performance than that of traditional RDBMS software.

However, relational database designs do not need to be complex. It is possible to model data multidimensionally in an RDBMS, thereby providing an intuitive presentation of data for end users while continuing to leverage investments in open technology. Moreover, strategies based on this data model enable relational databases to outperform multidimensional databases—particularly on very large data warehouses. This database design paradigm is known as "dimensional modeling." The technical concepts behind dimensional modeling are discussed in this article, as are the strategies that leverage this paradigm to achieve high performance in the largest of data warehouses.

Dimensional Modeling

Dimensional modeling is a technique developed to structure data around natural business concepts and to provide a foundation for performing sophisticated data analysis. Traditional ER models describe "entities" and "relationships." This strategy focuses on breaking up information into a large number of tables—each describing exactly one entity. An entity might be a physical object (for example, a product or a customer) or a transaction (for example, a sale or an order's line item). Entities are interrelated through a complex series of joins.

In dimensional modeling, data structures are organized to describe "measures" and "dimensions." Measures are the numerical data that is tracked. Measures are stored in central "fact" tables. Dimensions are the natural business parameters that define each transaction. Dimensions are stored in satellite tables that join to the central fact table. Classic examples of data stored in fact tables include sales, inventory, magazine subscriptions, expenditures, and gross margins data. Classic dimension tables include time, geography, account, and product data. The focus in dimensional modeling is to organize information according to the way that analysts intuitively think about their business and to minimize the number of joins required to retrieve the information into meaningful, integrated reports.

Note the example of a marketing analyst who examines sales data via the following queries: "Sales by product line manager over the past six months," or "Sales by account for April, 1994." In such scenarios, the data model can consist of a fact table used to track sales information. Each sale can be associated with a record storing the quantity ordered, price, and extended price—among other variables. The satellite or dimension tables can include account, product, and time information—the natural dimensions of sales information.

In this scenario, every sales record can possess a key that joins it to each dimension table. Thus, the fact table can store the quantity ordered, sales, account code, time code, and product code; see Figure 6-2. Generally, fact tables are fully normalized, meaning that there is no duplicate data storage within the table.

Information in the dimension tables is used to specify subtotal break points in reports, as well as standard query constraints. A typical query might ask for "Sales by brand by month for all retail stores in the western region." In this case, sales are found in the fact table,

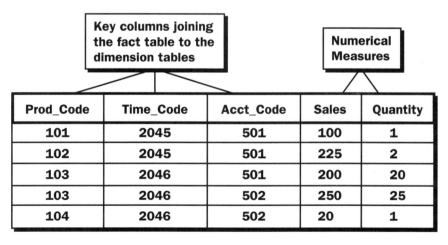

Figure 6-2 *Data from a sample fact table.*

which is joined to the product, time, and geography dimension tables. Product (brand) and time (month) are used as break points in the report, while geography (region) is used as a query constraint.

The dimension tables store all information associated with a particular dimension. Primarily, the tables provide for:

• Tracking the hierarchical relationships of each dimension; and
• Tracking the descriptive attributes of each dimension.

Dimensions are often organized into hierarchies. Each level of a hierarchy is said to "roll up" to the next. For example, within the time dimension, days roll up to weeks, which roll up to quarters. For the product dimension, products roll up to product lines, which roll up to brands.

Hierarchy is very important to dimensional modeling because it provides the framework for "drill down" and "drill up" functionality. Drilling down is the process of requesting a more detailed view of a data set. For example, a query might present sales by region. Upon viewing a spike in one region, a user might drill down to see the sales in that region by state. Drilling up is the opposite of drilling down; it involves a more summarized view of data.

Note that not all hierarchies roll up as neatly as those described here. For example, days roll up to weeks and months. Since months do not divide evenly into weeks, weeks cannot roll up to months, but both weeks and months roll up to quarters; see Figure 6-3. In many instances, hierarchies are significantly more complex than this. One of the challenges of hierarchical modeling is accounting for such structural complexity.

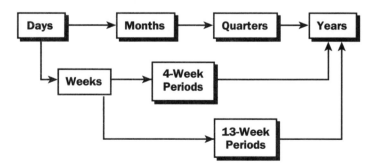

Figure 6-3 *Multiple time hierarchies. Dimension elements roll up in several different combinations, resulting in hierarchies that are substantially more complex than the structure pictured above.*

Dimension Elements

A "dimension element" is a special category of data that represents a particular level in the dimension hierarchy. There is one dimension element for each hierarchy level. Thus, for the product dimension, there might be three dimension elements: product, product line, and brand. In this model, the dimension element "product" represents the lowest hierarchical level in the product dimension, and "brand" represents the highest level.

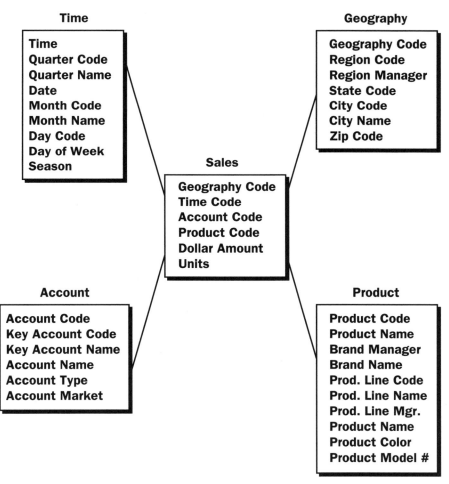

Figure 6-4 *A sample star schema. This schema is simplified; tables tend to have many more columns than what is shown in this example. The actual number of tables (five) is exactly the same as it would be in any four-dimensional information warehouse.*

Dimension Attributes

Dimension attributes describe particular dimension elements. For example, "brand manager" might be a dimension attribute that describes the dimension element "brand." "Flavor" might be a dimension attribute that describes the dimension element "product." Dimension attributes allow users to categorize nonhierarchical data.

The Star Schema

The physical architecture of the dimensional model is described by the star schema. As Figure 6-4 illustrates, the star schema can be represented as a fact table at the center of the star, with surrounding dimension tables at the star's points.

Denormalization of Dimensions

A defining characteristic of a star schema is that dimension tables are denormalized. Denormalization is a database design approach in which data is repetitively stored in individual tables for the sake of the design's simplicity and performance. Thus, a dimension table can store dimension attributes repetitively—depending on which level of the dimension hierarchy the attributes describe (compare Figures 6-5 and 6-6).

Product_Code	Product_Name	Product_Color	Brand_Code
101	Widget	Blue	XYZ
102	Gadget	Blue	XYZ
103	Snicket	Orange	ABC
104	Graplit	Orange	ABC

Brand_Code	Brand_Mgr
XYZ	J. Smith
ABC	T. Jones

Figure 6-5 A normalized representation of sample product data.

Product_Code	Product_Name	Product_Color	Brand_Code	Brand_Mgr
101	Widget	Blue	XYZ	J. Smith
102	Gadget	Blue	XYZ	J. Smith
103	Gadget	Green	XYZ	J. Smith
104	Snicket	Orange	ABC	T. Jones
105	Graplit	Orange	ABC	T.Jones

Figure 6-6 The same product data, denormalized.

For example, consider a company with 100 separate products, each rolling up to a total of five brands. For each product listed in the dimension table, its corresponding brand is also listed, as are all attributes of the brand. Brand manager information is stored for every record in the product dimension. The same holds true for brand name and all other brand attributes. In a normalized data model, brand attributes are ordinarily stored once in a brand table, and only the foreign key to that table is referenced repetitively.

Advantages of Star Schema in Dimensional Modeling

The simplicity of the star schema in dimensional modeling confers four important advantages:

1. It allows a complex, multidimensional data structure to be defined with a simple data model. This makes it easy to define hierarchical relationships within each dimension and simplifies the task of creating joins across multiple tables.
2. It reduces the number of physical joins that the query must process. This greatly improves performance.
3. Simplifying the view of the data model reduces the chances that users will inadvertently submit incorrect, long-running queries that consume significant resources and return inaccurate information.
4. It allows a data warehouse to expand and evolve with relatively low maintenance. The star schema's simple and powerful dimensional design provides a flexible foundation for a data warehouse's growth.

Aggregation

Aggregation is the process by which low-level data is summarized in advance and placed into intermediate tables that store the summarized or "aggregated" information. These aggregate tables allow applications to anticipate user queries, and the tables eliminate the need to repeat resource-intensive calculations that are otherwise performed each time the summary information is requested.

Aggregating the Multidimensional Data Warehouse

A typical data warehouse architecture begins as a massive store of transactions at the lowest, or "atomic" level. Measures are stored in the main fact table in their most detailed form, for use in the latter phases of data analysis and reporting.

However, extracting data from the most atomic level does not yield optimal performance—even with leading-edge software and hardware. Fact tables tend to be very large and present serious performance challenges. Accessing millions of rows takes a long time—no matter what software or hardware is used and no matter how well the data warehouse has been tuned.

A significant percentage of queries against the data warehouse call for the summarization, or aggregation, of data elements. A typical user might ask, "Show me the total of sales for this month." This request can be interpreted by the database as "Add up all the sales for each of the days that this month contains." If there is an average of 1,000 sales transactions per day in each of 1,000 stores and data is stored at the transactional level, this query must process 30,000,000 rows to return an answer. Obviously, a summary-intensive query like this consumes significant resources.

For commonly accessed data, presummarization is often useful. It enables the use of intermediate results or "aggregates," significantly reducing the resources required to deliver the final query results. To appreciate the value of aggregates, consider a request for sales in August. If an aggregate table exists to track monthly sales by store, the query must process only 1,000 rows (August's total for each store). Compare this number to the 30,000,000 rows that the same query must process with data stored at the transactional level. It is obvious that the resource savings are of several orders of magnitude. In fact, since query response time in a well-tuned warehouse is roughly proportional to the number of rows that the query must process, the improvement in performance can be close to a factor of 30,000.

How Much to Aggregate?

Most existing technologies offer database users a drastic choice: no aggregation at all or exhaustive aggregation for every possible combination of queries. Performing no aggregation is generally out of the question for substantive data warehouses. Aggregating in every possible combination achieves the best possible query performance—but with significant storage, maintenance, and load-time costs. First, storing summary information at every level consumes enormous amounts of disk space, increasing the storage requirements by a factor of five or more. Second, typical data warehouses

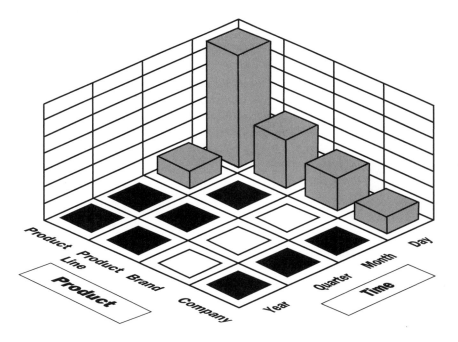

Highly Summarized Data

Figure 6-7 Selective aggregation. By creating a product-by-month aggregate, an intelligent data warehouse engine can deliver dramatically improved performance for all queries at higher levels of summarization.

contain thousands of combinations of dimension elements. Thus, creating a table, or tables, to hold the aggregates for all combinations is an overwhelming maintenance task. Finally, it is time consuming and resource-intensive to build aggregates each time that new information is added to the fact table. Often, the load window required to make the warehouse operational is unacceptably long.

It is best to use a query engine that uses aggregates intelligently. For example, consider a query that asks for sales summarized by year. Further, consider that sales are stored by transaction in the fact table, and by month in an aggregate table. The query should be issued against the monthly summary and should add up the 12 records for the 12 months that are stored in the aggregate—instead of adding up the thousands of transaction records from the fact table; see Figure 6-7. If the engine can make such a decision, it is unnecessary to create the "sales-by-year" aggregate—since summarizing 12 rows is trivial. Such intelligent query optimization is performed by Informix Dynamic Server with the MetaCube™ ROLAP Option, the engine that drives the family of decision-support software products.

With the option's query optimizer, the data warehouse architect has a choice of which aggregates to build since the optimizer automatically retrieves information through the best available route. Furthermore, the warehouse architect can change the way that data is aggregated—based on usage patterns, the addition of new applications, or changing informational needs. The architect can then add or delete aggregates, without changing a single line of code in the front ends that use the engine.

Choosing the Right Aggregates

There are two main considerations to keep in mind when determining what aggregates to create:

- Data density: Where is the data concentrated, and in which dimension elements do the number of rows steeply increase?
- Usage patterns: Which aggregates most improve the performance for end users' most frequent queries?

If a given dimension element represents a large number of rows as compared to other elements in the hierarchy, aggregating by that dimension element drastically improves performance. Conversely, if a dimension element contains few rows or if it contains hardly more rows than the superseding dimension element, aggregating by that dimension element is less efficient.

This analysis becomes more meaningful—and more complicated—as dimensions combine with one another. Defining a data request by multiple dimensions not only decreases the range of data retrieved but also the density. It is rare, for example, that every product sells in every store, every day. For many products, there may in fact be few sales records for any given day, and thus, the daily product sales data will be sparse. However, if all or many products sell in every store, every day, the data is classified as relatively dense. Data density complicates the calculation of how many records a query engine must process. A sizing simulation based on the facile assumption that every possible record exists—in other words, the data is perfectly dense—skews the performance analysis of each aggregate.

When determining, for example, whether to compile an aggregate summarizing product line sales by region, the number of different products sold in each store within the regions is crucial. Consider a simplified database containing four stores in each of two regions (a total of eight stores), with those stores selling four products in each of two product lines (a total of eight products).

If only one of the products in a product line sells in each region on a daily basis—sparse data—the number of products in the product line for that day effectively shrinks to one. For the query, "Daily product line sales by region," one product row is retrieved for each product line (two) in each region (two), for a total of four rows. Similarly, if products are aggregated into a sales-by-product line aggregate and the same query is posed, the same number of rows are processed: four. In this instance, the aggregate offers no performance advantage whatsoever.

If, at the other extreme, dense data—every product in every product line sells in every store, every day—this query must process four products for each of two product lines and for each of the four stores in both regions, for a total of 64 records. But an aggregate summarizing product line sales by region can process this query using only four records—reducing the number of records processed by 16-fold. In a typical database representing thousands of stores and products, the performance advantage is substantial. An analysis identifying optimal aggregates favors a product line aggregate in this instance.

Informix has developed software to perform this analysis. While the analytic process is sophisticated, the methodology that Informix uses to approach this problem is straightforward. The question that must be answered at each step is "Which aggregate will reduce the average number of rows that a query in this data warehouse must process?" The algorithm recursively calculates this answer and stores it, along with the supporting evidence in the database.

Informix tools audit user queries—collecting information on which data is requested most often, who requests it, how long the query takes to process, how many rows are retrieved, and other criteria. This information is used to further tune the data warehouse.

Sample Aggregation Sizing

To determine the optimal number of aggregates to create in any given data warehouse, it is possible to conduct a "sizing simulation." The main factors to consider are the total amount of space occupied by the aggregates (cost of disk) and the total number of aggregate tables (cost of load window and maintenance). This section describes an actual simulation that Informix conducted for a sample data warehouse.

Simulation Procedures

The following steps are performed during the sizing simulation:

1. A database is loaded with a representative sample of data. This sample fact table contains enough low-level data to produce statistically significant test results.
2. A series of SQL statements that query every possible combination of dimension elements is generated and saved on the server for execution by a background process.
3. The SQL statements are executed, and information about the number of rows returned from each statement—as well as the time to execute each statement—is recorded in the database.
4. The resulting "aggregate cost matrix" is extracted from the database and fed into Informix's software, which implements the optimization algorithm. The software lists the top 100 aggregates and uses them for sizing and performance analysis.

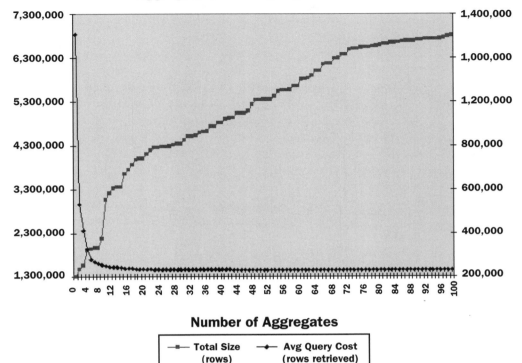

Figure 6-8 *Aggregate size versus query performance.*

Simulation Results

After application of the optimization algorithm to the sample database, the best aggregates can be selected from the overall pool. Figure 6-8 illustrates the effect of additional aggregates on the following criteria:

- Average query cost; and
- The total number of rows dedicated to aggregates—roughly correlated to aggregate storage requirements.

In Figure 6-8, the horizontal axis represents the number of aggregates created (best aggregates are added first), increasing from 0 (fact table only) to 100. The left vertical axis represents the total number of rows stored in the database. The scale starts at 1.3 million —the size of the fact table in this sample. The right vertical axis represents the computed average query cost (in rows processed), using the algorithm described in this article.

The improvement in the average query cost for this example is exponential and quite dramatic. After seven to eight aggregates, additional aggregates do little to improve the average query cost, while adding significantly to storage, maintenance worries, and load time. On the basis of the information in this chart, Informix recommends the creation of only seven aggregates to prepare this sample data warehouse for random, ad hoc access.

Clearly, the information in Figure 6-8 is incomplete, mainly because of the assumption that the usage of the data warehouse is random. The final step of the aggregation analysis is to incorporate information about which queries are most frequently run by end users.

Incremental versus Full Aggregation

As mentioned earlier, one disadvantage associated with the aggregation process is the time window required to build the aggregates. For end users with very large databases and significant aggregation requirements, a tremendous amount of time and computer resources is required to build all necessary aggregates. Each week, as more information comes into the data warehouse, the aggregates are outdated and must be recalculated. One option is to simply recalculate the aggregates from scratch by performing the summary operation on the base fact table. However, in situations where the aggregation time window is a serious problem, this is an impractical solution. To address this issue, Informix has developed MetaCube Aggregator™. A program that updates existing aggregates based on incoming atomic data, MetaCube Aggregator can be used to help avoid unnecessary resource utilization; see Figure 6-9.

Extending Dimensional Modeling

There are situations in which the simplest implementation of dimensional modeling—the star schema—is not ideal. There are two possible reasons for this:

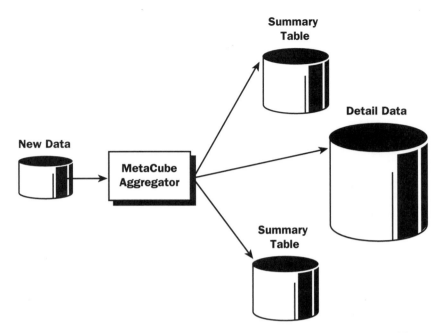

Figure 6-9 Incremental aggregation. The MetaCube Aggregator adds new data to existing aggregates. By dealing with much smaller quantities of data, incremental aggregation reduces the load window by many order of magnitude smaller than reaggregation.

- Denormalized schema may require too much disk storage; and
- Very large dimension tables can adversely affect performance, partially offsetting the benefits gained through aggregation.

Normalizing the Dimensions

Denormalization is an effective method to simplify data design and improve performance through the reduction of table joins. However, there are instances where the disk storage costs may be too high.

For example, consider a product dimension in which there are 100,000 products rolling up to fifteen product lines and five brands. In a star schema, the corresponding dimension table could have 100,000 rows, and each row could store all of the relevant information for each level of the hierarchy above or equal to its own level (brand manager 100,000 times, product line category 100,000 times, etc.). Refer to Figure 6-10.

Prod_Code	Prod_Name	Prod_Color	P_Line_Code	P_Line	Brand_Code	Brand_Mgr
101	Widget	Blue	805	Widget	XYZ	J. Smith
102	Widget	Red	805	Widget	XYZ	J. Smith
103	Gadget	Blue	890	Gadget	XYZ	J. Smith
104	Gadget	Green	890	Gadget	XYZ	J. Smith
105	Snicket	Orange	770	Misc Prod	ABC	T. Jones
106	Plunket	Orange	770	Misc Prod	ABC	T. Jones
107	Graplit	Orange	770	Misc Prod	ABC	T. Jones

Prod_Code	Time_Code	Acct_Code	Sales	Quantity
101	151	507	$100.00	2
102	151	507	$100.00	2

Figure 6-10 *Sample star join for product dimension.*

In some cases, the number of attributes stored for each dimension element can be substantial. In the case of the above product dimension, every kilobyte of attribute data elements consumes 100 megabytes of disk space.

Normalizing the dimension table avoids this additional disk storage requirement. In a normalized model, the primary dimension table could have 100,000 rows, but might have only three columns: product_id, product_line_id, and brand_id. In this case, the dimension could contain three additional tables: one for brand attributes, another for product line attributes, and one for product attributes. The brand table could store the brand_id, brand manager, and all other brand attributes. The product line table could store product_line_id, product line category, and all other product line attributes. In a dimension table of 500,000 rows, saving just two megabytes per row through the normalization of the star saves a full gigabyte of disk space; refer to Figure 6-11.

The Snowflake Schema

Normalized dimension tables turn star schemas into "snowflake schemas," so named for their added structural complexity.

To understand how snowflake joins improve performance, consider the following scenario. In the sample database, assume that aggregates exist for sales by product line and brand. Assume also that the fact table contains roughly 10-million rows.

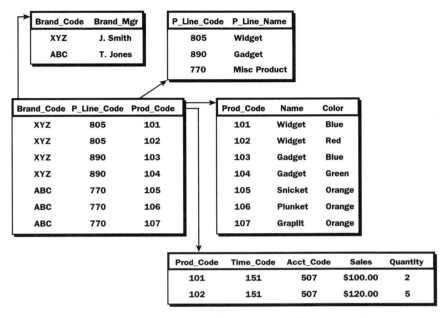

Figure 6-11 *A sample of a normalized product dimension. As the number of products increases to 100,000, the brand and product line tables barely grow in size. Where many attributes are tracked, the disk savings can be substantial.*

Now, consider a query that returns sales by product line manager. In the case of either a star or snowflake, the query retrieves the sales information from the product line aggregate table. However, in the case of a star, the 100,000-row product dimension table must be joined to the star to retrieve the product line manager information. In the case of a snowflake, the product line attribute table is separated out from the entire 100,000-row product table. The query can thus obtain the product line manager information needed from the product line aggregate table and the 15-row product line attribute table—a substantial performance advantage; refer to Figure 6-12.

To summarize the snowflake architecture, each dimension table stores one key for each level of the dimension's hierarchy (that is, for each dimension element). The lowest level key joins the dimension table both to the central fact table and to the attribute table that contains the descriptive information about the lowest level's dimension element. The rest of the keys join the dimension table to the corresponding attribute tables; refer to Figure 6-13 (page 118).

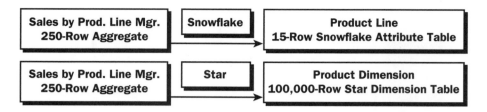

Figure 6-12 Star versus snowflake processing: sales by product line manager. The snowflake join depicted at the top is orders of magnitude faster than the star join depicted at the bottom.

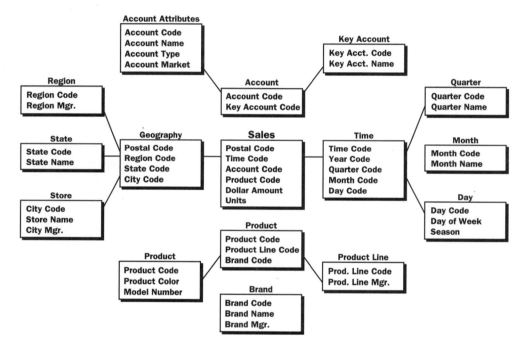

Figure 6-13 An example of a snowflake data structure.

Disadvantage of Normalization

The main disadvantage of snowflake versus star processing is the relative complexity of the normalized snowflake data structure. When MetaCube products—or custom applications built using MetaCube's OLE object interface—are being used, the structure's complexity is not as critical because MetaCube can interpret snowflake structures as easily as it interprets star structures. However, if users generate queries by using typical database ad hoc query tools, it is more difficult for them to navigate through the snowflake. In addition, load programs and overall maintenance become increasingly difficult to manage as the data model becomes more complex.

Partial Normalization

The performance gains and disk storage savings provided by snowflake designs are often worth the price of marginally higher complexity. However, as shown earlier, the value of a snowflake join is greatest for dimensions in which:

- There are many rows—in the tens or hundreds of thousands; and
- There are many attributes stored at low levels of the dimension hierarchy, and disk space is a significant problem.

Thus, the best solution is often to normalize one or two dimensions and leave the rest of the dimensions in a simple star format. This design is referred to as a partial snowflake.

Conclusion

Traditional entity-relationship data models function effectively in the OLTP world, driving most of today's operational, RDBMS-based applications. Due to the success of these data models, the first graphical DSS and EIS systems were implemented using similar designs. As these DSS databases grow larger and more complicated, performance degrades and systems become more difficult to use and maintain.

Dimensional modeling—the database design approach discussed in this article—improves DSS performance by several orders of magnitude. By presenting information in a format that parallels the multidimensional business environment, dimensional modeling offers an easy-to-navigate data model that is also intuitive. Moreover, the structural simplicity of dimensional modeling facilitates application maintenance and provides the flexibility to expand the data warehouse. Finally, this approach to data warehousing leverages investments in open, relational technology.

About the Author

Jonathan Kraft is director of Business Development, Data Warehousing Business Unit, at Informix Software, Inc., Oakland, California.

A Data Mining Tutorial

by Alice Landy

Introduction

Since the dawn of the computer age, corporations have been accumulating enormous amounts of data about customers, transactions, inventory, finances, and operations. With technology for gathering and storing data steadily increasing in availability and sophistication, corporations collect massive amounts of data at accelerated rates and in ever-increasing detail. Until recently, most of this data was stored on tape and in storage vaults and thus was not easily accessible to users throughout the organization.

Today, corporations are beginning to realize that their huge warehouses of data contain untapped knowledge that can give them a competitive edge. They are eager for tools to help them comb through data for patterns and relationships that predict customers' buying habits, identify clients likely to default on loans, anticipate unusual demands on inventory, or find perpetrators of fraud. Businesses use this information to develop marketing strategies, target mailings, adjust inventories, minimize risk, and eliminate wasteful spending, in short, to increase return on investment.

Scalable Data Mining and Knowledge Discovery

The process of digging through large databases to extract information is called *data mining*. Data mining software analyzes huge databases to discover new patterns, extract hidden information, and predict future trends. It finds subtle relationships and shifts among billions of pieces of data, then uses this information to generate predictions that answer such questions as:

- Can we cut our direct mailing budget in half by limiting our next mailing to just the right customers?
- For which patients is this new medical test most likely to be cost effective?
- Which products will be the biggest sellers in our Louisville store next November, and why?
- Which clients are likely to switch to new credit cards next month, and why?
- Which insurance claims in our database are likely to be fraudulent, and which policy holders are likely to perpetrate fraud?

With advanced data mining techniques, decision makers can obtain the knowledge they need to create business strategies, compare scenarios, evaluate risk, and set policy.

Scalability in Data Mining

The term *scalable* refers to a tool's ability to take full advantage of multiple processors. A scalable tool can run 16 times as fast on 16 processors as it can on one. In practical terms, scalability also demands the ability to handle large data sets during computation and to work directly with existing databases.

Parallel Processing

In parallel processing, the workload of a program (that is, its data) is divided among multiple processors, with the processors carrying out each stage of the job in parallel. The data may be held in shared memory or in the local memory of each processor. If each processor has its own memory, then each typically carries out computations on its own portion of the data—sharing results with the other processors as needed. This technique provides obvious advantages when working with gigabyte-sized data sets. If one "fully loaded" processor can handle X records in Y seconds, then N processors should be able to handle NX records in Y+Z seconds. Z represents the additional cost of communication among the processors —a sort of "shipping and handling" charge. When data sets are large enough to derive significant benefit from parallel processing, the communication cost is very small in comparison to the processing time saved.

For true scalability, the number of processors should be flexible. Today's users expect their data mining software to shape itself to their site's demands on computing power. Users want to prototype a data mining application on one processor and perform production runs on multiple processors. They want to run an application on two or four processors during the day when the system is heavily loaded, and run large jobs on larger numbers of processors during nonpeak hours—at night or on the weekend. Similarly, volumes of data collected over different time periods may vary, and thus, different numbers of processors might be most efficient for each.

Out of Core Processing

Traditional data analysis tools use only as much data as can fit in main memory (in core) at one time. Such tools are much easier to code than those which handle data from disk. Even with today's larger-memory systems, however, some data sets are too large to fit into memory. To handle these data sets efficiently, a data mining tool must make good use of core processing techniques.

Working with Databases

Traditionally, data analysis and data mining tools require that data is presented in the form of flat files, usually with fixed-length records. For companies that work with large databases, creating these files on disk is a burden, both in man-hours and in disk space. Today, there is a demand for data mining tools that work directly with existing databases. Users who work inside the data mining application must be able to connect to a database (perhaps through the medium of some connectivity package) and use SQL queries to construct a table that holds the desired data—organized as they need it; and subsequently, the data must be fed from that table directly into their learning and analysis tools as their data set. Eventually, the data set thus formed may be physically copied to a flat file for future use—often a wise precaution if the database itself is subject to change—or it may be "saved" only as a series of instructions within the data mining application, from which it can be re-created at some future time.

Using All the Data

Traditional statistical methods of data analysis bog down when the database size approaches the gigabyte range. Until recently, corporations circumvented this problem by attempting to guess which small subset of information in a database was most relevant to the problem at hand, analyzing only that portion of the data, and discarding the rest. In practice, this often means discarding the vast majority of data. But discarded variables often contain key information: correlations that aren't obvious, unexpected patterns, or unusual fluctuations which are normally overshadowed by larger trends.

The speed of modern data mining techniques when linked with parallel processing techniques fundamentally changes the way users solve problems. Now, in many cases, businesses obtain answers based on large amounts of data in a few minutes or hours—instead of waiting until days later, when there is a risk that the questions become obsolete.

Knowledge Discovery and Deployment

In the past, most corporations employed one expert who performed data mining on individual research projects. Today's best data mining systems, on the other hand, meet the needs of larger corporations by offering two approaches: knowledge discovery and deployment.

Knowledge discovery presents a centralized model in which one group of people perform all data mining operations in a single "flow." They prepare data, build and evaluate models, and apply the gathered knowledge.

Knowledge deployment presents a decentralized model. Typically, several groups are involved. For instance, data preparation may occur at a data warehousing facility that is functionally distinct and geographically distant from other groups. From this location, data sets may be sent to headquarters, where analysts create, evaluate, and refine models. Because sophisticated data mining models are complete, discrete items, the analysts can then send completed models to any number of field offices. Then, these models can be applied to new data in specialized applications.

Note that the end users of the specialized applications do not need expertise in data mining; they simply need to know how to use the finished applications, which are often simple and easy to use.

Using Data Mining Software

For all its usefulness, data mining has not yet advanced to the level at which the user simply points the tool at a database, says "Increase my profits by 200 percent," and receives instantaneous and useful instructions. User participation—often in the form of careful and focused thinking—is still required.

Figure 7-1 depicts the steps involved in using data mining software. Please note, however, that this is an iterative process. Predictions gained from data mining lead to the implementation of decisions. This, in turn, generates new data—which leads to a new round of data mining (starting back at the top of the figure).

Define the Business Problem

Most corporations begin by identifying a business question in the form that will directly produce an answer. For example, note the following questions:

- How much of items X, Y, and Z should be ordered for next quarter's stock?
- What is the best way to identify which potential credit card customers will be good credit risks?
- How can losses due to equipment failure be reduced?
- How can the next product introduction be targeted?

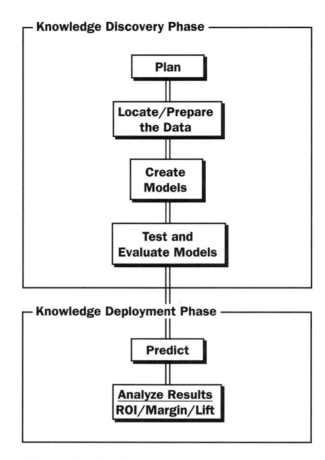

Figure 7-1 *The data mining process.*

At the same time, the corporations define the conditions under which the problem should be solved. Ensuring clarity at this first step helps to set the direction for the selection and preparation of data, the design of the analysis, and judging the quality and utility of results. As a starting point, consider the following questions:

1. What business problem is to be solved?
2. What in-house data can be used to find the solution?
3. When is the solution needed?
4. What resources can be used?
5. What costs (actual costs of lost profits) are incurred by not solving the problem?

6. What is the minimum level of improvement needed from the analysis?
7. What costs can be incurred as a result of incorrect analysis? In particular:

   - How much cost will each false positive incur?
   - How much cost will each false negative incur?

Costs and Benefits

Potential costs and benefits influence business decisions. The key questions in deciding whether to perform a data mining project are:

- What is the return on investment (ROI) for the minimum level of accuracy which is acceptable?
- How will the ROI change with greater accuracy? For every percentage increase in accuracy, what is the return?

More precisely phrased considerations can be factored into prediction models, as well. For this purpose, the basic cost considerations are as follows:

- How much benefit will be gained from a correct positive prediction? For example, how much revenue is likely to be gained as a result of sending a direct-mail piece to someone who responds to it?
- How much loss will an incorrect positive prediction (a *false positive*) incur? For example, how much does it cost to send a mailing to someone who does not respond?
- How much benefit will be gained from a correct negative prediction? For example, how much is saved by not sending mail to someone who will not respond to it?
- How much cost will an incorrect negative prediction (a *false negative*) incur? For example, what potential revenue is lost by not sending the mailing to someone who would respond?

Each data mining tool has its own method to allow for the specification of how (and whether) costs should be factored into the classification process.

The Time/Perfection Tradeoff

Data mining is usually an iterative procedure: Try something, look at the results, see something that might make an improvement, try a somewhat different model, and so on. Or, make several models and test them against each other, and learn how to improve the models in the process.

Users provide parameters for this process by identifying practical constraints and expectations. Performing this analysis before the start of the modeling process helps to identify any necessary trade-offs between getting results "today" and getting the "best possible results."

Locate the Data

After identifying what business question must be answered, locate the data that is potentially relevant to the question. Examples include the following:

- A company's billing records for the last three fiscal years;
- Credit records for a group of people—from initiation of the records to the current date; and
- Data on equipment failures for the last year for a company, plant, or department.

The *historical* data that is mined for information helps to provide focus on the decisions governing current and future actions. This is the data that *trains* the learning tools, providing the information to build models which will be used later to answer business questions.

Organize the Data

Data mining tools view data exclusively in terms of records and fields. Each question posed to a data mining tool must have an answer that can be contained in a single field. This field is known as the *target field* (or the *response field*), and the expected answer(s) are known as *target values* (or *response values*). The target field is also sometimes referred to as the *dependent variable*, since the value predicted for it depends on the values of the other fields—the *independent variables*.

Dimensions

In addition to fields, users frequently see *dimensions* in their data records. A dimension represents a single type—or area—of information, as it relates to a given study. It may contain one field or a group of fields. For instance, the dimension *weather* might include fields for temperature, precipitation, and wind. Moreover, the fields within a dimension may change from one study to another. For instance, depending on the study, the dimension *location* might refer to a town, a zip code, a service district, a store, or a hospital.

When planning a particular data mining study, therefore, start by setting out the dimensions to be included, and then examine the data to determine what fields must be included for each dimension. It may be that one set of records contains all the fields needed, in the desired form; or, it may be necessary to prepare data by making changes to the data's format. For instance, it may be necessary to combine fields from several sets of records in order to create the record format needed for a study.

Prepare the Data

Having established a basic sense of a business problem and the sort of data which is anticipated, decide how to use existing data to solve it. Properly organized data is important to achieve good data mining results. Preparing data may include cleaning, as well as organization. Figure 7-2 describes the questions that can be answered at this stage.

Cleaning Data

Three major issues in cleaning data are noise (or incorrect values), missing values, and the improper use of delimiters.

Noise in the data is frequently the result of typographic errors. In numeric data, it may appear as out-of-range values: numbers that are either too large or too small. In categorical data, noise in data may appear as a unique or meaningless value. Values that are obviously incorrect should be corrected, if possible, or if that correction is not possible, such values must be nulled out.

Missing values should be replaced by a set value that does not appear elsewhere in that field. For instance, given a field that con-

General Questions:
1. How much data do I have?
2. What period does it cover?
3. How clean is the data?
   - Do I trust its accuracy?
   - Are there likely to be missing values?

Setting Out the Problem:
4. How much of the data do I want to use?
5. Do I want to create a data set for this one problem only, or do I want a more general data set that can be used for other problems as well?
6. What data dimensions do I need to analyze my problem?
   What is the correct granularity for each?

Specific Questions:
7. In what form is the data currently held?
8. What is the current record format?
9. Can I use the data as is, or should I reorganize it in some manner for this particular analysis?
10. What fields should the records contain?
11. What will be the target field?

Figure 7-2 Questions regarding data.

tains values from 0 to 1000, do not use 0 to indicate a missing value. While this rule may seem obvious, it is a surprisingly common error and can create wildly inaccurate predictions.

Delimiters can also cause problems. For example, if a text file contains commas within any of its fields, it must not also use commas for delimiters, and vice versa. If commas are delimiters in a text file, then one comma in an address field is interpreted as the end of that field; thus, all entries thereafter are read into the wrong field. This example concludes with a record that contains more fields than it should. When choosing delimiter characters for a data set, choose a character that will never appear in the data. Try exclamation points (!), vertical lines (|), curly braces ({ }), or whatever is safest.

Organizing Data

There are many occasions when users want to create data sets with record structures that differ from those of the original data. This objective requires thinking through the problem and performing some data preparations.

Some examples of situations that might require changing record formats are as follows:

- Security of privacy issues may require either the removal of meaningful identifiers or their replacement with encoded or encrypted identifiers.
- Some categories of discrimination are illegal in certain situations. Fields that contain information that might lead to illegal discrimination should either be removed from the data or should be labeled in some legible way so that the field can be omitted, if necessary, at some later time.

For example, one strategy would be to first build the model including all fields, then build a second model excluding the illegal fields; then, compare the results of the two models. This design will indicate whether retaining the questionable fields would change the results of the analysis in any way.

- A record of sales might include the bin number for each item of merchandise. Such information would be useless for marketing research and can be removed to save space.
- Sales by quarter for various items may have been recorded as:

```
item_code, Q1_sales_target, Q1_actual_sales, ...
```

For some analyses, it may be preferable to look at what percent of target was met during each quarter:

```
item_code, Q1_percent_target_achieved, ...
```

In this case, it is necessary to perform calculations on fields in the original data to create new fields for the data set.

- A data field may carry too much information. For instance, when a model is being built to determine which users are likely to cancel a service, the termination dates of those who have canceled cannot be part of the record used to build the model.

- An analyst might wish to study patterns of purchases in order to discover which items are commonly purchased together. In the original data, each item purchased might have its own record. In the data set, all items that were purchased at the same time would share a record. The original records may be similar to the following records:

```
store_code, bill_number, date, line_number, dept_code,
item_code, quantity, price, discount, value
```

The records for the data set might look as follows:

```
store_code, bill_number, date, item_code_1, quantity_1,
item_code_2, quantity_2, ... item_ code_n, quantity_n
```

In this case, the analyst would select and group fields from a number of records to create each new record for the data set.

Create a Historical Data Set

A data set is created from the historical data. A data set may be a disk file or a table resulting from a database query. In most cases, the data set is divided into sections: one section each to train, test, and evaluate a model.

Create a Model

After creating the data set, use one or more learning tools to create and evaluate a model that will provide the answers for a business problem.

A model identifies:

- The target variable;
- The costs of incorrect predictions;
- Information about value distributions, biases, etc.; and
- Any other choices made—such as choices among algorithms, functions, etc.—when creating the model.

Data Mining Models

The central facet of today's sophisticated data mining techniques is the creation and use of intelligent models. Various types of models exist, each based on a different set of algorithms. Common examples include the following:

Decision Trees
A method that generates rules for making predictions by repeatedly dividing historical examples of data into smaller and smaller subgroups.

Neural Networks
Techniques that make predictions by analyzing the relationships among data elements in historical data. The name is derived from the fact that artificial neural networks are similar in structure to biological neural systems.

Genetic Algorithms
Techniques that use the principles of genetics and evolution to make increasingly accurate predictions about a given database.

Memory-Based Reasoning
A technique for classifying records in a database by comparing them with similar records that are already classified. Also called the *k*-nearest-neighbor (*k*NN) technique.

Models are created from historical data, that is, data in which the values of all fields or variables are already known. These models can also be applied to new data, in which the critical value (the dependent or response variable, or target field) is not yet known. Models can be applied either to a file of new data (for instance, in a weekly run) or to an individual item (for instance, at point of sale). Ideally, the user of a model does not have to know how the model was created or what technology lies behind it; the user simply enters the data and "pushes the button."

Multiple Learning Tools

Some data mining products offer only a single learning tool. Others provide multiple tools. Multiple learning tools allow a data mining product to handle varying collections of data and to work with many different types of prediction and learning problems. Because each problem and each database are different from all others, no one tool is optimal for all problems. Indeed, one cannot necessarily know in advance what algorithm will serve best for each problem.

Experimentation is sometimes needed, especially when people are beginning to work with a new database, and the ability to test one algorithm against another (a tree against a neural network, for example) can be extremely useful.

Guidelines exist. Each learning tool has special strengths and limitations. Note the following examples:

Decision trees are particularly suited for problems that have (or appear to have) high dimensionality (a large number of fields or variables). Trees are the method of choice in cases where it is necessary to display the rules produced by the model.

Neural network learning tools are particularly useful for problems that require forecasting exact values. Thus, neural networks are often used for regression problems, as well as for binary and multi-class prediction problems.

Memory-based reasoning algorithms are excellent for handling idiosyncratic data and for discovering cluster-type patterns in data ("islands" as opposed to "trends").

Build Models

Models are created, trained, and evaluated in an iterative process. The four phases of this process are *training*, *testing*, *evaluation*, and *prediction*.

With relatively small numbers of variables or fairly predictable problems, all four phases are typically performed in a simple sequence. For complex problems and knowledge discovery and for cases where large numbers of variables and/or data records may be used, the process is often better performed in two steps.

First, preliminary studies are performed on a relatively small subset of records to test and refine the planned method of attack and to discover, by examining the first models produced, which are the important variables for this particular model. Trees, since they provide visible rules, are particularly helpful in this early phase.

Second, based on the results of these preliminary studies, a new data set is created. The new data set will omit fields that proved to be of little or no use. It may also contain fields that present data in new ways, such as by summing, averaging, merging, or splitting fields. The full four-phase process is now carried out on large numbers of records, and the true production models are created.

A closer look at three of the most popular learning tools in use today—trees, neural networks, and match models—shows the similarity of tools which use radically different mathematical bases.

One particularly useful form of a decision tree is the Classification and Regression Tree (CART). A classification tree is a representation of the rules by which the independent fields in a data set determine the target values. For example, a classification tree might represent the following rules:

- If age is greater than 40 and balance is greater than or equal to 7250, then the applicant is a good risk with a probability of 85 percent.
- If age is less than or equal to 13, balance is less than 0, and head_of_household = 0, then the applicant is a poor risk with a probability of 80 percent.

These rules are illustrated in the partial tree shown in Figure 7-3. The probabilities shown in the tree are the probabilities that the classifications (rules) are *incorrect*.

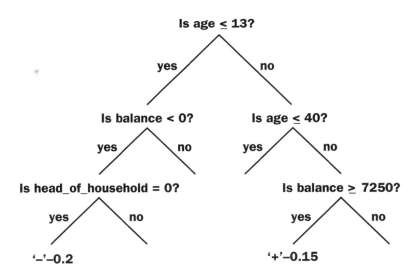

Figure 7-3 A partial tree representing two rules.

One way to understand classification trees is to think of a tree as a game of "20 Questions." The tree asks a series of questions about the values of the independent fields in a record, with the goal of making an educated guess as to the target value. Each question has a form like, "Is the value of `field_1` equal to *x*, *y*, or *z*?" or "Is the value of `field_2` less than *u*?" The answer, which can only be "yes" or "no," places the record in one of two categories. When applied to a set of records, any given question splits the set into two distinct subsets.

A classification tree begins with the full data set (the *root node* at the top of the tree) and asks successive questions to split the data set repeatedly. Each question forms a *node* of the tree. The splitting continues as long as there are "good" questions—questions that will help predict the response value—left to ask. Note that one of the most important considerations in growing a classification tree is how to select the questions (splits) to minimize the probability of misclassification. At the end of the splitting process, the terminal nodes (called *leaves*) represent a partitioning of the data set into distinct subsets. The records at each leaf are classified (as + or -, in our example) with a specified probability that the prediction is incorrect.

Figure 7-4 is a partial representation of a tree created from a training data set in a sample credit risk problem. Each node that is not a leaf is labeled with the condition (question) that splits the records at that node. For example, the first split, at the root node, is defined by the condition "Is `a9` a member of the set {'t'}?" Each leaf is labeled with the class to which the records at that leaf are assigned, followed by the probability of misclassification. For example, the two nodes at the bottom of the tree are assigned classes - and +, each with the probability 0.333333 of misclassification.

Pruning a Tree and Testing the Subtrees

A classification tree created for a particular data set is likely to include some splits that reflect the idiosyncrasies of that sample. Therefore, the optimal tree to predict the response variable is usually a pruned subtree of the full tree. A pruned subtree is a subset of the full tree, formed by removing one or more branches. A branch consists of a node and all the nodes below it.

The next step in creating a tree model, therefore, is to create a set of pruned subtrees, apply them to a specified data set, and examine their relative error rates. Typically, after growing a tree using the training data set, test the pruned subtrees on a separate test data set. Figure 7-5 shows a pruned subtree produced from the tree shown in Figure 7-4, using a test data set.

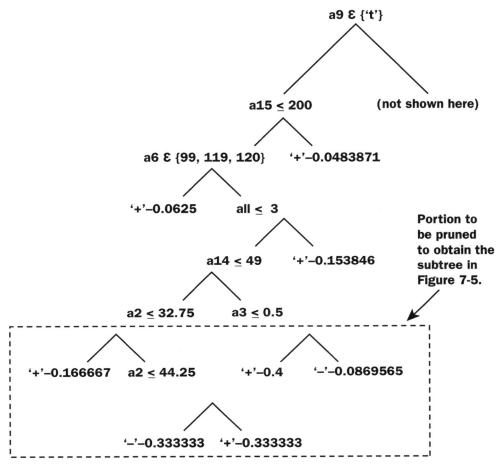

Figure 7-4 A partial representation of a simple binary classification tree.

Evaluating a Subtree

Even the relative error rates that are obtained by testing subtrees on the test data set may not reflect the performance that can be expected from the subtrees on the unclassified data set. Again, idiosyncrasies may have affected the results. Thus, a fresh data set is needed. After testing the pruned subtrees on the test data set and selecting the one that performs best, evaluate the performance of the best subtrees once again, this time applying the subtrees to an evaluation data set and examining the error rate of the selected subtrees.

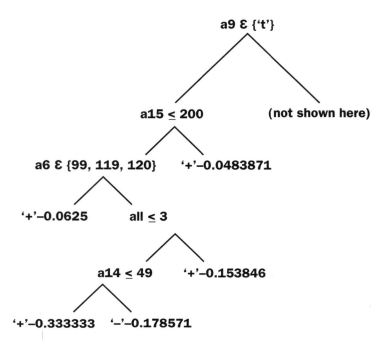

Figure 7-5 A pruned subtree of the tree shown in Figure 7-4.

Predicting the Response Variable

Finally, use the best subtree to predict the response variable in your unclassified data set. Prediction typically produces a new data set that includes, for each record, the predicted response value, the cost if the classification is incorrect, and the confidence of the classification.

Optimizing Trees

Tree models can be optimized in a number of ways:

• The proportion of target values in a training data set does not always reflect the proportions that exist in the real world. In these cases, provide the learning tool with "priors" information, which tells it what the true proportions of target values are in the population: that is, what the true probability is that any given record will have a particular target value.

- A simple method of growing a tree assumes that costs and profits are equal in all cases. This assumption is not always true. For this reason, the costs involved in making an incorrect decision can be specified, or the cost savings or profits involved in making a correct decision. This clarification can be useful when the cost of different misclassifications varies significantly: that is, when a false negative is much more costly than a false positive, or vice versa.
- If cost information is supplied, it requires a different pruning function than if cost information is not supplied. Pruning functions are used to define subtrees within the tree.
- Choose between alternative decrease functions, which determine how the learning tools decide which splits to make when growing the tree.

Try any or all of these optimizations while creating tree models. For instance, experiment with different costs to see how the model is affected.

Neural Networks

Neural networks attempt to imitate the human brain in that they work with clusters and patterns of facts, often in highly complex ways. They are "black box" tools: the data goes in at one end, the results come out the other end, and only the computer knows what happens in between.

Some sophisticated neural network algorithms can handle both binary and multiclass classification problems. They can also handle regression problems, or forecasting: these are problems in which the target value is "continuous"—for example, in which the value could be a number anywhere between 1 and 1,000,000.

Creating a Neural Network

A neural network is built in layers:

- An *input layer* containing *input units*, each of which corresponds to an independent field;
- An *output layer* containing *output units*. When used for forecasting or for binary predictions, a neural network has only one output unit, which represents the target (dependent) field. Networks used

for multiclass predictions have one target field per class; and

• Optionally, one or more *hidden layers*, with arbitrary numbers of units. These layers are used in the computation of the predicted response value.

Figure 7-6 shows a diagram of a very simple neural network.

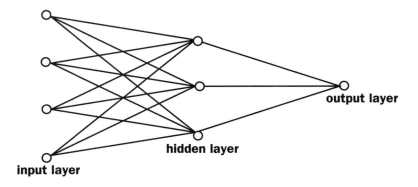

Figure 7-6 A neural network with one hidden layer.

To create a neural network, supply the number of hidden layers and the number of units in each network layer. The input layer has one unit for each independent field. For most problems, satisfactory results can be obtained with one or two hidden layers. The output layer has one unit for each target class or target field.

The number of hidden layers and the number of units in each layer are sometimes referred to collectively as the network topology, or structure. For this discussion, the layers of a neural network are ordered as follows: the input layer is followed by the hidden layers in increasing order, and the last hidden layer is followed by the output layer. An activation function is associated with each unit in the hidden and output layers.

Each unit in a neural network is logically connected to all the units in the adjacent layers. Figure 7-7 shows a simple neural network with its weights.

Training the Network

After creating a network, the next step is to apply it to the training data set in order to calculate the weights for the network.

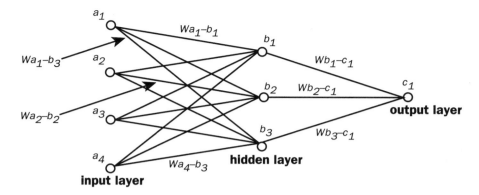

Figure 7-7 *A neural network with weights.*

Network Weights

For each record in a data set, a neural network uses the values in the input units to compute the output value—a predicted value for the target field. The element that changes during the training process is the set of numeric *weights* that govern the computation of the output value.

To start training, each connection between two units is assigned a weight. The starting weights come from a randomization process. In Figure 7-7, $w_{ui\text{-}vj}$ denotes the weight assigned to the connection between units ui and vj.

The computation of the output value begins with the input layer. The values in each layer are used to compute the values in the next layer. Specifically, the value of any given unit is computed as the weighted sum of the values of the units in the previous layer. If vj is a unit in the network and $u1$ through un are the units in the previous layer, then the value at vj is

$$V_j = \sum_{i=1}^{n} U_i \, W_{ui\text{-}vj} + B_{vj}$$

where B_{vj} is a *bias weight* associated with vj. vj passed through the activation function; the resulting value is passed on to the next layer in the network. The weights reflect the relative importance of the independent fields—and combinations thereof—in predicting the target field.

Training Algorithms

Numerous training algorithms for neural networks exist: for example, backpropagation, steepest descent, modified newton, conjugate gradient, and genetic algorithm. As an example, backpropagation works as follows:

1. The training function uses the input values and weights to compute output values for the first batch of records. "Batching" is typically based on available memory.
2. The training function then compares the computed output values with the target values for the first batch of records, computes the error rate, and adjusts the weights. Because the adjustments are performed backward through the network, this step is called *backpropagation*.
3. The training function repeats steps 1 and 2 for each batch of records.
4. Upon reaching the end of the data set, the training function begins again with the first batch of records. Typically, the user can specify the number of iterations the training function makes through the data set, or the user can specify that the training process should stop when the error rates stop declining and when the rates should begin to climb again—indicating that overtraining is beginning. Cross-validation may also be used.

The composition of the data can have an effect on which algorithm works best for a given problem.

Optimizing Neural Networks

Neural network algorithms utilize cost functions and activation functions. Different functions should be used for classification (prediction) and regression (forecasting) problems.

In addition, neural networks can be optimized by experimentation with different training algorithms—assuming that your data mining tool provides a variety of possible algorithms. It is also possible to provide different starting points for the network's weights, change the learning rate (on certain algorithms), and try out various network structures (or topologies).

Match Models

Match models use *memory-based reasoning* (MBR) to predict the response fields in a data set. Unlike classification and regression trees, and neural networks, which condense the patterns in a data set into a set of rules or network weights significantly smaller than the actual data set, *match models* incorporate an actual data set—called the *model data set*—in the model.

For each record in the unclassified data set, the match model identifies *k* nearest neighbors in the model data set. These nearest neighbors are the *k* records in the model data set whose field values are most similar to those of the input record.

After finding a record's nearest neighbors, the match model uses the target values of the nearest neighbors to classify the record. If the nearest neighbors do not all have the same target value, the model decides which value to predict, based on how many neighbors have each target value and how "near" each neighbor is to the input record.

For example, to solve a credit risk problem, a match model would classify each applicant as a good or bad credit risk by selecting the customers whose profiles are most similar to that of the applicant and by using the target values of these nearest neighbors to predict the applicant's behavior. Thus, if an applicant's nearest neighbors were good credit risks, the match model would predict that the applicant would also be a good risk.

Once the match model has classified all records in the input data set, it creates a prediction data set containing the predicted response value and the associated confidence for each input record.

Many match models are sensitive to individual records in the sense that the existence of even one record that closely matches the record to be classified affects the prediction. In contrast, the presence of any one record by itself would not be likely to affect the outcome of a tree model or a neural network classification.

Optimizing Match Models

Match models can be created and deployed by giving equal importance to all attributes in a record. However, improvements in accuracy can often be obtained by optimizing the relative importance given to each attribute. Relative importance is determined during the training process and reflected in the weight given to a field.

In addition, users can vary the number of nearest neighbors used to make a prediction and can set biases for the model. Typically, the tool can be instructed to bias results toward the positive if a false negative is considerably more costly than a false positive or if an unbiased model produces an excess of false negatives. A negative bias may be used if a false positive is more costly than a false negative or if the unbiased model produces an excess of false positives.

Use the Model

Some business questions are answered directly by modeling the historical data. Others require applying the model to new data before taking action. For instance, historical data by itself can help in the following cases:

- Looking at visualization of patterns of recent equipment failures can focus corrective efforts for maximum payback or provide earlier warnings of failures.
- Studying a decision tree could provide guidelines for a number of future actions. For example, a tree might discover hidden buying patterns among a subset of customers.

New data is not yet complete. Generally, predictive models are applied to new data to determine what decisions to make about it. For example:

- Given a new mailing list, what catalogs should be sent to specific list members to maximize the return on the mailing?
- Given a new applicant for credit, how much credit (if any) should be granted?
- Given a patient with a particular history and set of symptoms, what is the most likely diagnosis? What is likely to be the optimal treatment?

Analyze the Results

What can be gained from a data mining operation? Modern data mining tools provide answers in terms of lift, margin, and ROI.

Lift represents the benefit gained from a model's predictive ability. It can be thought of as the profits that accrue from an accurately targeted campaign: for instance, sending a direct mailing to only the 20 percent of customers who will provide 90 percent of the positive response.

Lift analysis predicts against actual values. It tests predicted values against actual values in known data. Thus, the analysis can be performed on a test population, to predict lift, or at the end of some period during which the predictive model has been in use and the data resulting from its use has been recorded.

To measure lift, the population according to the predicted value of each record is sorted:

- Records predicted to be responders, with a high probability of correct prediction, are first;
- Records predicted to be responders, with a low probability of correct prediction, are next;
- Records predicted to be nonresponders, with a low probability of correct prediction, are third; and
- Records predicted to be nonresponders, with a high probability of correct prediction, are last.

The population is then divided into quantiles, with the user setting the granularity by choosing the number of quantiles. The number of actual responders are then compared against the number that would be expected if responders were distributed randomly throughout the quantiles. Calculations are cumulative: thus, for a given quantile N, lift represents the results for all quantiles up to and including N.

When lift for a good model is expressed numerically, it begins with large numbers in the first quantile(s) and ends with the number 1.

Margin and ROI

Lift itself is a purely statistical measure and does not take costs or profits into account. The lift analysis lets users specify the profits or cost savings to be gained from a correct prediction and the costs (or lost profits) associated with an incorrect prediction. It then uses these numbers to provide two measures of monetary benefit: margin and return on investment (*ROI*).

Margin is a measure of the net profit associated with the use of each quantile of population, as predicted by the model. *ROI* is a measure of gross profit for the quantile: it sums the profit and the avoided cost for each correct prediction. For example, assume a company gains $20 in profit from each response to a direct mail campaign and loses $2 in costs for each nonresponder. Then, for each quantile, the margin for using that quantile is calculated on the basis of $20 per responder, while ROI is calculated on the basis of $22 per responder.

Most advanced data mining software includes a lift analysis providing both measures, allowing the user to pick the one best suited to each analysis.

Update Your Model

If an application deals with an ongoing business question, it is possible to periodically update (and potentially refine) the model. For instance, use a predictive model, based on data through 1995, to decide whether 1996 credit applicants were likely to be good risks. At the end of 1996, add the credit histories of the accepted applicants to the model for making decisions about 1997's applicants.

Measuring Success

The success of predictive models in the business world is measured not only by how accurate the models are but also by the amount of profit they create. For example:

- Company X reduces bad credit losses by N percent. Depending on the amount of credit Company X offers, the reduction can represent hundreds, thousands, or millions of dollars annually.
- Company Y uses a predictive model to target a direct mailing more precisely. By so doing, it spends only 40 percent of what it would normally spend on the mailing but generates 90 percent of its usual sales. Company Y has thus increased the lift on its mailing substantially: again, this can represent a wide range of savings, based on the company's costs and sales volumes.

Data mining software supplies the tools. The customer supplies the goals.

About the Author

Alice Landy holds a doctorate from Harvard University and has 17 years of experience in software technical writing and management. She is currently the documentation project leader for Darwin™— Thinking Machines Corporation's scalable data mining product.

About Thinking Machines Corporation

Founded in 1983, Thinking Machines Corporation revolutionized high-performance computing with its massively parallel supercomputing technology. Today, the company is focused on being a leading provider of high-end data mining solutions to the commercial market via the world's most powerful workstation and server platforms. Thinking Machines also markets software development tools for a variety of high-performance parallel processing technologies.

A privately held corporation, Thinking Machines employs nearly 200 computer engineers, customer support specialists, marketing personnel and other key staff at the company's Bedford, Massachusetts, headquarters and offices worldwide.

Darwin—from Thinking Machines Corporation—is an open, scalable suite of data mining software that enables businesses to analyze huge databases to discover new patterns, extract hidden information, and predict future trends. Scaling from workstations to SMPs to clusters, Darwin provides fast results by taking advantage of parallel processing. With several predictive and analytic modules to choose from, Darwin gives users multiple approaches for building highly accurate data mining solutions.

Thinking Machines Corporation is located at 14 Crosby Drive, Bedford, Massachusetts, 01730. For more information, call Thinking Machines at 617 276 0400, send email to alison@think.com, or access the following Web site: http://www.think.com.

Sampling: The Latest Breakthrough in Decision-Support Technology

by Jonathan Kraft

Introduction: Increasing the Demand for Information

In the early 1990s, when data warehousing began its meteoric rise in popularity and on-line analytical processing (OLAP) emerged as an ubiquitous application paradigm, databases on the order of tens of gigabytes were considered large. By today's standards, these are small *data marts*, the diminutive and subject-oriented form of a data warehouse. As information is made available across the enterprise, the demand for that information has increased dramatically. The result is that large data warehouses today are measured in terabytes, not gigabytes, and scalability has joined performance as a dominant issue among customers evaluating data warehouse technology.

At the same time, as decision support systems (DSS) solutions become increasingly targeted toward the end user, demand for these applications grows across a broader spectrum of user communities. It is no longer simply the power-user marketing analysts who access the corporate data warehouse. Today, managers at all levels of the corporate hierarchy, entire sales organizations, and virtually all decision makers across the enterprise are connected online. As a result, it is not uncommon to have many thousands of users linked to a single data repository.

This chapter discusses *sampling*, a new paradigm for decision support that addresses the issues of performance and scalability. Sampling is a statistical technique used to estimate results by querying a small sample of a total population. It has been popularized by functions such as election polling and the Nielsen ratings. While sampling has existed for much longer than data warehousing, it has never been used in the enterprise decision-support framework until its introduction as a paradigm by Informix in 1997. It is likely to be one of the most important performance and scalability breakthroughs in the history of enterprise decision support. After a brief introduction to general decision-support strategies, this article explains how sampling works, how it relates to a process known as aggregation, why it is a scalability windfall for data warehouse designers, and how several other of its key advantages benefit the enterprise.

Business Trend Discovery

If more and more users are accessing data warehouses, what are they looking for? The simple answer is business trends. Detailed data is a critical source of business intelligence and is often the end result of a series of decision-support investigations. However, most queries actually run against data warehouses, and data marts look for high-level information to guide detailed investigations. Typically, OLAP analysis starts at the top of the business hierarchies, searching for patterns and trends that might provide users with strategic insights, which often result in the need for even more detailed information.

Consider a retail bank that is attempting to determine product profitability. As a bank analyst, you might start by running a high-level report by product category. An initial report may reveal that safety deposit boxes are unprofitable. Continuing trend analysis may unearth other unpredictable business insights. For example, a profitability by branch report may show that the most profitable branches are those that sold the most safety deposit boxes. This would seem to be a paradox, until further customer profitability analysis reveals that customers with safety deposit boxes tend to be wealthy. Since customers don't like to move items from one safe place to another, safety deposit boxes may help to reduce churn among these high-income customers. Thus, while they are a cost drain on the surface, safety deposit boxes may actually be a relatively inexpensive way for banks to retain profitable customers who will eventually open large mutual fund accounts or purchase other profitable products from the bank. Starting with trend analysis helps to focus further inquiries into detailed data.

Drilling to Detail

Drilling down, a common practice in decision support, involves choosing a particular element of a report and seeking more detailed information about that element. For example, suppose in the example outlined previously, you weren't content with simply knowing that safety deposit boxes are linked to the customer category "High Income." That was interesting to learn, but now you want to drill down into your customer dimension and determine exactly which customers own safety deposit boxes and what additional products and services they currently use. Once you see that report, you may want to slice out the customers who do not have mutual funds but who have opened savings accounts, in order to conduct a direct mailing to those customers to determine if they might be interested in new investment opportunities.

The further down into the hierarchies you go, the larger the data volumes you must navigate. When you finally reach the most detailed data, system performance typically relies on the core parallelism, partitioning, and scalability of the underlying database and hardware systems. In fact, these are critical to any performance solution, regardless of whether you are going against detailed data or high-level summary data.

There is, however, an important new option for achieving extraordinary performance when performing high-level trend analysis. No longer are organizations forced to either dynamically summarize answers at the time of the analysis or to anticipate all possible analyses that users will perform by building a complex matrix of summary tables in advance. This is where sampling becomes interesting.

Sampling: A Usability and Scalability Breakthrough

The introduction of sampling into the OLAP arena comes at a very good time. Just as data volumes, warehouse schemas, and business hierarchies are becoming too large and complex for aggregation to be the sole performance solution, a new paradigm has arrived. Sampling allows users to estimate results based on a partial representation of detailed data and to accomplish this in a fraction of the time it would otherwise take to retrieve an answer. Results are derived by means of well-established, time-tested statistical techniques, and query performance is orders of magnitude faster.

Aggregation and Its Uses

Before delving into the intricacies of sampling, it is important to understand aggregation, a critical performance-enhancement strategy that works alongside sampling. *Aggregation* is the process of pre-summarizing transactional data within the data warehouse in order to lighten the resource load on the database that performs the dynamic calculations. Instead of requiring that the database dynamically add up millions of records each time a user requests summary information, aggregates enable commonly requested information to be precomputed and consolidated for faster access. For example, to run a quarterly sales report, you could either add up all of the transactions for a particular quarter—traversing millions of records—or you could have a presummarized aggregate table by month, for example, and simply summarize the monthly records for each quarter.

Aggregation is a critical part of any data warehouse solution, but as warehouse complexity and data volumes increase, aggregation as a total performance solution becomes less and less feasible. The reasons include load windows and storage/maintenance cost. One of the biggest challenges in building an effective data warehouse is discovering how to incrementally load and summarize data in an acceptable time frame each time the warehouse is refreshed. In theory, if a warehouse were fully aggregated, actual query performance would never be an issue. Producing user reports would largely be a matter of delivering them straight from the database while performing some basic analytical calculations. Why don't organizations aggregate exhaustively? Because it takes an enormous amount of resources to update these aggregate tables each time new detailed data is loaded into the base tables.

As an example, consider a data warehouse with the following business dimensions and hierarchies (Figure 8-1).

In this relatively simple five-dimensional data warehouse, how

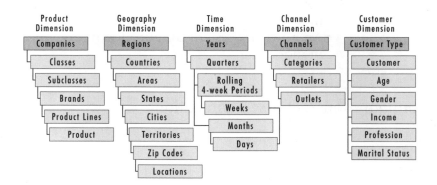

Figure 8-1 *A sample data warehouse with its specific business dimensions and hierarchies.*

should we determine which aggregates to build? There are two possibilities: build them all or figure out which is the optimal aggregate configuration and build only those kinds. Following are more detailed descriptions of these two possible configurations.

Configuration 1: Exhaustive Aggregation

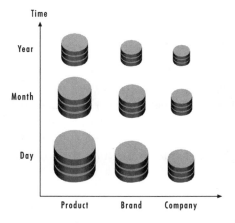

Figure 8-2 *Configuration 1 denotes exhaustive aggregation.*

The total number of aggregate tables (in this case 8,064) is calculated by multiplying the number of hierarchy levels in each dimension: 6*8*8*4*7. The advantage of this scheme is that nearly every query is returned in subsecond response time. However, the disadvantages include the following:

- Very long load times make the data warehouse difficult to maintain, even with the most flexible load windows; and
- An unwieldy system contains too many tables to effectively manage.

Configuration 2: Sparse Aggregation

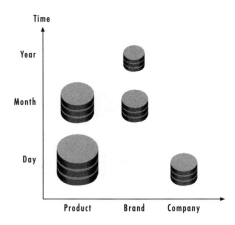

Figure 8-3 *Configuration 2 denotes sparse aggregation.*

Typically, a database administrator (DBA) must perform a complex analysis to determine the set of aggregates that provide the optimal balance between performance and manageability. Suppose such an analysis indicates that 45 aggregate tables provide fair coverage of the warehouse and enable a comfortable load window.

The advantages include the following:

- The warehouse is manageable; and
- Most reports are generated quickly, and users are pleased a majority of the time.

The disadvantage of this scheme is that many reports still take an unacceptably long time to run. The coverage provided by choosing only 30 aggregate tables from over 6,000 is not ideal.

The graph in Figure 8-4 visualizes this tradeoff. *Query cost*, the time it takes to run a report, is measured using an arbitrary unit of

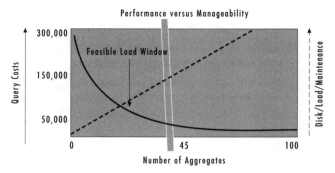

Figure 8-4 *A graph that indicates the tradeoff between performance and manageability.*

measure. The number 300,000 represents the average cost of running a query in this data warehouse, assuming all queries run against the fact table that holds the lowest level of detail. Query cost goes down, however, as aggregate tables are added to the data warehouse. Since aggregate tables are much smaller than the detailed data table, the cost of running queries against them is much lower. Therefore, with each additional aggregate, the average cost to run a query is diminished. The maintenance (load time and overhead) required on a data warehouse containing aggregate tables, however, increases as more and more aggregate tables are added to the data warehouse. This is represented in the above graph by the dashed line, which rises from left to right. No units of measure are listed as this line is a combination of multiple factors, including load windows, disk storage, and overall maintenance costs. In this graph, the optimal tradeoff falls at an average query cost of roughly 50,000, which means that approximately 45 aggregates are required to support this data warehouse. This number corresponds to the point on the query cost line where adding additional aggregate tables ceases to measurably improve the average cost to run a query.

Unfortunately, as the arrow indicates, this data warehouse is constrained by its load window and thus cannot handle more than approximately 20 aggregate tables. As data warehouses grow in size and complexity, more and more summary tables are required to deliver acceptable performance, and load windows become tighter and tighter. The problem with size is obvious: more detailed records mean more rows to crunch in order to generate the aggregate tables or to produce query results.

As hierarchies become deeper, as organizations break up their businesses into more dimensions, and as those dimensions become more complex, the number of aggregate tables required to provide dimensional coverage grows exponentially. *Dimensional coverage* is the ability to effectively answer a question at any level of the dimension hierarchy, using an aggregate table. With five business dimensions having four hierarchy levels each, the number of potential aggregate tables is four to the power of five (4^5), or 1,024 possible tables. If a sixth dimension is added, the number of possible aggregate tables climbs to 4,096. Add a seventh dimension and the number becomes 16,384. In the previous example, we ended up with 8,064 possible tables. It is not uncommon for production data warehouses to include over 20 dimensions. You can see that the problem of providing a high-performance data warehouse which is still manageable becomes increasingly challenging.

Sampling: A Scalability and Maintenance Windfall

Sampling is an effective, efficient, and simple way to attain maximum coverage and performance on any data warehouse. The use of sample tables can provide excellent response time on *any* query, mitigating maintenance headaches and concerns regarding load windows.

Sample tables contain data derived from base data by means of one of many possible random sampling techniques. User queries are directed to these samples instead of to detailed fact tables or precreated aggregate tables. The answers are retrieved very quickly, and estimates are provided to users, along with the degree of confidence they can have with those estimates.

Because the samples are based on the lowest levels of the hierarchy, data warehouses can be defined to be as complex as a business model might require, without impacting query performance or load windows. The only decision to be made is what size sample to use. This decision will dictate the accuracy of the answer, as later discussed.

Consider what sampling means from a maintenance standpoint. Instead of wading through several thousand aggregate tables to come up with the top 20 to 50, and instead of struggling with load windows and hoping you have the correct coverage, sampling allows you to build one or two samples, know you have complete

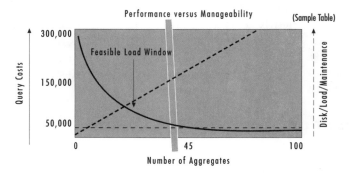

Figure 8-5 A graph that uses sampling to balance performance with manageability.

coverage, and choose only the most important aggregates to round out your warehouse tuning strategy.

Figure 8-5 expands on the previous graph, taking sampling into account. Note that without sampling, there is a constant tradeoff between performance and storage/maintenance costs, including load windows. Assuming load windows or other storage/maintenance factors were constrained, as indicated above by the arrow, it would not be possible to create the 45 aggregates previously said to be optimal for warehouse performance. Thus, performance could suffer dramatically. In many implementations, the actual situation is far more dramatic than this graph indicates. However, with sampling, there is always a constant level of performance, regardless of the number of aggregates. This provides the freedom to set load windows as the constraining factor (which they are in reality anyway) and modify the samples and aggregates to optimize the performance of the warehouse, thus assuring a manageable warehouse environment. This optimization is the first scalability windfall delivered by sampling.

The second scalability windfall comes from one of the least intuitive aspects of sampling: accuracy. The accuracy of a sample has more to do with the absolute size of the sample than it does with the ratio of the size of the sample to the size of the data source. What this means is that once a sample provides the accuracy needed and a comfortable level of confidence, it does not need to grow nearly as fast as the detailed data grows. Thus, consider a data warehouse with a base fact table of one billion records. Assume that a sample size of 500,000 delivers the required combination of accuracy, performance, and confidence. As the detailed data grows into the tens of billions of records, the sample will not have to grow nearly as fast, because it is the actual size rather than the size ratio that matters. Query results will remain accurate. While this is non-intuitive, it is well documented in statistical sampling texts, and it is a windfall for the data warehouse designer.

Accuracy and Confidence: A Complex Paradigm Made Simple

The terms accuracy and confidence mean very different things. In fact, they are completely separate concepts in sampling. Think of accuracy as the expectation of how close the estimate is to the actual answer. Confidence depends on two things: the accuracy (measured in part by the size of the base sample) of the estimate and the acceptable margin of error.

The accuracy achieved from a very small sample is not only incredibly high, it is so high as to be completely counterintuitive. For example, when TV networks are calling the national elections, any distinguishable margin can be declared insurmountable after only a small percentage of the voting precincts have reported. When pre-election polls are taken, often only a few hundred people are polled, and the confidence that viewers have in the results is typically 95 to 98 percent, plus or minus a few points (the error margin).

A tangible example will help to bring about a full understanding of the relationships between error margin, confidence, and accuracy. Consider again the retail bank that is attempting to establish how many of its customers, organized by age range, have purchased safety deposit boxes at each branch. Unfortunately (or fortunately, depending on how one looks at it), the bank has millions of customers, most of whom have made hundreds of transactions.

The bank does not want to spend the resources to ask such a complex, multidimensional question against so much data. Instead, it wants a random sample. Instead of running the report against a multibillion row transaction table, it is run against a statistically accurate sample of the data consisting of roughly 500,000 records. The bank wants to have significant confidence (95 percent) that answers are within the boundary of the report's error margin. The report indicates (via technology that uses advanced statistics to automatically calculate the important parameters) that the answer is 50,000 customers, plus or minus 500. This means that the bank can have confidence (95 percent) that somewhere between 49,500 and 50,500 customers have purchased safety deposit boxes.

In this example, 500 represents the error margin. Since the query ran so quickly, the bank decides to increase the accuracy by running the query against a larger sample, that is, one million records. This time, the answer returned is 49,790, plus or minus 270. Now the bank has the confidence (95 percent) that it sold safety deposit boxes to between 49,520 and 50,060 customers (a margin of error of 270). It is zeroing in on the answer. Just out of curiosity, the confidence setting is increased to 98 percent and the report is rerun. The answer comes back: 49,790 customers, plus or minus 400. The estimate was identical since the accuracy, or sample population, was identical. However, the level of confidence is now 98 percent that the answer is between 49,390 and 50,190 customers. Note that if you keep accuracy the same but want to increase your confidence that the real answer will fall within the sampled answer's margin of error, the margin of error is naturally increased.

Think in terms of holding two of the three concepts constant and letting the third be derived from the other two, in coordination with the actual data sample. Thus, for high accuracy (going against a large sample) and a confidencelevel of 95 percent, a query can retrieve results with an associated error margin (call it plus or minus X).

To take this example further, it is useful to examine actual data. Consider a complete, bidimensional report of customer count by region and age range. First, assume a very small sample (.01 percent) and specify a 98 percent accuracy rate. Table 8-1 shows a partial report:

Table 8-1 *A bidimensional report of customer count by region and age range.*

Region	Customer Age Range	Customer Count	Error Margin
Northeast	Under 25	6224	±373
	26 – 39	10666	±649
	40 – 49	8905	±532
	50 – 65	10340	±678
	Over 65	10480	±635
West	Under 25	6803	±456
	26 – 39	7750	±458
	40 – 49	6810	±308
	50 – 65	7430	±425
	Over 65	9270	±548

If these results are unsatisfactory (perhaps error margins are too high), use a larger sample, possibly .02 or .03 percent, maintaining the same confidence level. Table 8-2 shows a partial follow-up report:

Table 8-2 A bidimensional report of customer count by region and age range, using a larger sample.

Region	Customer Age Range	Customer Count	Error Margin
Northeast	Under 25	6105	±243
	26 – 39	10344	±641
	40 – 49	9317	±369
	50 – 65	10860	±397
	Over 65	10594	±373
West	Under 25	7262	±374
	26 – 39	8113	±297
	40 – 49	7140	±340
	50 – 65	7885	±311
	Over 65	8734	±366

The larger the queried sample, the smaller the margin of error, and the more accurate the estimate. Assuming these margins are acceptable, an analyst at the hypothetical bank might begin to initiate a program to boost sales of safety deposit boxes in the West among the age groups 40 to 49 and 50 to 65, and in the Northeast, among age groups 26 to 39 and 50 to 65. If, out of curiosity, the analyst were to run the full report just for confirmation purposes, the results would appear as shown in Table 8-3.

Table 8-3 A bidimensional report of customer count by region and age range, yielding target market statistics.

Region	Customer Age Range	Customer Count
Northeast	Under 25	6102
	26 – 39	10111
	40 – 49	9445
	50 – 65	10709
	Over 65	10928
West	Under 25	7096
	26 – 39	8053
	40 – 49	7309
	50 – 65	7775
	Over 65	8763

Informix has developed a way to make this entire process completely transparent to the end user, who simply asks to estimate a result and is told the margin of error based on a user-defined level of confidence. If users want more accurate estimates, they can adjust the accuracy, and the answer will simply be closer to reality with a lower margin of error. Refer to the following chart (Figure 8-6) for a sense of how close the sampled data sets are to the actual data in illustrative examples.

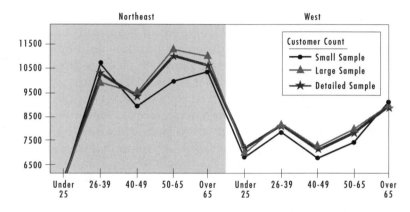

Figure 8-6 *An analysis of sampled data sets against actual data.*

Trusting Samples

One common question asked about sampling concerns its trustworthiness. OLAP users are making mission-critical decisions based on their discoveries and need to feel a high level of confidence in the query results before trusting their conclusions. There are two answers to this question, but both make the same assumption: the sample must be random.

Sampling is useless unless the technique that is employed yields a truly random sample, meaning that no bias is introduced into the sample population. A classic example of nonrandom sampling was the Truman versus Dewey presidential election in 1948. Gallup's last poll, conducted from October 15th to October 25th, showed Dewey ahead 49 percent to 44 percent of the vote. On November 2, Truman won 50 percent of the vote to Dewey's 45 percent. What was wrong with the poll? Sampling bias. The most likely explanation for this was that, in 1948, only people with higher incomes had phones. Thus, when Gallup called to ask people their voting intentions, they introduced an enormous bias into the poll:

individual wealth. As it happens, a larger percentage of wealthy individuals vote Republican than does the broader United States (US) population, hence the huge discrepancy in the 1948 polling result. As we address the issue of trusting sampled data, understand that a completely random sampling technique is a base requirement for this approach.

The first point of evidence on the issue of trust is the advertising industry. Businesses in this country spend billions and billions of dollars annually on advertising through television, radio, magazines, etc. Leading organizations, such as Nike and General Motors, sometimes spend hundreds of thousands of dollars advertising on a single television program. But how do they know which program to bet on? How do they know which ones attract their target demographics? The answer is the Nielsen ratings, which are based on a very small random sample of TV sets across the United States. Major advertisers look to Nielsen ratings for answers to questions that are virtually identical to many traditional OLAP questions: what are the top five programs (ranked) among viewers between the ages of 30 and 49? Which programs appeal to high-income couples in their late 20s? What are the top 10 programs by category by geographical region? The list goes on. This system has been in place for many years, and it works. Companies continue to put greater and greater trust in the Nielsen ratings and continue to ask more and increasingly innovative questions of their sampled data set.

The second point is that sampling is not meant simply to be used in a vacuum (although it can be trusted with multimillion dollar decisions, as evidenced by the Nielsen ratings) but should be your guide through the data warehouse. More than 90 percent of the time that many users spend on their decision-support applications is devoted to trend analysis. They evaluate patterns in the data until they see something that catches their attention. Then, they ask the detailed question. As we have seen, even lightly sampled data can provide accurate trending patterns. When it is time to ask the detailed question, users may not wish to utilize the sampling functionality of their data warehouse. In that case, they simply ask that final question of the detailed data, and the sampling functionality will have saved them hours of processing and waiting time while they discovered what that question should be. This time-saving is the real power of sampling in decision support.

Conclusion

Sampling has been used for decades as a paradigm for information analysis, but only now is its power being harnessed for enterprise decision support systems. Its implications for scalability are critical to today's corporate environments where information overload is the norm and demand for information is growing rapidly at every level of the organization. The Informix Dynamic Server with the Extended Parallel Option and Advanced Decision Support Option is the first relational database to leverage sampling. In addition, the MetaCube ROLAP Option is the first relational OLAP product to provide transparent end-user access to statistical samples and, just as importantly, to provide the critical information required for users to determine the accuracy of their estimates.

About the Author

Jonathan Kraft is director of Business Development, Data Warehousing Business Unit, at Informix Software, Inc., Oakland, California.

Part 3

Hardware, Storage, and Backup Issues in a Data Warehouse

Optimal Architectures for Enterprise-Class Data Warehousing

by Steve Deck

The Evolution to High-End Data Warehouses

Data warehouses are increasingly providing a competitive advantage for companies worldwide, primarily because data warehouses provide a means for companies to understand the customer better—data warehouses enable users to analyze customers' buying habits and trends. Understanding these trends allows companies to focus sales and marketing and to develop strategies that better match the products and services which are targeted to customers.

Data collected from operational systems—such as point-of-sale, telemarketing, manufacturing, and financial systems—is increasingly loaded into data warehouses. Subsequently, this raw customer data is transformed into strategic information. Large daily sales volumes populate the data warehouses, resulting in exponential growth. Thus, organizations are looking for a data warehouse architecture that can support warehouses in the multiple terabyte range. The well-known industry analyst group, Gartner Group, predicts that "databases of this size will allow companies from almost all vertical industry groups to become more actively involved in data warehousing" (1995, Gartner Group).

Businesses embarking on data warehousing strategies must ensure that a warehouse's foundation and tools are flexible enough to meet long-term data warehousing needs, as the warehouse continues to grow and evolve. Key features of a successful high-end data warehouse include the following:

- Parallelism—The platform should support the parallelization of queries and query traffic;
- Scalability and performance—It should be possible to incrementally add processors and storage drives as demand grows, without compromising performance;
- High availability—Features of high availability should be designed into the data warehousing project, including on-line backup and recovery, component redundancy, and fail-over; and
- Manageability—A good warehousing foundation incorporates performance monitoring, storage management tools, robust relational databases (RDBMS) tools, and network configuration utilities.

Informix Software, Hewlett-Packard (HP), and their business partners offer a complete data warehouse solution. This chapter focuses on two key components: an optimized parallel relational database management system and scalable, open systems hardware. It briefly defines the data warehouse and reviews the key benefits and challenges of adopting and implementing an enterprise-class data warehouse strategy. The chapter then compares and contrasts clustered symmetric multiprocessing solutions (SMP) to massively parallel processing (MPP) solutions for high-end data warehouses; addresses how the complementary architectures of the Informix and HP products—used in a clustered SMP environment—exploit the key features of a successful data warehouse; and demonstrates why HP and Informix provide an ideal data warehouse foundation which is flexible enough to meet the growing and evolving needs of an enterprise—ensuring long-term investment protection.

Data Warehouse Overview

Definition

A data warehouse is a separate database that is designed explicitly for decision support. Typically, a warehouse application tends to optimize query times and eliminates the impact on the production on-line transaction processing (OLTP) systems. It is a subject-oriented, integrated, time-variant, nonvolatile collection of data which supports management decisions. In simpler terms, a data warehouse stores a company's business data in an integrated database and provides a historical perspective of information for decision-support applications and business queries.

Planning and Implementation

A well-planned data warehouse enables businesses to better serve customers by empowering end users to make better decisions in a faster time frame through improved access to information. Corporate users' demands for information are pushing corporations to reengineer their information technology (IT) systems. As businesses look to reengineering, they must ensure that their IT infrastructure is flexible enough to adapt to the organization's evolving needs and that it will accommodate the emerging data warehouse technologies.

Building a data warehouse is a complex process that requires evolving towards an information—as opposed to a data—architecture. It involves thorough planning to determine how business objectives will be met, what information is necessary, where the data will come from, how the data will be used, who will have access to the warehouse, etc. The next step involves extracting data from various operational, historical, and external databases to populate the specialized data warehouse database. This step requires an extensive development effort to select, map, and transform the data that goes into the warehouse and also necessitates the use of a powerful front-end tool to allow users to easily retrieve and analyze the newly available information. In addition, building a warehouse requires expanding the limits of current technologies to accommodate fast, complex queries on databases that may grow to the multiple terabyte range.

Support and Management

Data warehouse support and management are interactive, ongoing processes. Success generally creates a series of interrelated increases:

• The number of users who want information;

- The demand for faster access;
- The size of the RDBMS behind the warehouse; and
- The complexity of the interacting components.

Quite often, the size of the data warehouse increases, as does the reliance of users on the information provided by the data warehouse. One of the key challenges of very large data warehouses is maintaining performance as the databases continue to grow. It is imperative that the supporting technologies are flexible enough to accommodate both the growing demands of the end-user population and the technical requirements of data warehouses which may grow to the multiple terabyte range.

Clustered SMP versus MPP in Data Warehousing

There is an ongoing debate about which system environment is best suited for managing high-end data warehouses: either symmetric multiprocessor systems (SMP) or massively parallel processor systems (MPP). Currently, both clustered SMP and MPP environments are used in the deployment of large data warehouses.

Massively Parallel Processors

MPP systems are designed for flexibility, manageability, and scalability. These are large, mainframe-sized systems connected by a high-speed communications mechanism or interconnect. Each node consists of a CPU, and its own memory and I/O subsystem—together, these elements create a single, closed environment. The interconnect provides multiple point-to-point connections which scale with the addition of more nodes. These systems are known as *shared-nothing* since they share nothing across nodes. Data and messages must travel across the interconnect.

Although scalable with the MPP shared-nothing approach, the addition of more nodes and users creates a potential bottleneck across the high-speed interconnect. Therefore, as the system scales to higher numbers of CPUs, performance may be compromised, as requests must travel along the "interconnect highway"—from CPU to CPU—to execute tasks that process data and return results. The higher number of nodes in an MPP environment can also pose a potential systems management issue.

Clustered Symmetric Multiprocessors

Symmetric multiprocessor systems have evolved over the past few years as a cost-effective solution for environments that require a robust and scalable solution. Clustered SMP extends this environment by grouping two or more symmetric multiprocessor systems to allow for the efficient utilization of systems resources, with minimal common overhead. The clustered SMP environment is ideal for enterprise-class data warehouses.

Clustered SMP systems combine shared-nothing and shared-everything technologies to provide infinite scalability, while reducing potential bottlenecks. Like MPP, clustered SMP environments employ a shared-nothing technology of passing data and messages between systems via high-speed fiber optic interconnects. Yet unlike MPP, clustered SMP systems also employ a shared-everything environment that utilizes fewer, faster, and more intelligent nodes with fewer interconnects. Each interconnect links supernodes which house multiple CPUs. Each supernode is intelligent and allows data, operating system code, and memory to be utilized within the system.

SMP systems generally provide superior performance because of their ability to share resources within a node. The use of clustered SMP nodes permits the highest performance within a node, while minimizing the amount of traffic between nodes. Higher-performance nodes require fewer nodes to achieve performance goals, simpler management, less partitioning requirements, and more flexible queries.

To accomplish comparable tasks, an MPP system needs to utilize

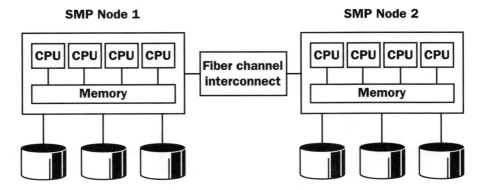

Figure 9-1 A clustered SMP environment requires only one fiber channel connect between nodes.

more less powerful nodes with exponentially more interconnects. For example, in a clustered SMP environment with four CPUs per node, one fiber channel connection is required to communicate with another SMP node; note Figure 9-1.

However, in an MPP system, the same number of processors requires 10 interconnects. Similarly, 16 CPUs require 24 interconnects for an MPP system; see Figure 9-2.

Informix and HP in Enterprise Data Warehousing

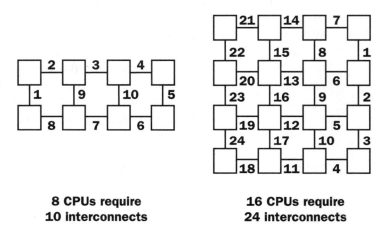

8 CPUs require 10 interconnects

16 CPUs require 24 interconnects

Figure 9-2 MPP systems require more interconnects than clustered SMP systems.

Informix Dynamic Server with the Extended Parallel Option and Advanced Decision Support Option, and the Hewlett-Packard Enterprise Parallel Server™ (EPS) clustered SMP environment provide an ideal infrastructure to support enterprise-class data warehouses. These products' core internal parallelism and complementary architectures provide optimal scalability, real-world performance, availability, and manageability. Organizations can cost-effectively expand from a single processor, to SMP systems, to clustered SMP systems—as data warehouse needs grow and evolve—while still using the same system management infrastructure. This approach to data warehousing supports a gradual evolution that ensures long-term investment protection in a heterogeneous environment.

In contrast to the clustered Informix/HP SMP environment for data warehousing, MPP-based data warehouses typically involve adopting new management technologies that require substantial retraining, more complex management schemes, and greater maintenance efforts. Performance, availability, and manageability can be compromised due to the lack of vertical parallelization in a shared-nothing environment—resulting in an increased need for interconnects and management protocols.

Complementary Architectures

A data warehouse requires a combination of a high-performance server and database software that is flexible enough to meet the growing and evolving needs of the enterprise. HP's industry leading HP-UX® Precision Architecture-Reduced Instruction Set Computer (PA-RISC) architecture and Informix's core internal parallel architecture, Dynamic Scalable Architecture™ (DSA), were designed to provide highly scalable parallel performance. Each is optimized to run in both shared-everything and shared-nothing environments. Informix Dynamic Server with the Extended Parallel Option and Advanced Decision Support Option and HP EPS extend the inherent advantages of each architecture in a clustered SMP environment to effectively address the unique demands of the enterprise-class data warehouse.

Informix Dynamic Server with the Extended Parallel Option and Advanced Decision Support Option

The successful implementation and management of a data warehouse depend in large part on the database software system that supports the warehouse. Infinite scalability, optimal performance, high availability, and the ease of system management are all mandatory features. Achieving these optimal characteristics requires a database engine that is designed at the core to address each interdependent feature—the engine must be infinitely parallel by design, and not by afterthought.

DSA: Parallel Origin

In response to the quickening pace in the development of today's databases and the increasing number of decision-support and OLTP applications, Informix reengineered the architecture of its database engine to support parallelization at the core—taking full advantage of multiprocessor environments. DSA, developed in 1991 and released in 1993, provides parallel processing capabilities at the core of Informix's RDBMS kernel, thereby exploiting a range of multiprocessor environments.

Informix Dynamic Server with the Extended Parallel Option and Advanced Decision Support Option

Informix Dynamic Server with the Extended Parallel Option and Advanced Decision Support Option extends DSA to loosely coupled or shared-nothing computing architectures, including clusters of SMP systems, to completely utilize all available hardware resources. Informix Dynamic Server with the Extended Parallel Option and Advanced Decision Support Option is a next-generation parallel database architecture that delivers mainframe-caliber scalability, manageability, and performance (see Figure 9-3).

Like the hardware architecture that it supports, Informix Dynamic Server with the Extended Parallel Option and Advanced Decision Support Option takes a shared-nothing approach to managing data. This approach greatly minimizes operating system overhead and reduces network I/O. To achieve this level of

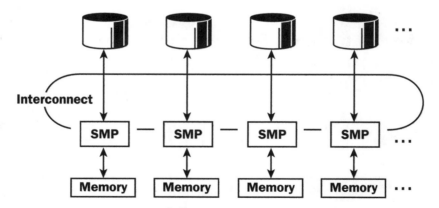

Figure 9-3 Informix Dynamic Server with the Extended Parallel Option and Advanced Decision Support Option features a shared-nothing architecture that delivers almost infinite scalability. Additional SMP nodes can be easily added to accommodate the demands of growing data volumes or additional servers.

independence, each node runs its own instance of the database, which consists of basic services provided by Informix Dynamic Server with the Extended Parallel Option and Advanced Decision Support Option to manage logging, recovery, and buffer management. This instance of the database server is called a *co-server.*

Each co-server owns a set of disks and the partitions of the database that reside on these disks. A co-server typically has physical accessibility to other disks owned by the other co-server(s) for failover purposes; however, in normal operation, each co-server will access only those disks.

Co-servers can interact and coordinate activities with other co-servers on the Informix Dynamic Server with the Extended Parallel Option and Advanced Decision Support Option system. For example, if a co-server receives a request to perform a join, other co-servers in the Informix Dynamic Server with the Extended Parallel Option and Advanced Decision Support Option may be called upon to perform the scan and join and sort tasks, to speed up the query.

Informix Dynamic Server with the Extended Parallel Option and Advanced Decision Support Option ensure that all SQL operations are optimized to enable all nodes within a loosely coupled cluster or MPP architecture to execute tasks in parallel. Informix Dynamic Server with the Extended Parallel Option and Advanced Decision Support Option is the only open database today that provides the ability to perform a comprehensive set of SQL operations in parallel. Additionally, the Informix Dynamic Server with the Extended Parallel Option and Advanced Decision Support Option is one of the few databases to offer the ability to perform hash joins—an invaluable method which is ideal for performing join operations without indices on the join columns. Additionally, this functionality enhances the performance of the RDBMS—without the purchase of additional CPUs—thereby increasing the return on the investment in hardware.

Informix Dynamic Server with the Extended Parallel Option and Advanced Decision Support Option is particularly well suited for the data-intensive tasks that are associated with high-end data warehousing, decision support, and other VLDB applications. Its unique parallel processing and management capabilities provide an order-of-magnitude improvement in performance by automatically distributing tasks across systems and minimizing operating system overhead.

HP 9000 Enterprise Parallel Server

Just as scalable parallel software is a key component of the data warehouse, a scalable, open systems hardware platform that supports the features, benefits, and advantages which are inherent in the RDBMS architecture is critical. The HP Enterprise Parallel Server (EPS) encompasses essential hardware characteristics and is fully complementary to Informix's DSA—exploiting the benefits of each and providing core internal parallelism, optimal scalability, real-world performance, high availability, and superior manageability, with the security of proven technologies.

HP-UX Operating System/PA-RISC Architecture

The HP-UX operating system and the PA-RISC platform provide an ideal foundation for flexible data warehouse solutions. The HP 9000™ performance growth over the past ten years demonstrates a continuing high-performance evolution which maps to businesses' needs to evolve the data warehouse environment. First, HP uniprocessor systems were designed with parallel architecture to provide a strong high-performance CPU foundation (PA-RISC 7100, 7200, and 8000). Next, HP increased performance with the best-in-class SMP systems—HP 9000 models T-Class and K-Class—to offer optimal performance scalability with multisystems and parallel processing.

Hewlett-Packard Enterprise Parallel Server

HP's recent addition of fibre channel interconnects for system-to-system communication is merely an extension of the capabilities and design of HP's architecture. HP's EPS supernodes are by nature parallel: intraserver communication between subtasks residing on the same SMP node takes place via efficient shared-memory pointer passing. The clustered SMP environment provides highly parallel, four- to twelve-way supernodes for the greatest flexibility in fine-tuning performance for real-world, mixed-query, enterprise, DSS, and specialized transaction processing workloads. Supernode, high-performance capacity also reduces data partitioning requirements and minimizes dependency on node interconnect—minimizing the potential of bottlenecks (see Figure 9-4).

HP 9000 Enterprise Parallel Server
Highly Parallel Processing

Supernode

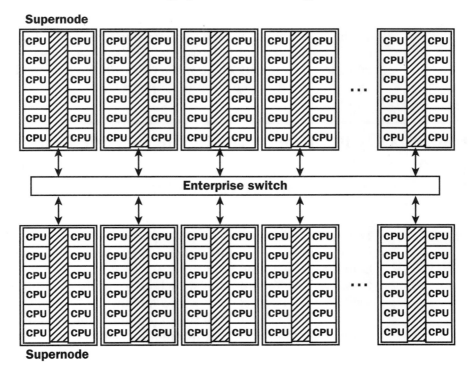

- **Higher performance capacity per 4- to 12-way supernode**
- **More flexible for mixed, complete queries of real-world DSS**
  - ✓ **Structured and sequential queries**
  - ✓ **Ad hoc and random (sml. read/writes) queries**
- **Minimized data partitioning requirements**
- **Minimized dependency on node interconnect bandwidth**
- **Scalable resources (RAM, I/O)**
- **Reduced node-to-node bottleneck potential**

Figure 9-4 *The HP 9000 Enterprise Parallel Server is designed for real-world, large-scale DSS and specialized processing environments.*

The efficiency of HP's EPS solution is enhanced by the following features:

- Evolution to 1 GB/second high-speed fiber channel system interconnect for high-bandwidth, node-to-node switching;
- Modular upgradability for easy scale-up of systems resources;

- Central management and performance monitoring for simplified systems management and optimization; and
- High availability for business-critical computing.

The EPS architecture is a cost-effective solution for large-scale data warehouses and fully supports the inherent benefits of parallelization in Informix Dynamic Server with the Extended Parallel Option and Advanced Decision Support Option.

Informix Dynamic Server with the Extended Parallel Option and Advanced Decision Support Option, and the HP EPS Clustered SMP Environment

The core internal parallelism of a clustered SMP environment is infinitely scalable—providing optimal performance, redundancy for high availability and fault tolerance, and superior manageability. Clustered SMP environments, such as Informix Dynamic Server with the Extended Parallel Option and Advanced Decision Support Option on HP EPS, are well suited to handle the unique challenges of the enterprise-class data warehouse.

Scalable RDBMS

To fully leverage a loosely coupled or clustered SMP environment, the RDBMS must be scalable to accommodate the growing numbers of users and hardware peripherals. Adding CPUs can increase the power of a system, but only if the software is designed to take full advantage of the SMP. Informix Dynamic Server with the Extended Parallel Option and Advanced Decision Support Option supports very large system requirements, including the most demanding OLTP applications and multiterabyte data warehouses. Informix Dynamic Server with the Extended Parallel Option and Advanced Decision Support Option provides multiprocessor support and the ability to add database servers, storage devices, and memory, as required. Data or users can be added without degrading response times.

This almost infinite scalability is achieved through the employment of a configurable pool of database server processes, *virtual processors*. Virtual processors specialize in different resource management tasks, such as CPU work, client/server communication, disk I/O, and database administration. Virtual processes occur at the database level in the form of multithreading, in contrast to other database products which perform these functions at the operating-system process level. Multithreading enables Informix Dynamic Server with the Extended Parallel Option and Advanced Decision Support Option to transparently and dynamically divide these tasks into subtasks. The subtasks can be routed to multiple CPUs without any unnecessary operating-system overhead, enabling infinite scalability.

Open Systems Hardware

In addition to a scalable RDBMS, scalable open systems hardware is essential for the continually changing business demands placed on the enterprise-class data warehouse. The data warehouse platform must process huge amounts of data quickly and efficiently. Businesses must have the capability to add computing resources and users—without affecting the availability of existing data and applications. The database server must be able to schedule tasks to use available resources. A parallel processing server, such as HP EPS, makes full use of SMP systems by dividing end-user requests and queries into subtasks that are performed in parallel. The database can easily scale or grow with future hardware enhancements.

HP enables organizations to seamlessly upgrade from current uniprocessor or SMP systems to clustered SMP systems as needs grow and emerging data warehouse technologies evolve. HP provides a wide range of computing solutions—from standalone uniprocessors to Enterprise Parallel Servers—supporting a broad range of needs through easy hardware upgrades. During a progression through these upgrades, the customer's investment in programming is protected through the binary compatibility of code throughout the product line. SMP nodes permit software to utilize shared-everything techniques which usually require few changes to the code from the uniprocessor implementation. Operating system upgrades are virtually transparent to the operating environment and are frequently accomplished with little or no interruption of the data center.

Real-World Performance

The near-linear scalability of HP's clustered SMP solution, when running on Informix Dynamic Server with the Extended Parallel Option and Advanced Decision Support Option, enables organizations to incrementally increase processing power without compromising performance, as follows:

- Four-way supernodes provide the best price/performance per node at the lowest entry cost;
- Twelve-way supernodes handle work loads with heavy single-node performance requirements; and
- Future scalability to 32 nodes (384 CPUs) is supported.

Through parallel processing, infinite scalability yields enhanced performance. Just as tasks are divided and routed for parallel processing, data and control of the data are divided, or partitioned, to ensure maximum performance and the elimination of bottlenecking.

The use of clustered SMP nodes permits the highest performance within a node, while minimizing the amount of traffic between the nodes. Higher-performance nodes, in turn, mean that fewer nodes are required to achieve performance goals, simpler management, fewer partitioning requirements, and more flexible queries (Figure 9-5).

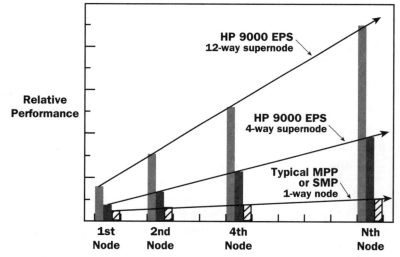

Figure 9-5 HP 9000 EPS provides greater performance capacity per node than MPP or SMP platforms.

Data Partitioning

Data partitioning, also known as *data fragmentation*, provides the basis for the parallel execution of all SQL operations by partitioning large tables and indexes into smaller sections, also known as *fragments*. By breaking down the database into finer granularity, operations such as scans, joins, and sorts can be distributed and executed across multiple CPUs and disks in parallel. Data partitioning minimizes I/O bottlenecks by allowing balanced I/O operations across all nodes and disks within a system (Figure 9-6).

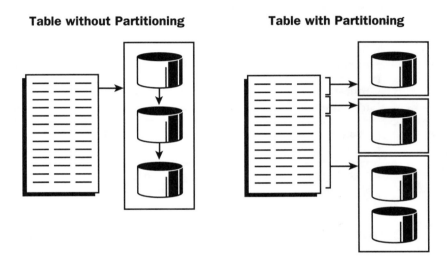

Figure 9-6 *Data partitioning conquers very large databases. A table without partitioning requires serial access, whereas a partitioned table can be accessed in parallel—greatly reducing response time.*

Control Partitioning

Control partitioning minimizes locking, logging, and schedule bottlenecks. Control is partitioned by means of function-shipping algorithms, data partitioning, and advanced query optimization within Informix Dynamic Server with the Extended Parallel Option and Advanced Decision Support Option. Requests are sent only to the node where the data resides. Each node manages the logging, recovery, locking, and buffer management for the database objects that it owns. This approach avoids the bottlenecks caused by central lock management architecture and makes the most efficient use of memory because the database buffers are partitioned.

Query Execution

Finally, queries are broken down into subqueries and executed in parallel (vertical parallelism or intraserver). These subqueries can be further broken down into subtasks that can be executed in parallel on multiple co-servers (horizontal parallelism or interserver). The results of a particular scan can then be pipelined to join a subtask before scans have been completed. Additionally, the results of the join can be pipelined to other subtasks before the join is completed.

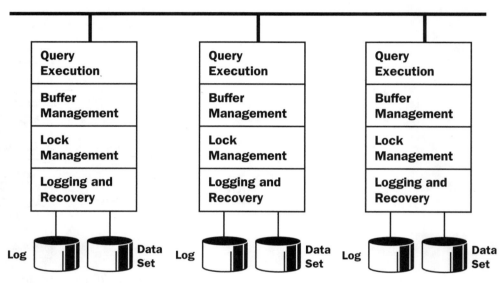

Figure 9-7 *The Informix Dynamic Server with the Extended Parallel Option and Advanced Decision Support Option enables all nodes to manage the control of partitioned data. This eliminates lock-management bottlenecks, thus increasing the efficiency of operations.*

Intraserver Communication

Intraserver communications between subtasks that are located on the same SMP node take place via efficient shared-memory pointer passing. Interserver communications between subtasks on different nodes are achieved by use of networked messages across a high-speed interconnect. The coupling of both interserver and intraserver communication increases performance exponentially as the system scales, since it avoids the blocking or bottlenecking problems generated by the central-system architecture of competing products.

High Availability

As dependency on data warehouses increases, high availability becomes more critical. Should the data become unavailable due to a hardware or software failure, the supporting business functions cease. A clustered SMP environment inherently provides many characteristics of a fault-tolerant system from a hardware perspective since the architecture consists of many independent nodes. Fast detection and automated response to component failures minimize application downtime, as well as provide protection from both planned and unplanned downtime. Rolling upgrades and on-line replacement of key components are easily supported. Informix Dynamic Server with the Extended Parallel Option and Advanced Decision Support Option takes advantage of the fault-tolerant nature of this environment to extend high availability to the database.

Dual-Ported Disks and Other Disk Solutions

In Informix Dynamic Server with the Extended Parallel Option and Advanced Decision Support Option, each co-server owns a set of disks and the portions of the database that reside on disks. In hardware platforms that support dual-ported disks, these disks are dual-ported to other co-servers in the Informix Dynamic Server with the Extended Parallel Option and Advanced Decision Support Option system to guard against unexpected failures. Should a hardware or software problem bring down a co-server on a node, alternate co-servers in the system will take over the disks of the failed node. Recovery procedures will be implemented to ensure that the data is available and accessible after recovery and that the transactions of the failed node are restored to physical and logical consistency. Similarly, if a disk in the system fails, Informix Dynamic Server with the Extended Parallel Option and Advanced Decision Support Option supports database mirroring and logs to provide continuous availability of the failed disk; see Figure 9-8.

Data Replication/Data Skip

In hardware platforms that do not support dual-ported disks, Informix Dynamic Server with the Extended Parallel Option and Advanced Decision Support Option provide data replication and data skip as mechanisms to access data from failed nodes or disks. Data replication places a copy of the database or a portion of the database on a different node—when a node fails, the data is recoverable on another node. Data skip allows for the data on the failed

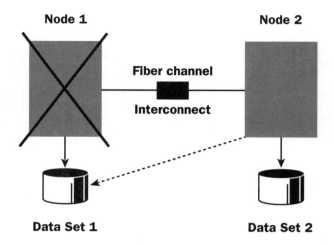

Figure 9-8 *Dynamic data fail-over between nodes provides high availability. If Node 1 fails, Node 2 automatically takes control of Data Set 1.*

node to be passed or skipped, returning a limited number of results to keep from canceling the query.

These levels of fail-over depend on the hardware as much as the software. Protection from disk failure is available through the use of Redundant Array of Independent Disks (RAID) devices. Even greater protection and potentially higher performance are available through the use of HP-UX's Logical Volume Manager and Disk Mirroring. Protection from system failure is accomplished through HP's MC/ServiceGuard™, which permits groups of up to eight systems (sixteen in the next release) to provide fail-over facilities for each other. An open, scalable, parallel, multiway hardware system, such as HP's EPS, works in concert with Informix Dynamic Server with the Extended Parallel Option and Advanced Decision Support Option to ensure high availability and fault tolerance through its complementary architecture.

Systems Management

Database system availability is affected by factors other than system hardware and software faults. Today's data warehouses require that systems be available to users 24 hours per day, 7 days per week, 52 weeks per year. The lack of access to data because of administrative operations is the equivalent of a fault.

On-Line Administration

To minimize the downtime associated with administrative operations, Informix Dynamic Server with the Extended Parallel Option and Advanced Decision Support Option allows database administrators to perform administrative functions without forcing the system to be brought down. These operations include the ability to repartition tables, add and drop columns, add and drop indexes, back up and restore, and change the physical disk or node layout. With the ability to perform these administrative functions on-line, continuous access to data is maintained.

Single-System View

To make these tasks efficient to administer, Informix Dynamic Server with the Extended Parallel Option and Advanced Decision Support Option provides a single-system view. A single-system view enables database administrators to manage multiple database objects that reside on multiple nodes from a single console. This capability is especially important in clustered SMP environments, where data is likely to be partitioned across multiple nodes for maximum database efficiency. The single-system view enables database administrators to configure, monitor, control, and install all database objects in the network from one centralized location, thus dramatically decreasing the amount of time required to manage this multinode environment. Informix Dynamic Server with the Extended Parallel Option and Advanced Decision Support Option supports Simple Network Management Protocol (SNMP) environments such as Hewlett-Packard's OpenView™, as well as a number of lower-level Application Programming Interfaces (APIs) and the industry-leading Tivoli Management Environment™ (TME) from Tivoli Systems.

Improved Manageability

HP has a broad range of enterprise management and performance monitoring tools to facilitate the management of Informix Dynamic Server with the Extended Parallel Option and Advanced Decision Support Option on EPS. For example, HP OpenView provides a framework that permits a graphical, single view of the enterprise, including simplified task execution, advanced problem detection and management, and unattended parallel backup for large databases. Within the OpenView framework, a number of solutions from HP and other solution providers facilitate the management of the enterprise.

Intelligent nodes and minimal communication via fiber channel connections make HP's clustered SMP data warehouse environment easy to manage. Also, little or no retraining of system administrators is necessary because HP's clustered SMP environment allows businesses to add to, as opposed to replace, current systems. By minimizing the number of nodes necessary, the EPS architecture provides considerable flexibility and ease of administration for Informix database administrators and designers.

Early Benchmark Results

Early tests show that Informix Dynamic Server with the Extended Parallel Option and Advanced Decision Support Option on HP's Enterprise Parallel Server is an ideal infrastructure to support enterprise-class data warehouses. The combined Informix Dynamic Server with the Extended Parallel Option and Advanced Decision Support Option/EPS solution demonstrates impressive results—both in the area of database scalability and in database speedup.

The following tests were conducted at the joint HP/Informix Advanced Development Lab at Informix's Menlo Park facilities. The goal was to test the initial scalability and speedup of Informix Dynamic Server with the Extended Parallel Option and Advanced Decision Support Option on HP EPS clusters, using a combination of complex queries common in decision-support environments. A 100-GB database (350 GB total disk) was tested on an HP EPS20 cluster, using fiber channel interconnect technology and nodes with four PA-RISC 7200 (100 MHz) processors. The database was partitioned across eight Fast/Wide SCSI-2 disks on each node. Data was fragmented across disks, using fragmentation techniques internal to Informix Dynamic Server with the Extended Parallel Option and Advanced Decision Support Option. No LVM disk striping was used.

In the first test, both the number of nodes and the size of the database were doubled. For linear scalability, one would expect the load and query times to remain constant. These tests indicated database scalability between 95 and 97 percent.

Table 9-1 First benchmark test.

	1 node/4 GB (hh:mm:ss)	2 node/8 GB (hh:mm:ss)	Scalability
Database Load Time	0:27:52	0:28:40	97.13%
17 Decision-Support Queries	3:12:10	3:20:16	95.78%

In the second test, the number of nodes was doubled, but the database size remained constant. One would expect the load times and query execution times to be reduced by 50 percent. These tests indicated a database speed up of 94 percent.

Table 9-2 Second benchmark test.

	1 node/4 GB (hh:mm:ss)	2 node/4 GB (hh:mm:ss)	Speedup
17 Decision-Support Queries	3:12:10	1:41:33	94.31%

For the above two tests (Tables 9-1 and 9-2), data load rates were in excess of 2.2 GB/hour/CPU. As such, a one-node system with a total of four CPUs sustained a load rate of 8.8 GB/hour. An eight-CPU system, distributed over two nodes, sustained a load rate of 17.3 GB/hour.

In the third test, a multiuser data warehouse benchmark test with very complex queries was used to test disk-access rates, load rates, and fiber channel switch throughput on a four-node EPS20.

Informix Dynamic Server with the Extended Parallel Option and Advanced Decision Support Option traffic across the fiber channel interconnect consisted of an average 8.3K packet size, with 250–500 packets going in each direction from every node. As such, aggregate throughput through the switch averaged 16 MB/second (four nodes x 500 packets/second/node x 8.3K packet size). Disk access rates averaged 9 MB/second/node. Peak rates were higher.

Informix Dynamic Server with the Extended Parallel Option and Advanced Decision Support Option on HP's Enterprise Parallel Server provides a powerful platform for enterprise-class data warehouses. The combined Informix Dynamic Server with the Extended Parallel Option and Advanced Decision Support Option/EPS solution provides near-linear scalability, as well as database speedup.

Conclusion

The complementary architectures of Hewlett-Packard Enterprise Parallel Server and Informix Dynamic Server with the Extended Parallel Option and Advanced Decision Support Option offer businesses an ideal foundation for enterprise-class data warehousing. The core internal parallelism in both hardware and database software provides optimal performance—exploiting the inherent benefits of each—to enable near-linear scalability, high availability, and ease of management.

Ongoing joint development efforts at the HP and Informix Advanced Development Lab ensure that the architectures of Informix Dynamic Server with the Extended Parallel Option and Advanced Decision Support Option and HP EPS are optimized to exploit parallelism and to maximize performance and scalability. Early results indicate near-linear intranode and node-to-node scalability.

Both Informix and HP provide leadership in protecting the investments of their customers. The HP-clustered SMP environment provides unprecedented investment protection, enabling customers to add to their current uniprocessor or SMP implementations as their needs grow—without investments in new technology or the retraining of personnel. HP and Informix are industry leaders, with proven track records in the delivery of state-of-the-art technologies. Businesses can feel safe in investing in these products, confident that HP and Informix will meet their current and long-term enterprise-class data warehouse needs.

About the Author

Steve Deck is the Hewlett-Packard Business Development manager at Informix, Menlo Park, California. He has 13 years of experience in the high-technology industry and has co-authored several books on business management and strategies, including *Strategic Corporate Alliances, The Protectionist Threat to Corporate America, The Management of Corporate Business Units,* and *Corporate Financial Planning and Management in a Deficit Economy.* Steve holds a Bachelor of Science degree in Operations Research and Industrial Engineering from Cornell University.

Chapter

10

Data Warehousing and the Value of 64-Bit Computing

by Marvin Miller

Introduction

We live in a very exciting time in the computer industry. The promises of the past 15 years are being realized in the form of advanced PCs, the unprecedented connectivity of the Internet, and the vast improvements in system performance and software features.

Today, huge volumes of data can be cataloged, indexed, combined, and analyzed to uncover hidden relationships about seemingly unrelated facts, to provide information about group behavior, and to coordinate the activities of organizations' worldwide sales forces.

An example of this power comes from D. Wayne Calloway, CEO of Pepsico, who gave the following presentation several years ago at a stockholder meeting. It is indicative of how far data warehousing systems have progressed:

"Ten years ago I could have told you how Doritos were selling west of the Mississippi. Today, not only can I you how well Doritos sell west of the Mississippi, I can tell you how well they are selling

in California,
in Orange County,
in the town of Irvine,

in the local Von's supermarket,
in the special promotion,
at the end of aisle 4,
on Thursdays."

The purpose of this chapter is to acquaint the reader with the uses for data warehousing. This chapter also discusses how a data warehouse is built, the technical trends that support data warehousing, and the expected future growth of data warehousing.

The explosion in data warehousing activity has spawned a new and sometimes entirely separate computing culture with distinct products, performance measurements, schema design, and capacities. 64-bit computing is central to this growth.

The chapter concludes with examples that demonstrate how 64-bit computing enables this growth in the areas of very large data sets, improved performance, and the ability to handle problems of higher complexity.

Business Work Flow

Work Flow for Operational Data Systems (OLTP)

Computer systems and applications have evolved over the last 30 years. Both applications and system hardware were initially developed to solve specific problems. Usually, this meant solving a particular need—since engineering resources were scarce and the technology extremely limited and costly by today's standards.

Thus, applications evolved to support clerical processes, especially the processes which kept the parent business running—writing checks for Accounts Payable, balancing the General Ledger, and other accounting functions. Over time, a large number of applications were developed, and they amassed large amounts of historical data. However, most of this data was archived since the needs of the business only dictate a 6- to 18-month history for the recall of most data.

Operational data systems (ODS) mirror the primary accounting functions: A/P, G/L, A/R, Payroll, etc. ODS are involved with transactions, which allow users to update or retrieve specific pieces of information in answer to specific queries. Most of these queries are not flexible, and the generated reports are fixed in design because the reports' uses are repetitive.

Finally, these ODS systems usually run at or near capacity and are finely tuned and maintained to provide optimal performance for the investment that they represent. In summary, the ODS runs the business, and every precaution is taken to keep the ODS system running efficiently—since the health of the business relies on their daily performance.

Work Flow for OLTP and DSS

Computer systems are becoming more abundant because of reduced prices. In addition, these newer systems offer increased capacity and performance. Software applications—notably, the relational databases such as Informix Dynamic Server™—are more robust and capable of handling large volumes of information. As a result, Decision-Support Systems (DSS) have grown in popularity and influence.

Data warehousing and DSS systems are now used to analyze corporate data instead of running the daily business. The results of the analyses are used to guide the business, resulting in new and improved policies and procedures. Figure 10-1 shows how the business cycle is completed by the use of both operational and DSS systems. The operational systems run the business, and the decision-support systems guide the business.

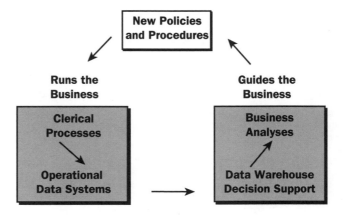

Figure 10-1 Work flow for OLTP and DSS.

Data Warehousing's Hidden Relationships

One of the exciting uses for data warehousing is in discovering the hidden relationships from mountains of data. These relationships explain phenomena and can be used as rules for a variety of strategic planning and business evaluations. Several examples follow which illustrate this point.

Examples

Market-Basket Analysis

A well-known small market chain looked for ways to improve their use of floor space. After an extensive market-basket analysis—analysis of the contents of a customer's purchase—a very high correlation between sales of disposable diapers and beer on Friday nights was revealed. In the analysis, it was determined that fathers of infants and young children stopped on their way home to pick up additional supplies for the weekend. Based on this input, the store moved the diapers next to the beer and sales rose for both items.

Buying Patterns

A famous clothing chain performed a similar analysis and combined weather data with sales receipts. It found a high correlation in the purchase of dark clothes on rainy days. The chain directed its stores to move the clothes racks containing dark clothes to the front of the store on cloudy or overcast days. Sales rose by approximately 70 percent.

The Relation of Samples to Prescriptions

A famous pharmaceutical company analyzed the results of giving drug samples to doctors and the subsequent prescriptions that were written by the same doctors. Those who did not write new prescriptions against the samples were visited less frequently.

The Value of Data Relationships

These anecdotes are interesting and entertaining; however, the value of discovering hidden data relationships and putting the uncovered information into practice creates significant benefits for business. For example, the drug company realized a million-dollar payback in only ten weeks. The data warehousing system investment was completely recouped in that brief duration. The three-month pilot was put into production immediately.

The clothing store chain realized a 70-percent jump in sales when the store layout was matched to the daily weather pattern. There are many other examples of the power inherent in this kind of analysis: stolen phone cards can be detected in one day or less, purchasing behavior can predict significant life-style changes, including an impending bankruptcy, and so on.

Clearly, the business advantage generated by these analyses is even more critical as competitive pressures grow. The efforts to reduce costs, improve efficiency, and improve competitive position all drive the need for this form of analysis. To use a metaphor from Marshall McLuhan, we can no longer navigate by looking through the rear-view mirror of life. We must find the hidden relationships in data and change business behavior to improve or take advantage of such relationships.

Data Warehouse Examples

Table 10-1 lists only a sampling of the more popular areas for analysis.

Table 10-1 *Examples of popular analyses.*

How Is the Hidden Relationship Found?

- Frequent-Shopper Programs
- Market Basket Analysis
- Product Affinity Analysis
- New-Market Identification
- New-Market Creation
- Multiaccount Incentives
- Product Profitability
- New-Product Demand
- Margin-Based Delivery
- Dynamic Price Markdowns
- Rapid Distribution Response
- Store-Level Forecasting
- Supply Chain Integration
- Micromarketing Programs
- Demand Profiling Analysis
- High-Value Relations Mgmt.
- Affinity/Gap Targeting
- Churn Analysis/Retention

Successful data warehousing analyses are:

- Cross-functional—Spanning different departments or disciplines. Sales data can be matched with production data and even external data, such as marketing demographics.
- Derived from ad hoc queries—The analysis follows no set formula or pattern.
- Complex—Several different variables are combined in the hopes of discovering hidden relationships.
- Involved with large data sets—Historical data must be available to produce successful and meaningful results.

The idea is to "think large"—using more data helps to build a more complete analysis—and to "think with varied data"—using data from several sources to identify the root causes for business patterns.

Linking the ODS and DSS

There are fundamental differences in the evolution, usage, system configuration, and performance between operational and decision-support systems. The ultimate purpose for the DSS is to guide the business, rather than to run it on a daily basis. Data warehouse systems use separate computing resources from the operational systems, run specific applications, require deeper historical archives, and call for specialized tuning.

However, the two systems—operational and decision support—are linked by a fundamental requirement: the same data source must be used to make the two systems truly symbiotic. To be useful, the data used by the data warehousing system must be pulled from the operational system, verified, and occasionally transformed and consolidated. The data stored in the DSS system is processed in a different way and is not stored with the same schema as an OLTP system.

Finally, a feedback loop must link the people who perform the analysis—the power users—to the extant policies and procedures. With this link, new rules can be invoked and supported quickly. Fortunately, one characteristic of data warehouse systems is that such systems are often supported by senior management because of the extraordinary business results that are provided.

Following is a summary of DSS requirements:

- Use selected operational data—Extracted, cleansed, and transformed;
- Use a separate computer for performance—Operational systems at or near maximum;
- Store data in a form ready for any query—Denormalized;
- Create a feedback loop to use analysis results—Take into account power users and new policies and procedures; and
- Obtain the support of executive management.

Accessing the Operational Data Store

Which Data Is Needed?

When a data warehousing system is being built, the system must be stocked with data from the organization's business. However, the operational system has been accumulating data for years. This data is now stored in vaults, on tape, or on some other archive material. The evolution of the computer industry has generated many different forms of data storage, access methods, programming languages, and even transaction-processing monitors. Figure 10-2 highlights the popular methods used to store legacy data, organized by decade.

Legacy data is often enmeshed in a series of business processes and resulting programs that have evolved over 30 years. What is legacy data? It is simply the data that must be used every day. This does not necessarily mean "old" data.

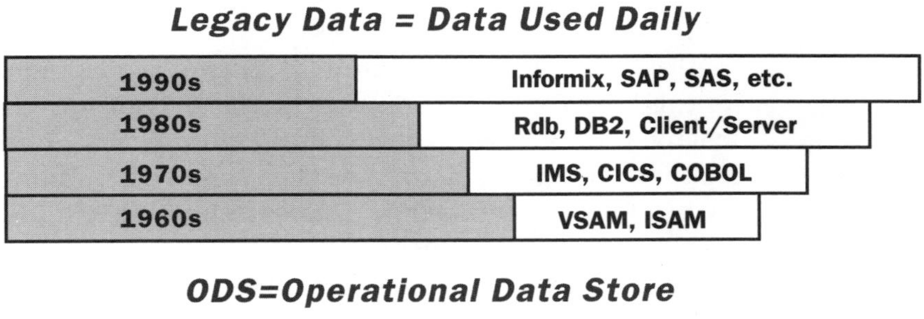

Legacy Data = Data Used Daily

1990s	Informix, SAP, SAS, etc.
1980s	Rdb, DB2, Client/Server
1970s	IMS, CICS, COBOL
1960s	VSAM, ISAM

ODS=Operational Data Store

Figure 10-2 Popular data storage mechanisms by decade.

Although its sources and uses may be quite varied, legacy data is integral to the functioning of the business. It is extremely difficult to change the programs or usage of this data. This evolution, in turn, creates a new meaning for ODS—the "Ossified Data Strata."

Legacy data presents a significant question to the builders of new data warehousing systems: "Which data do I use?" The answer is that portions of all data are needed to populate the data warehouse. The data warehousing system must be updated frequently by the ongoing results of the operational system, and the data warehousing system also stores data for longer periods than the existing operational systems; note Figure 10-3.

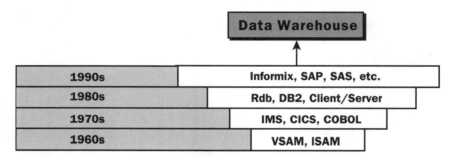

Figure 10-3 *Moving legacy data into the data warehousing system.*

A Different Data Design for Ad Hoc Queries

Operational data systems are designed and optimized in most cases to handle high-transaction volumes. This means that each data item must be accessible from a variety of different programs at any one point in time. Linking data items can cause delays or even inconsistencies when processed incorrectly.

For these reasons, most RDBMS systems for operational systems that support OLTP use a database schema that is highly optimized for this "piece by piece" approach. This is known as a normalized schema, or a schema which is in the third-normal form—all of the redundancies in the data have been removed, and the individual pieces of data are linked by a series of indexes, via the RDBMS.

DSS systems do not use the data in a piece-by-piece manner. Instead, the DSS traverses entire tables, joins entire tables, and even uses tables to search against other tables. For these reasons, the DSS is cumbersome and slower to rely on than many indexes to reach data that is related in some form.

Data warehousing systems actually combine some of the data items, or denormalize the data, to gain efficiencies when an entire table is processed. A common example of this process is known as a star schema. In a star schema, a central fact table is linked or controlled by several dimension tables. The facts are the sales receipts, for example, and the dimensions are the boundaries, such as "Customer," "Salesman," "Time Period," etc. Note Figure 10-4.

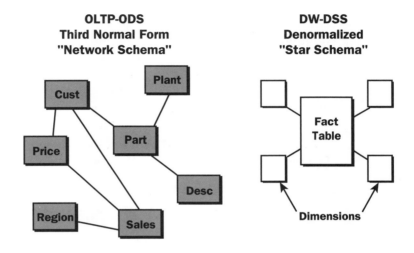

Figure 10-4 *Different data design for ad hoc queries.*

Future Needs

Explosive Growth

Once a data warehousing system demonstrates success—especially in real business terms—its growth is almost explosive. More users appear almost daily with requests to access the new analysis tool. This success usually translates to more queries from more departments—remember, the key to the analysis is in using cross-functional data. Ultimately, the query becomes more complex; users want to access data in increasingly novel ways: four-way, five-way, and n-way joins. Finally, additions to the data itself sometimes occur, including deeper histories and more sources.

This growth is good for the business—since more accurate analysis leads to more accurate business goals and practices. However, such growth places a strain on the data warehousing system, to say the least.

The amount of growth for data warehousing systems cannot be forecasted at the current time. Similarly, the impact of the data warehousing system on business cannot be predicted. The DSS causes a fundamental change to the organization. Once discovered, it is not possible to turn back.

Finally, the organizational reach of the data warehousing system cannot be predicted. Presently, several businesses are changing the boundaries of their departments to handle the new business dynamics. The traditional "stove pipe" departments are being swept away, and new, refocused organizations are taking their places.

Traditional computer systems—such as SAP R/3 or PeopleSoft—can be planned for and their growth managed, and therefore, such systems can be implemented gracefully over a given time period. A data warehousing system can literally take off and consume large amounts of computer resources in a short period of time; note Figure 10-5.

- **Cannot predict the impact of a data warehouse**
- **Cannot predict the organizational reach of the data warehouse**
- **Data warehouse growth is unpredictable, without precedent and has executive support**

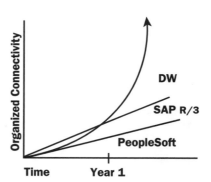

Figure 10-5 The explosive growth of data warehousing systems.

Technical Trends

What are the underlying computer trends needed to support data warehousing? How can the systems of today and beyond begin to cope with the explosive growth which is forecast for data warehousing? Can the RDBMS systems of the future—such as Informix Dynamic Server—support large capacity and complex queries and provide significant performance to match the increasing needs and pace of business analysis? The following trends support data ware-

Data Warehousing with Informix: Best Practices

housing growth and the expansion of sophisticated RDBMS tools like Informix Dynamic Server:

- CPU power will continue to grow.
  More MIPS are always needed. Systems like Digital's AlphaServer will continue to lead the industry in clock speed (currently at 350 MHz) and resulting application performance.
- The WAN will become as fast as the LAN.
  New technologies in both compression and transmission will make remote systems appear closer.
- Memory will offset limited disk performance growth.
  As working sets grow, as applications become more complex, and as more users are added, system memory will continue to be the best value for improving overall system performance.
- Denormalization uses more disk storage.
  Introducing some redundancy in data will consume more disk space, and the addition of deeper histories and more sources of data will also contribute to higher data capacities on a given system.

These trends suggest a centralized system resource for the data warehousing system. Concentrating the expensive resources—memory, disk, and CPU—in one system makes sense from a cost standpoint. Clearly, Informix Dynamic Server already supports the large volumes of data needed for data warehousing.

The "fat server/skinny client" approach is compelling since it is cost effective, easier to manage, and supports multiple users from a common data source.

The Value of 64-Bit Computing

Previously, most computer systems were based on 32-bit architectures; file sizes could be as large as 2 GB, and many hundreds of users could work on a given SMP system. However, a data warehousing system needs files and system memory well in excess of 2 GB in order to traverse the huge tables and create the five-way (or larger) joins that are required for business analyses. The answer lies in the next step for computer architectures: 64-bit computing.

What do 64-bit applications provide? They provide the ability to handle huge amounts of data without limitations of size, complexity, or performance. For example, 64-bit applications currently run databases that are several times larger than the largest 32-bit system is capable of processing. 64-bit database responsetimes actually improve as the complexity of the query increases. As for performance, 64-bit databases can in some cases exceed the performance of 32-bit databases by over 1,000 times.

Technically, 64-bit computing affords more bits, which application developers can use for internal tables, broader indexes, and the ability to literally catalog any amount of data in a single file or database. Beyond the simple arithmetic of adding more bits of address space, 64-bit computing offers economies of scale as well.

64-bit architectures are being developed by the leading hardware manufacturers. A few are even including 64-bit CPU chips in their system offerings. Digital Equipment Corporation, however, has shipped a complete system—hardware, operating system, compilers, libraries, and 64-bit based applications—on its 64-bit computing platform, the Alpha® family, since 1991.

64-bit computing is not limited to the CPU chip or its supporting hardware system. The applications must be developed for 64-bit computing as well, to achieve the performance and scaling benefit. In fact, the operating system, compilers, and runtime libraries must be developed, coordinated, and tuned so that the overall system is a success.

After the system and system software are designed and built, as outlined above, the next step in the development process is to work closely with the relational database to take full advantage of the underlying 64-bit architecture. When this is completed, the potential for application growth in size and speed is enormous.

The power of 64-bit computing is the next evolutionary step for data warehousing and large computing problems.

Large Data Set Capacity

As mentioned previously, 64-bit computing allows for larger internal tables and bigger indexes, and ultimately solves bigger problems. One example is the Supply Chain Decision Support™ application from Manugistics. Their software is used for demand, distribution, manufacturing and transportation planning not only across an enterprise, but throughout the entire supply chain. An underlying RDBMS is used to store detailed data—such as Stock Keeping Units (SKUs) and Demand Forecasting Units (DFUs).

Using 64-bit computing, the size of the database used by Manugistics can be expanded significantly beyond the range of 32-

bit systems. This expansion allows the application to store significantly more SKUs than ever before.

With the advent of vendor-managed inventory and efficient consumer response programs, growth is a critical need. Growth will force the need for larger and larger numbers of SKUs and DFUs in the future. An example of this heightened capacity and the resulting performance through the use of Digital's 64-bit architecture is shown in Figure 10-6. In this example, a 250,000 SKU database was built and tested on Digital's AlphaServer. Previous SKU sizes were limited to less than 100,000 SKUs. Not only is the AlphaServer capable of running the larger database, it runs in less time than smaller SKU databases using 32-bit technology.

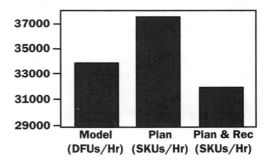

Manugistics—Supply Chain Decision Support

- **No other vendor can support a 250,000 SKU database.**
- **No other vendor has published 100,000 SKU numbers.**
- **No 32-bit vendor can come close to offering these results.**

Figure 10-6 *Supporting large data set capability.*

Application Performance

64-bit computing creates application performance benefits as well as size benefits. Informix and other RDBMS manufacturers have developed 64-bit versions of their products for the Alpha family of systems. Significant performance gains occur when the 64-bit version is invoked.

Figure 10-7 clearly shows the boost in performance—1,200 times—over the 32-bit version of the same RDBMS. In this example, a hypothetical breakfast food manufacturer must analyze shelf-space allocation for future planning.

This performance is achieved by use of both the inherent gains of

64-bit computing and the Very Large Memory (VLM) option available with Digital's AlphaServer family. Since there are no constraints regarding file size or memory size, large amounts of physical memory can be configured on Alpha systems. In other words, very large data sets and very large databases (VLDBs) can be built and run in system memory. In this case, 6 GB of physical memory were used to run the complete problem in three seconds, compared to the original one hour to run with the 32-bit version of the RDBMS.

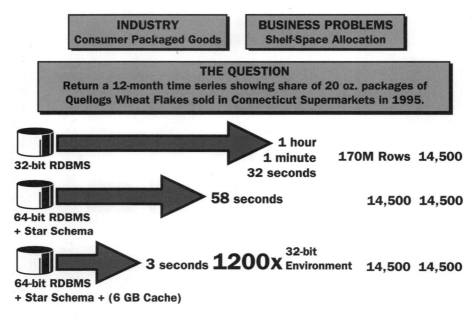

Figure 10-7 *VLM64 application performance.*

Increased Performance As Complexity Grows

As described earlier, business analyses will continue to increase in complexity. This increase results in a much harder challenge for the supporting RDBMS—both in performance and management. Three-way, four-way, and five-way joins are becoming increasingly popular and will be extended as soon as computer systems are able to support extensions of the current technology.

64-bit computing on Digital systems not only supports complex joins, but the performance actually increases as the joins become more complex. Figure 8 shows these results. Informix ran identical tests, using a 32-bit version and a 64-bit version of their product. As the number of joins increased, the performance increased by a large margin—up to 251 times.

To put this in perspective, if the 1:251 ratio is converted to linear distance, for every foot traveled by the 32-bit version, approximately one football field is traversed by the 64-bit version.

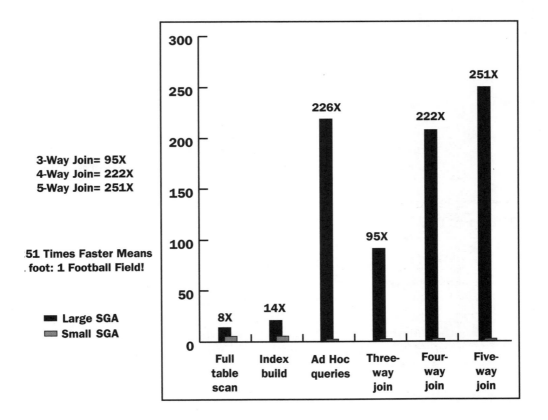

Figure 10-8 *Higher performance as complexity grows.*

Conclusion

Data warehousing can provide business analyses that create competitive advantages, improve productivity, and lower costs. The size, complexity, and frequency of data warehousing queries continue to grow at a rapid pace. 64-bit computing is the only viable environment for large and complex queries and also provides performance benefits that equal or exceed those of yesterday's computers.

The two industry forces—data warehousing and 64-bit computing—are well matched. When combined, these two forces afford continued growth and higher levels of performance for large-scale computing problems. This combination results in a competitive business advantage for companies that use 64-bit computing.

About the Author

Marvin Miller is a senior consultant for Digital Equipment Corporation, where he works closely with Informix on large-scale data warehousing opportunities. He has 25 years of experience in the computer industry, including large-scale system design, benchmarking, and migrations. Special thanks to Scott Semple, president of NewTHINK, Inc., for his significant contributions to this article.

About Digital Equipment Corporation

Digital Equipment Corporation is the leading worldwide supplier of networked computer systems, software, and services. Digital pioneered and leads the industry in interactive, distributed, and multivendor computing. An international company, Digital conducts more than half its business outside the United States, developing and manufacturing products and providing customer services in the Americas, Europe, Asia, and the Pacific Rim.

The Use of Storage Subsystems in Data Warehousing

by Rob Nicholson and
Nancy Ann Coon

Introduction

The implementation of a data warehouse can provide a competitive edge to companies. It is also a major undertaking and requires thoughtful and competent project management in order to ensure success. This article focuses on an aspect that is often taken for granted in a data warehouse, the physical repository of the data itself: the storage subsystem. It also highlights the successful Informix Dynamic Server with the Extended Parallel Option and Advanced Decision Support Option™ data warehouse at MCI®, implemented on an IBM® RS/6000 SP™ with terabytes of data on IBM SSA disks.

Components of a Data Warehouse

As with any computer application, a data warehouse consists of software and hardware components. A data warehouse is likely to be mission critical, almost by definition. If the data being warehoused were not of value, the effort required to organize it into a warehouse would not be justified. Therefore, the most important aspect of any data warehouse is the data itself. By processing this data quickly and accurately, companies can be rewarded with tremendous competitive advantages.

This processing ability is provided by the other components of the data warehouse: the database software and the computer itself. Often, the focus on the computer is on the processing capabilities of the CPU. Equally important is the storage media where the data resides—the disk storage subsystem. The ability to quickly feed data from the physical repository to the CPU, where the database software can unlock its secrets, is a very important aspect of a balanced data warehouse. Initial decisions about how to arrange the data on the disks and what type of disk subsystems to use can be very important to end results. This chapter discusses these issues as they relate to Informix Dynamic Server with the Extended Parallel Option and Advanced Decision Support Option, a parallel database optimized for MPP environments such as IBM's RS/6000 SP.

Hardware and Software Overview

Let's look briefly at the hardware provided by IBM's Massively Parallel Processor (MPP) product. The IBM RS/6000 SP consists of between 1 and 512 processor nodes. Each processor node is a stand-alone system, with its own memory, running a copy of AIX®, IBM's industrial-strength UNIX operating system. The nodes can be uniprocessors or symmetric multiprocessors (SMP) and are connected by a high-bandwidth, low latency, interconnect fabric known as the SP Switch. Each node may have one or more adapters within it that give it access to a storage subsystem of some type. The choice of a storage subsystem is the issue addressed by this chapter, and options range from directly attached disk drives to complex out-board RAID storage subsystems. Throughout this chapter, we use the term *storage subsystem* to mean any one of these options (see Figure 11-1).

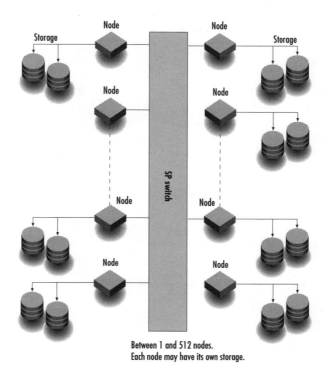

Figure 11-1 *Block diagram of IBM RS/6000 SP architecture.*

Informix Dynamic Server with the Extended Parallel Option and Advanced Decision Support Option exploits this architecture, using a true shared-nothing parallel database server architecture. Each node runs its own instance of the database, which consists of the basic Informix Dynamic Server with the Extended Parallel Option and Advanced Decision Support Option services to manage logging, recovery, locking, and buffer management. This instance of the database is called a co-server. Each co-server "owns" a set of disks (or part of a storage subsystem) and the partitions of the database that reside on those disks. A co-server will typically have physical accessibility to other disks owned by other co-servers for fail-over purposes; however, in normal operation, each co-server accesses only the disks that it owns (see Figure 11-2).

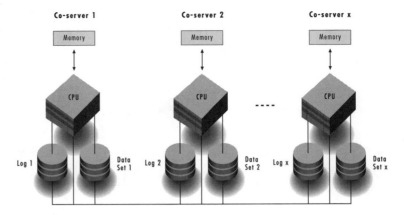

Figure 11-2 *The architecture of Informix Dynamic Server with the Extended Parallel Option and Advanced Decision Support Option.*

Data Placement

To exploit the opportunities for parallelism provided by a massively parallel processor (MPP) such as IBM's RS/6000 SP, Informix Dynamic Server with the Extended Parallel Option and Advanced Decision Support Option partitions data. That is, it spreads the data from each table across many co-servers and across several disks on each node. This means that a single query may involve many nodes in retrieving data. On any individual node, partitioning means that multiple disks will receive I/O requests in order to satisfy a single query. It follows, therefore, that the best overall performance will be achieved if the I/O system is able to accept these multiple concurrent I/O operations without introducing contention between the operations for resources.

A database administrator (DBA) knows very well that the placement of data on disks is critical to database performance. In order to maximize database performance, a DBA will typically perform the following steps:

1. Place the root dbspace, logical log, and physical log in separate dbspaces on separate disks.
2. Assign temporary tables and sort files to separate disks.
3. Place heavily used tables on separate disks.

Each of these measures aims to maximize performance by increasing parallelism and minimizing contention for any particular resource, thereby optimizing the use of the available I/O bandwidth. To further minimize contention, critical resources may be spread across multiple disk controllers. As we explain later, the requirement to do this depends somewhat upon the storage technology chosen.

Another measure often taken by the DBA to improve performance is to place the most critical data in the middle partition of the disk drive, that is, midway between the inner and outer tracks of the disk. This placement reduces the disk head movement required to reach the most frequently accessed data. The time taken to move the head to the required track, known as *seek time*, is an important part of the *response time*—the time measured from the point at which the database requests an I/O operation and the time that operation completion is communicated back to the database.

Traditionally, placing data in the middle of the disk is one of the few activities that the database administrator can perform to reduce response time, but as we discuss later, the choice of storage subsystem is also very important in this area.

The Elements of Response Time

The term *response time* describes the total time between the application requesting an I/O operation and receiving notification of the completion of the I/O operation. For a simple disk access, the components of response time include:

1. The time taken for the operating system to process the request and submit it to the adapter.
2. The time taken for the adapter to convey the request to the disk drive.
3. The time taken for the disk drive head to seek to the required track on the disk (seek latency).
4. The time taken for the data which needs to be read or written to rotate under the disk head (rotational latency).
5. The time taken to transfer the data.
6. The time taken to pass completion status from the disk drive to the adapter.
7. The time taken for the operating system to pass the completion status back to the application.

To improve performance, one or more of these seven components of response time must be improved, or two or more of them may be overlapped with one another.

Bandwide and Response Time

Bandwidth and response time are two important attributes of a storage subsystem. Depending upon the workload, one variable may be more or less important than the other. However, in many cases, it is important to optimize both.

Bandwidth is the measure of the rate at which the storage subsystem or device can transfer data, such as 10 MB/second. Bandwidth, however, says nothing about the length of time between the application asking for the data and the data arriving. It merely indicates how fast the data will flow once it starts flowing.

Response time is the measure of how long it takes the storage subsystem to complete an I/O. Response time depends upon many factors, including several aspects of the workload and the bandwidth. It is also quite difficult to measure response time on many UNIX platforms. For these reasons, response time is rarely quoted in advertising literature or reviews. It is important nonetheless.

Disk-Access Patterns in Data Warehousing Applications

Data warehousing applications have very characteristic disk-access patterns, which are quite distinct from those found in online transaction processing (OLTP) applications. From a disk point of view, the workload can be split into two distinct categories:

• Database load; and
• Query.

Query can be further subdivided into the following:

• Complex query; and
• Data mining.

Database Load

Database load is highly write intensive. Typically, a database load involves a number of distinct streams of I/O to different tables, which ideally will have been placed upon different disks. Each stream behaves as follows: it reads some data from the input media, possibly processes it in some way, and then writes it to the storage subsystem. While the storage subsystem is transferring the data out of system memory, the process stops. Only when the storage subsystem signals that it has finished the write does the process continue by reading more data from the input device. Since the database load process waits for the storage subsystem each time a write occurs, the time taken to load the database is highly dependent upon the overall time taken to write the data, the write response time, and not solely the available bandwidth.

Complex Query

A complex query involves long reads. Often, whole tables must be read into memory in order to execute a complex query. As we have seen, Informix Dynamic Server with the Extended Parallel Option and Advanced Decision Support Option contains complex partitioning algorithms which allow it to spread the data as evenly as possible across all the disks and CPUs used for the database. This means that, provided the storage subsystem can handle it, a complex query should result in all disks—which make up the database—transferring data simultaneously into memory on multiple servers. This high degree of parallelism should result in excellent performance; however, this result depends upon the storage subsystem's ability to efficiently transfer multiple data streams.

Informix optimizes its queries in order to minimize the rereading of data. This optimization is pertinent to the use of read caches for Informix databases. It means that a complex query application running on Informix Dynamic Server with the Extended Parallel Option and Advanced Decision Support Option is unlikely to be accelerated very much by the provision of an outboard read cache.

Where very large tables must be joined or sorted, Informix may find that they are too large to be placed entirely in memory. In this case, Informix will make use of a temporary dbspace. This temporary space will, of course, receive writes as well as reads. In this case, the performance of the I/O device used to support the temporary space is critical to the performance of the application as a whole.

Data Mining

The I/O patterns which result from data mining are similar to those of complex query, perhaps with a greater proportion of long reads.

Available Storage Technologies

We have seen that the performance of the database system as a whole can be critically affected by the choice of storage subsystem. There are many parameters to consider when choosing a storage product. The two most important are probably the choice of the interconnect technology, such as SCSI or SSA, and the way that the data is protected against hardware failure, using mirroring or a redundant array of independent disks (RAID). It is also important to consider the effect of caching upon the performance of the system.

Let's look first at the available interconnect technologies. For commercial UNIX MPP machines today, the main alternatives are serial storage architecture (SSA) and small computer systems interface (SCSI).

Parallel SCSI

For many years, the bulk of the storage attached to open systems platforms has been attached via parallel SCSI buses. The original SCSI bus, which dates from the early '80s, was 8-bit wide and ran at a nominal data rate of 5 MB per second. Later, the clock rate was doubled (FAST-SCSI), and the width of the data bus was increased to 16 bits (WIDE-SCSI), so that today's "Fast and Wide" SCSI bus runs at a nominal data rate of 20 MB per second. Over the last few months, Ultra SCSI adapters have started to appear for attachment to PC platforms. Ultra SCSI adapters for UNIX platforms will undoubtedly appear in the near future. Ultra SCSI again doubles the clock rate on the bus, allowing an 8-bit-wide bus to transfer at a peak data rate of 20 MB per second and a 16-bit-wide bus to transfer at up to 40 MB per second.

Parallel SCSI operates as a bus (Figure 11-3). To put it simply, this means that there is a single set of wires or signals which are connected to all devices on the bus. Since there is only one set of signals, only one piece of information may be carried by the bus at a time. When a device wishes to use the bus, it must arbitrate with the other devices on the bus for permission to do so. If two devices ask for the bus at the same time, a predetermined set of priorities decides which device will win control. This priority system is based upon the device's "SCSI-ID," which also serves as an address. Once a device has successfully arbitrated for the bus, it must get the attention of the device (that is, "select it," in SCSI terminology) with which it wishes to communicate before sending either a command or data.

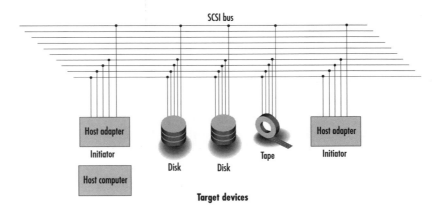

Figure 11-3 *SCSI bus with attached devices.*

The rate at which most SCSI devices can store or retrieve data is well below the maximum data transfer rate of the SCSI bus. Modern SCSI disks can store and retrieve data from the disk at approximately 10 MB per second; however, a SCSI fast/wide bus can transfer data at around 20 MB per second. Clearly, it is inefficient to transfer data across a bus capable of 20 MB per second at a mere 10 MB per second. Indeed, if this were what happened, there would be little benefit in producing a SCSI bus that ran faster than the fastest device on that bus.

For this reason, SCSI target devices typically have a data buffer that is used to stage data so that the bus bandwidth can be used more efficiently. In SCSI terminology, a device such as a disk drive or a tape that receives commands is known as a target, whereas a device that initiates I/O, such as an adapter, is an initiator. When data is written to the device, it is transferred into the buffer at the bus data rate before being destaged from the buffer to the medium at the media data rate, which is often much slower. In the case of a read, data is transferred from the media into the data buffer at media data rate, and only once a sizeable chunk of data has accumulated in the data buffer does the device arbitrate for the bus and begin emptying the buffer across the bus.

To reduce the response time parameter (identified as Component 5 "The Elements of Response Time"), most modern SCSI devices are capable of transferring data into the buffer at the same time as transferring data out of it. Another technique to reduce the response time for writes is to begin transferring data into the device's internal buffer before the disk arrives at the correct location on the disk surface at which to write it. That is, the data transfer is overlapped with the seek time and rotational latency.

If the buffer is not large enough to accommodate the data for an entire I/O operation, it may be necessary for the device to disconnect from the SCSI bus and reconnect later, once it has data to send (in the case of a read) or buffer space into which to receive data (in the case of a write). A target may disconnect and reconnect several times during a long data transfer. Each time it reconnects, it arbitrates for the bus before transferring data at a high data rate until either the receiving buffer is full or the transmitting buffer is empty, whereupon it promptly disconnects and allows another device onto the bus.

This ability to disconnect and reconnect allows a crude multiplexing of the SCSI bus between a number of devices. Due to the length of time taken to perform arbitration, SCSI devices will attempt to minimize the number of disconnects and reconnects, and this limits the effectiveness of the multiplexing which can be performed in this way. Typically, SCSI devices will perform 32-K to 64-K transfers before disconnecting. During these transfers, no other data transfer can occur on the bus.

The SCSI standard specifies that multiple SCSI adapters may be connected to a SCSI bus, and allows highly available hardware configurations of the type supported by Informix to be created. Each of the two SCSI adapters may be located in a different host system or in a node of an MPP, allowing a backup node or system to take over from a failed node or system and obtain access to the failing node's disks. In practice, one must be very careful when connecting multiple adapters to a SCSI bus to use only adapters designed for this purpose.

Weaknesses in Parallel SCSI

The very nature of the parallel bus means that only one data transfer can be active at any one time. As has been demonstrated, the ability of a target to disconnect and reconnect allows a crude form of multiplexing; however, this still causes the SCSI bus to be tied up for long periods of time with no opportunity for any other device to access it. This can lead to a poor response time. If the SCSI bus is free at the time a host wishes to initiate a new command to a device, it takes a certain amount of time to arbitrate for the bus and select the target device. This takes much longer than the equivalent process for SSA. If, however, the bus is in use when the adapter tries to arbitrate for it, then it must wait until the target disconnects before it can send the new command. This is important because it artificially lengthens Component 2 (in the section entitled "The Elements of Response Time") of the response time. Storage technologies that have the ability to send a new command in parallel with receiving data have a clear advantage.

As mentioned earlier, the device that "wins" the arbitration phase on the SCSI bus is the device with the highest "ID." This creates an artificial "pecking order" between the disks. Informix goes to great lengths to spread the data across the available disks in an even way so that each of the disks is evenly loaded. This artificial priority tends to lead to certain records taking longer to read or write than others.

This fact can be significant. Consider an application that needs data from four disks, numbered 1 to 4. Disk number 4 has a low priority on the SCSI bus. If the load on the SCSI bus is significant (making it probable that Disk 4 will have to wait significantly), then Informix Dynamic Server with the Extended Parallel Option and Advanced Decision Support Option will consistently receive the data from Disks 1, 2, and 3 first and will wait for the data from Disk 4. This skew wait time will tend to slow down the entire database since a process is only as fast as its slowest link.

Serial Storage Architecture (SSA)

In contrast to parallel SCSI, where a cable containing many wires carries the data bits "side by side" in parallel, serial attached storage uses a serial link. Serial link cables, which may be either copper or fiber optic, carry the data bits one after the other, serially. Although it may at first seem more efficient to carry the bits side by side, the difficulties of keeping all of the bits synchronized with one another indicates that the data can be transmitted serially just as fast or faster than as with a parallel bus.

Serial storage architecture (SSA) is a standard developed by the American National Standards Institute (ANSI) committee X3T10.1. SSA is based upon an earlier protocol, used in IBM's proprietary 9333 Storage Subsystem, which first shipped in July 1991. While SSA is relatively new compared with SCSI, it is based upon tried and tested technology. Hardware manufacturers with an interest in SSA have formed the SSA industry association, which currently has 35 corporate members. (For more information, access the following Web site: http://www.ssaia.org). Several vendors are now shipping adapter cards, and IBM Corporation recently announced that it has shipped more than one petabyte (1,000 terabytes, or a million gigabytes) of SSA storage since it was first announced in August 1995. SSA storage has been successfully attached to a growing list of leading Open Systems platforms, including IBM RS/6000, Hewlett-Packard®, Sun Microsystems®, and The Bull Group®.

SSA disks all have the same performance optimizations as SCSI disks; indeed, they are based upon common hardware and embedded software, with only small changes to accommodate the serial nature of the link. The performance advantages of SSA over SCSI come from the way that data and commands flow over SSA links.

SSA Nodes and Links

Unlike SCSI, SSA does not use a bus where each device must arbitrate for access. Instead, it uses a system of independent, full-duplex, point-to-point serial links (Figure 11-4).

Devices that connect to SSA links contain one or more SSA nodes.

Figure 11-4
Point-to-point SSA serial link.

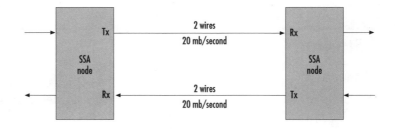

Data Warehousing with Informix: Best Practices

Architecturally, SSA nodes can have any number of ports; however, for the purposes of this chapter, we consider only two port nodes since all the SSA hardware in current use consists of two port nodes (Figure 11-5).

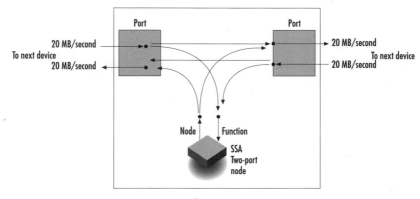

The six possible data flows at an SSA two-port node.

Figure 11-5 *An SSA two-port node.*

A two-port node consists of two bidirectional ports and a "node function." In the case of a disk drive, the node function would be the disk drive data buffers; in the case of a host bus adapter card, the node function would be the host bus itself or the data buffers used to transfer data across the bus. The six possible data paths are illustrated in Figure 11-5. Data can flow through the node from one port to the other in either direction without entering the node function, or data can flow into the node from either port, and it may leave the node by either port. All of these six data paths can be active simultaneously.

These point-to-point links and two port nodes can be assembled together into strings or loops as shown in Figure 11-6.

How Data Travels Over an SSA Link

Data flowing over an SSA link is not sent as raw data bytes; rather, it is encoded by an 8-bit/10-bit encoding scheme. This means that each byte of data is converted from its normal 8-bit representation into a 10-bit representation. There are many reasons why this is

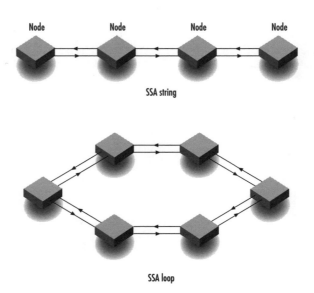

Figure 11-6 *SSA loops and strings.*

considered useful, and these reasons are beyond the scope of this chapter. However, one of the benefits is that this allows several "special" characters to be defined. These are patterns of 10 bits that do not represent any byte value. These can be used for other functions. They are used by SSA to implement flow control, synchronization, and low-level error detection and recovery, and to delimit frames.

Data flowing over an SSA link is split into frames. Each frame can contain up to 128 bytes of application data, plus some SSA control bytes. The beginning and end of frames are identified by one of the special characters provided for the 8-bit/10-bit encoding used in SSA.

Frame Multiplexing

Each frame contains addressing information that indicates the destination for the frame. Because this is present in every frame, different frames can have different addresses. This allows data flowing over an SSA link to be multiplexed between a number of separate data streams. Since the frame size is so small, at 128 bytes, an initiator that wishes to send a command to a target while another data transfer is ongoing is not prevented from doing so—as it would be on a parallel SCSI bus. As has been demonstrated previously, the performance advantages yielded by Informix Dynamic Server with the Extended Parallel Option and Advanced Decision Support Option's highly parallel nature depend upon the ability of the subsystem to sustain concurrent I/O to multiple disks simultaneously. SSA's ability to efficiently multiplex multiple data streams over the same link makes it well matched to the task.

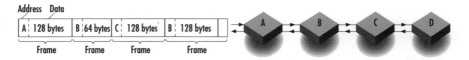

This diagram shows a simplified representation of the traffic on the SSA link flowing into Node A. Frames destined for Nodes A, B, and C are interleaved on the link.

Figure 11-7 _Frame multiplexing._

Spatial Reuse

Once data reaches the node for which it is intended, it is removed from the SSA link and not propagated onwards, thus giving rise to one of the most important features of SSA: spatial reuse (Figure 11-8).

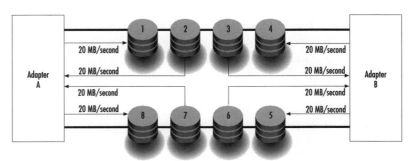

Figure 11-8 _SSA network and two adapters._

Consider the SSA loop shown in Figure 11-8. Spatial reuse means that Adapter A can be writing to Disk 1 at 20 MB per second while Adapter B is reading from Disk 3 at 20 MB per second. Even though these two data flows are in the same direction, they do not compete with each other for bandwidth because of spatial reuse.

Putting together the concepts of spatial reuse and bidirectional independent links, one can see that the total bandwidth of the system shown is 160 MB per second. This is calculated as follows: Adapter A could be writing to Disks 1 and 8, and reading from Disks 2 and 7 at 20 MB per second each. Adapter B could be writing to Disks 4 and 5, and reading from Disks 3 and 6 at 20 MB per second each.

For clarity, it is assumed in the previous example that disks which can sustain 20 MB per second to the media are widely available. Since this is not the case, it would perhaps be more accurate to show more disks in the diagram, thus reducing the data rate per disk. Of course, this is perfectly possible with SSA's efficient frame multiplexing.

Redundant Paths

The SSA loop topology not only allows multiple simultaneous transfers on different parts of the loop, it also provides a great deal of fault tolerance. In a correctly formed SSA loop, there are two alternative paths between any two devices. If a device cable or connector fails, the SSA loop becomes a string. Since all the devices are still connected by the string, two-way data flow can still occur.

Fairness

It is important for application performance that the storage interconnect be fair. What this means is that if there is a conflict for bandwidth, the conflict should be resolved so that each conflicting device receives an appropriate share of the available bandwidth. SSA uses an algorithm called SAT to implement fairness. The full details on how SAT works are outside the scope of this chapter; however, it is based upon passing a token, called the "SAT token," around the SSA loop. The token limits the number of frames that a node can initiate when there is a conflict for the available bandwidth. The scheme is carefully designed so that it does not limit the available bandwidth when there is no conflict.

Cut-Through Routing

SSA uses cut-through routing. This is a rather graphic name for a very simple concept which deals with the way that frames are passed when received. One way to pass frames would be for each node to wait until a whole frame was in a buffer within the node, before deciding whether to pass it to the next node or route it to the node function. If this were accomplished, it would introduce a 6.4 microsecond (the time taken to transmit 128 bytes at 20 MB per second) additional latency into the data transfer time per node that the data must travel through. For a transfer to a distant device, this would introduce a significant unnecessary latency. SSA does not do this. Each node receives the first few bytes of the frame, which contain the addressing information that it needs in order to decide if the frame should be passed. Once the node has the addressing information and has determined that the frame is not destined for its node function, but for some other node, it will start passing bytes to the outbound port, before receiving the whole frame. In this way, the latency, introduced by each node through which a frame must travel, is kept well below one microsecond.

Future SSA Developments

IBM recently announced that it has successfully manufactured silicon for SSA-160. This feat leads to a doubling of the unidirectional link speed to 40 MB per second, allowing a dual port node to maintain a cumulative 160 MB per second, using its two bidirectional links.

Fiber Channel and Fiber Channel Arbitrated Loop

Fiber channel arbitrated loop (FC-AL) products are not yet commercially available but will become so over the next few months. Let's take a brief look at the characteristics of FC-AL.

Fiber channel began its history in 1988 as an initiative by the ANSI committee X3T9.3 (now X3T11) to define an entirely new computer peripheral interface that would allow speed and distance beyond anything else which had previously existed.

The history of Fiber Channel itself is long, involved, and complicated. It now comprises a family of interrelated standards, which at the hardware level contain mappings to twisted pair, coaxial cable, and fiber optic links of various quality, and at the protocol level, contain mappings to traditional disk interface languages, such as SCSI and IPI, as well as communications protocols such as Internet Protocol (IP, as in TCP/IP).

Basics of FC-AL

FC-AL, like SSA, is based upon serial links, wired in a loop and transmitting data in frames using 8-bit/10-bit encoding, and running at a data rate of up to 100 MB per second—depending upon the type of cable used. An individual FC-AL link is unidirectional; however, since the devices are wired as a loop, two-way data flow can take place.

The FC-AL loop does not allow frame-level multiplexing in the way that SSA does; instead, it operates more like a bus in the same way that SCSI does. That is, just as with SCSI, in order to use the bus, a device must arbitrate, and once arbitration has completed, the destination for the data transfer must be selected. Just as with SCSI, an amount of data is then transferred across the bus before disconnecting and, as seen with SCSI, this disconnect-reconnect strategy is a compromise. Since arbitration takes some time, if too little data is sent, then the arbitration time will limit the bandwidth, and if too much data is sent, the bus is tied up for too long, causing poor response time.

Since FC-AL operates as a bus, there can be no spatial reuse. Once two devices are connected, no other device can access the loop. The 100 MB per second bandwidth is therefore shared among all of the devices on the FC-AL loop (Figure 11-9).

The unidirectional nature of FC-AL links means that the failure of a device, cable, or connector causes the loop to become broken and unusable. For this reason, FC-AL loops will almost always be used in pairs to provide some redundancy in the event of a failure. Even with dual loops, however, there is an exposure because the failure of a device could break both loops and prevent any of the other devices on the FC-AL loops from communicating with one another. For this reason, if a system with no single point of failure is desired, a bypass circuit must be provided for every FC-AL device. The bypass circuit is activated in the event of a device failure.

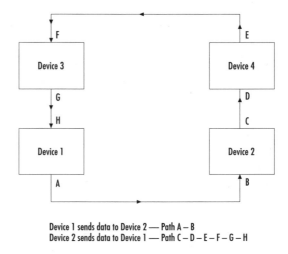

Device 1 sends data to Device 2 — Path A – B
Device 2 sends data to Device 1 — Path C – D – E – F – G – H

Figure 11-9 *A single FC-AL loop.*

RAID

In addition to taking regular backups, many installations also guard against failure within their storage subsystem by using some form of redundancy or duplication. Besides giving them a measure of data security (that is, safeguarding against data loss), this strategy may also yield improved availability (access to the data is not lost)—provided it is planned and implemented carefully. The simplest way to do this is to "mirror." When data is mirrored, two copies are written to different disks. Twice as much disk space is therefore required than for unprotected data; thus, this can be quite an expensive option. Mirroring tends to impact write performance slightly since two copies of the data must be written. However, this can actually improve read performance by exploiting the fact that two copies of the data are available.

If the goal is to build a highly available system, then it is important when planning and implementing mirroring to ensure that there are no single points of failure—that is, a single hardware component which, if it fails, results in a loss of access to data. This means, for example, that it is important that the mirror copies are placed upon different SCSI buses if SCSI is the implementation technology.

The alternative to software mirroring is some form of RAID, which is typically implemented in an outboard storage controller or storage adapter. There are various RAID levels, each with its own characteristics. The RAID levels commonly used for relational databases are RAID levels 1 and 5. RAID 1 is essentially mirroring implemented in hardware, and thus it warrants no further discussion.

RAID 5 reduces the quantity of the storage needed to implement redundancy at the cost of write performance and slightly worse data security features. Instead of maintaining a duplicate disk for every data disk as does RAID 1, RAID 5 combines the data from several data disks, using a logical exclusive OR (XOR) operation to form parity information. It writes the parity information to a single parity drive. In this way, the data on several disks can be protected by a single parity disk. A full description of RAID 5 is beyond the scope of this chapter; however, the performance characteristics are interesting. Due to the complex way in which the data is protected, there is a severe performance penalty for write operations. A single write operation to a RAID 5 disk array usually results in two reads and two writes being performed by the subsystem. This can drastically reduce the write bandwidth that is available to applications. RAID 5 will, however, typically improve read performance. The data in a RAID 5 array is spread or striped across all data disks. This means that the loading on the data disks is very even, yielding the maximum possible parallelism from the available disks.

Centralized Storage Controller or Independent Disks?

A number of products on the market today are based upon an outboard storage controller to which the disks are attached. This controller is then linked by some storage interconnect technology to adapters in a number of host machines. There are a number of advantages to this approach. It can be used to provide a centralized cache; it provides a way to implement RAID on multiple SCSI buses; and the controller can be easily connected to multiple platforms. There is, however, one key problem with this approach when applied to a parallel application running on an MPP: it does not scale very well. Outboard controllers are typically quite costly, so it is often not economical to install one outboard controller per node. Instead, several nodes may be connected to a single outboard controller. The danger with this approach is that the outboard controller becomes a point of contention between the otherwise independent nodes. The hardware and software that make up the parallel database server are carefully designed to eliminate shared resources, so that performance scales proportionally with the number of installed nodes. Unless carefully planned, the use of shared outboard controllers can jeopardize this scalability.

Cache

There are products on the market today that combine standard SCSI technology with large read and write caches. MCI chose not to use such a product, and additional details on the MCI installation are provided in the case study at the end of this chapter. For the moment, let us look at how cache can improve I/O performance and why it does not always do so.

Read Cache

Read cache is useful only if data that is in the cache is accessed, termed a *cache hit*. Some applications reread the same data over and over again without storing the data in system memory. Such applications benefit from a read cache. Informix Dynamic Server with the Extended Parallel Option and Advanced Decision Support Option, however, goes to great lengths to avoid rereading data.

Another use of read cache is to support relational databases that use a shared disk architecture. In a shared disk architecture, the database servers each have a logical or physical connection to a shared common pool of disk storage. In this architecture, a read cache can be useful because there is a high possibility that data read by one server may be read soon after by another server. A centralized, common-read cache is useful here since it allows the second access to be served from read cache. Informix Dynamic Server with the Extended Parallel Option and Advanced Decision Support Option does not use a shared disk architecture; instead, it uses a true, shared-nothing architecture, so this use of read cache as a central repository for recently read data is not helpful.

Write Cache

When an I/O subsystem uses a write cache, instead of data from the application being directed to the disk, it is placed first in the write cache before being destaged to disk later. This is beneficial because data can be written into the write cache far faster than it can be written to disk. Once the data is in the write cache, completion can be given to the write operation and the application can proceed. There are storage subsystems on the market which do this and which do not provide any backup in case of a hardware or power failure. If such a subsystem is used and power fails, the only way to restore the database is to restore from a recent backup. Ideally, a write cache should be battery backed and contain redundant hardware to make the probability of data loss remote.

Write cache is useful for applications that are very sensitive to write response time. For data warehousing, there is very little write activity except during database load. The provision of a write cache is therefore useful for data warehousing applications, mainly during database load.

Write cache is useful only provided that it does not fill. If the application writes a large amount of data to the I/O subsystem and this fills the write cache, the cache is likely to be counterproductive. Once the cache is full, new data can be written into it only after the data is destaged to disk. It follows that data cannot be written from the application any faster than the disk data rate; however, the situation is often worse. The overhead of routing the data through a write cache to the disk often reduces the I/O bandwidth of the storage subsystem to a level far below than if the write cache had not been present. This rapid drop-off in performance in itself can be a problem. In some environments, it is important that the I/O response time remain fairly predictable. The rapid drop in I/O performance which can result from a full write cache can be a problem.

To summarize, write cache is useful and improves the throughput of applications that are sensitive to write response time. However, the filling up of the write cache (as happens if there is a large volume of data to write) can be counterproductive.

Data Warehousing at MCI: A Case Study

MCI's strategic marketing system is a very good example of a successful data warehouse implementation using Informix Dynamic

Server with the Extended Parallel Option and Advanced Decision Support Option on the IBM RS/6000 SP with SSA disk. In recent years, the battle for competitive advantage has brought about a dramatic shift in marketing strategy for the telecommunications giant, MCI. The company's existing computer environment limited its efforts to obtain the customer information necessary to develop the services that customers required. MCI implemented its new Strategic Marketing System (SAMS) in order to pinpoint market segments and tailor its campaigns accordingly.

As the infrastructure for its planned multi-terabyte data warehouse application, MCI's Mass Markets unit selected the new, high-performance scalable database server from Informix running on the IBM RS/6000 SP with the IBM 7133 Serial Storage Architecture Disk Subsystem. "In the past, MCI's marketing efforts were based primarily on a single demographic piece of data, which provided limited information about a specific household," recalls Chip Grim, senior manager of SAMS. "But we also maintain valuable marketing information about our customers and prospects in a number of different legacy systems at MCI.

"So, we decided to create a single, corporate repository for organizing and managing this information—and make it available to MCI sales and marketing decision makers. The goal is to make it easy for the decision makers to query a database quickly and then make immediate, detailed follow-up queries to explore for useful nuggets of marketing information in the volumes of available data. What makes decision support successful is being able to ask your question, then use the answer to drive your next question, until you get to where you need to go—without having to wait a day or two each time.

"Using this approach, they [decision-makers] can make conclusions as to which products and services might have the greatest value—and then create campaigns for presenting them to those customers and prospects with the greatest, long-term value to MCI. We call it 'database marketing.'

"At the time we were developing SAMS, we had about two terabytes of data stored in our legacy systems. We knew the database would double in size as soon as we began tracking more specific data on customer segmentation. MCI is no longer just a long-distance company. We are now a full-service communications company. We needed to grow the systems environment to support new aspects of our business. That meant using a system that could store tremendous amounts of data and deliver it effectively. Data only becomes information after you get it into the hands of the people who drive the business—and get it there in a timely fashion."

In putting together its new data warehouse, MCI ran extensive benchmarks on processors, databases, and, of course, disk subsystems. Says Grim, "We felt that if we had the fastest machine running the fastest database using the fastest disk subsystem, then we had the fastest warehouse." MCI found that, with the exception of IBM's 7133 SSA Disk Subsystem, all of the various disk subsystem offerings were basically the same thing—fast-and-wide SCSI connection. "Fast-and-wide SCSI is fast-and-wide SCSI," Grim states. "It doesn't matter how much cache you put on it. The end results are the same. The overall results from vendor to vendor were practically identical, until we looked at IBM's 7133 SSA Disk Subsystem with full-duplex SSA technology."

The 7133 SSA Disk Subsystem impressed MCI with its speed. "It ran three or four times faster than anything we had seen with the SCSI devices," Grim explains. "When we benchmarked SCSI devices, the IBM RS/6000 SP processors were continually idled down. But with the 7133, the processors remained 100-percent busy, and we never got into an idle wait state. That was critical because it meant we were fully utilizing the processing power of the SP."

In addition to speed, MCI has found that the most important benefits of the 7133 SSA Disk Subsystem are its availability and the fact that the footprint is very small for the amount of storage it provides. "Our computer room is small, and getting that much storage into a single cabinet was very valuable," Grim notes. "Availability is key, of course, because we have so many different spindles running in this environment." Currently, the SAMS data warehouse contains six terabytes of mission-critical data, stored by the IBM 7133 and running with Informix Dynamic Server with the Extended Parallel Option and Advanced Decision Support Option on an IBM RS/6000 SP.

"Our data warehouse will put critical consumer information at our fingertips, allowing us to make faster strategic business decisions," says Rob Geller, director of consumer marketing and sales systems at MCI. "For example, the combination of the IBM RS/6000 SP and Informix Dynamic Server with the Extended Parallel Option and Advanced Decision Support Option will allow us to better understand our customers' needs, which will give us a competitive advantage in the market."

Scalability of both the hardware and software components was an important aspect of MCI's decision. "A database incorporating data—and, in the future, audio and video information as well—

could quickly grow to multiple terabytes and conceivably have to handle 30- to 40-million updates a week," says Grim. "The new system had to serve hundreds of end users simultaneously. What's more, each user needed to be able to pose follow-up questions immediately, not one hour or twenty-four hours later. After benchmarking two systems, we concluded that IBM's RS/6000 SP would scale to our needs."

Parallel processing on the SP links from 2 to 512 RS/6000 processors to perform numeric-intensive and data-intensive computations. The SP running MCI's Strategic Marketing System uses 104 processors to run the Informix Dynamic Server with the Extended Parallel Option and Advanced Decision Support Option database.

Grim believes that with the IBM 7133 SSA Disk Subsystem, the RS/6000 SP, and Informix Dynamic Server with the Extended Parallel Option and Advanced Decision Support Option, MCI has what it needs to support new lines of business and new market initiatives. "We're getting into wireless and local markets, as well as making long-distance products and services better, faster, and cheaper for our customers," he says. "As we grow, the SAMS environment can grow right along with us. This year, we plan to enlarge the system by 45 percent, adding another three terabytes of SSA disk storage. Beyond that, who knows? Whatever areas of business we enter in the future, we now have technology that can grow with us."

Summary

We have shown that in making a data warehouse decision, the choice of a disk subsystem can be critical to overall performance and reliability. There are many offerings by various vendors in the marketplace, predominantly based on SCSI architecture. We have shown the advantages of the serial storage architecture (SSA) over SCSI and other technologies.

In addition, we have provided a case study of MCI, where the combination of the Informix Dynamic Server with the Extended Parallel Option and Advanced Decision Support Option and the IBM RS/6000 SP and SSA disk has provided significant competitive advantage. In environments where scalability, performance, and reliability are key decision criteria, IBM and Informix offer a winning data warehouse combination.

About the Authors

Rob Nicholson graduated from Aston University in the United Kingdom with a Master of Engineering degree in Electronic Systems Engineering. He has worked for IBM's Storage Systems division for seven years—initially on IBM's proprietary 9333 storage subsystem and later focusing on SSA. Rob was involved in the development of SSA from the outset and worked in the group that made the initial SSA proposal to ANSI before its acceptance as a standard. He is currently working on the architecture of IBM's future serial storage products.

Nancy Ann Coon graduated magna cum laude from the University of Utah with an Honors Bachelor of Science in Chemical Engineering and an Honors Bachelor of Arts in Chemistry. After spending time as a Process Engineer in Chevron's Richmond refinery, Nancy joined IBM in 1985. She has had assignments in manufacturing engineering, systems engineering, sales, and services. She is currently a member of the Open Systems Storage worldwide marketing team.

About IBM Corporation

IBM is the world's leading supplier of information technology solutions in the areas of hardware, software, networks, consulting, integration services, maintenance, and post-implementation services. Introduced in February 1990, IBM's RS/6000 family has been successful both as a commercial platform and as a technical/scientific platform. The RS/6000 family scales from notebook systems and workstations through uniprocessor, symmetric multiprocessor, massively parallel processor SP servers, all of which run AIX. More information about IBM is available on the Web at the following location: http://www.ibm.com.

Chapter

12

The Backup and Recovery of Very Large Databases

by Daniel A. Wood

Introduction

The techological advances of the Informix Dynamic Server with the Extended Parallel Option have enabled the storage and processing of vast amounts of information. With this new power come new challenges for the database administrator.

With databases reaching hundreds of gigabytes and terabytes in size, a new challenge is to maintain a backup copy of the data to protect against data loss. It is no longer as simple as putting in a tape and backing up the whole database every day. Full backups can easily span many high-capacity tapes and take more than 24 hours to complete even for moderately sized VLDBs.

Companies now require whole backup solutions that are fast, easy, and reliable. Additionally, the backup solution must offer the flexibility to integrate with a wide variety of storage management solutions to support high-end, specialized features, such as support for autochanger devices, lights-out operation, networked and distributed operation, file compression and decompression, and data encryption and decryption.

Backup and recovery utilities have always been an integral part of Informix's database product strategy. With the introduction of Informix Dynamic Server, Informix provided optimized backup and recovery utilities, including ON-Archive and ON-Tape. These utilities offer capabilities such as parallel, on-line, and partition-level backup and restore, point-in-time recovery, and incremental backup, for maximum performance and availability.

To support increasingly large databases, Informix introduced a new backup and restore utility called ON-Bar. In addition to promoting performance and availability, ON-Bar includes features to enhance manageability, reliability, and flexibility, thus bringing a highly advanced backup and restore utility to address companies' growing needs.

What Are Database Backup and Restore?

Database backup is the process of copying the data stored in the database to stable storage media used to restore a database in the event of an emergency. *Restore* is the process of applying the data from the backup media to re-create the database to a known state. Database backup is especially important in an on-line transaction processing (OLTP) environment where companies rely on data to run their day-to-day business. Without a proper backup strategy to guard against unexpected failures or data corruption, companies can suffer a loss of revenues and customers.

Database Backup

Database backup can involve both physical backup and logical backup. Physical backup entails the copying of all or some portion of the database objects stored on disk to secondary storage. These database objects can be one or multiple dbspaces or blobspaces.

While physical backup guards against the loss of static data stored on disk, it may not protect transient data that is undergoing modification. Modified data is first stored in logical log files prior to being flushed to disk. In the event of a failure, these logical log files are used to roll forward all transactions that have been committed, as well as to roll back any transactions that have not been committed. To protect the data stored within logical log files, administrators can perform a logical backup, which is the process of copying one or many logical log files to secondary storage (see Figure 12-1). To guard against failures, businesses may choose to back up all

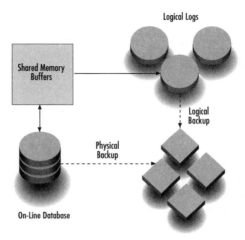

Figure 12-1 *Database and logical log backup.*

dbspaces daily. This process is sometimes referred to as full-system backup. However, performing full-system backups can be time consuming, depending on the size of the database. For example, while it can make sense to back up a 10 GB database daily, it would be too time consuming to back up a 500 GB database daily. For this reason, many companies with large databases try to minimize the number of full-system backups performed.

Instead, to protect from data loss, companies rely on logical backups to recover the transactions that occur between backups. However, depending on the number of days that elapse between full system backups, there may be a large number of logical log files. The process of applying all logical log files during recovery can be extremely time consuming.

In a data warehouse environment, this time expenditure may be acceptable. Many data warehouses do little updating of the data. The transaction logging that does occur is generally related to the periodic loading of new data and to queries that create and manipulate temp tables. Various techniques can be used to further reduce the amount of logging activity:

• Load new data to nonlogging "raw" tables.

Since raw tables are not recoverable from an archive, a database administrator should either back up the individual dbspace(s) in which the raw table was created or should maintain a copy of the source data to be reloaded in the event of a failure.

- Use nonlogging "scratch" temp tables where possible.
- Create and use temp dbspaces or dbslices(XPS).

When logging activity is reduced, full archives need not be accomplished as often.

While one way to alleviate the recovery of logical logs is to perform full-system backups more frequently, Informix provides an innovative feature that administrators can use to incrementally back up only the data that changed since the last backup. Referred to as incremental backup, this feature allows administrators to reduce the amount of time spent on database backup, while offering the same level of protection against data loss as a full-system backup.

After a backup is created, the backup medium should be stored off line, meaning that it should be removed from the computer so that it is not subject to being overwritten or damaged. An off-line location is called a secondary storage location. Ideally, the secondary storage location should be a secure location that is separate from the building in which the computer resides.

Database Restore

Restore is the process of applying the data from the backup media to re-create the database to a known state. The database is re-created by the data being copied from the backup media. A database restore typically involves two phases: the first phase is the physical restore, which restores lost or corrupt database objects by copying them from the secondary storage media created from the last physical backup. The second phase is the logical restore, which uses the logical backup storage media to re-create any database transactions that were applied to the database after the last backup.

Physical and logical restore constructs a copy of the database close to the time of the failure. However, it may not reflect the latest database transactions residing in the logical log files, which may not have been backed up. Therefore, for a database to be created with the most current activities, the transactions stored within the logical log files must also be applied to the database.

To illustrate, suppose a full-system backup was performed on

Sunday at 10:00 P.M., and logical log backups were performed daily at 10:00 P.M. On Wednesday morning at 11:00 A.M., the system suffers a mishap that corrupts the database. To restore the database, the administrator uses the full-system backup storage media from Sunday night to reconstruct the database up to that day. The logical log backup storage media from Monday and Tuesday are then used to roll forward any transactions that occurred up to Tuesday 10:00 P.M. Finally, the logical log files, which may still be on disk, are used to roll forward any transactions that were committed between Tuesday 10:00 P.M. and Wednesday 11:00 A.M.

Informix Backup and Restore: ON-Bar

Informix's next-generation backup and restore utility, ON-Bar, was developed specifically to address today's database needs. ON-Bar takes advantage of the features provided by Informix's industry-leading database architecture, Dynamic Scalable Architecture (DSA), to deliver mainframe-class backup and restore capabilities to open systems. Ideal for databases of any size, ON-Bar offers the following key advantages:

• High performance;
• High availability;
• Reliability;
• Manageability; and
• Flexibility.

High Performance

Because system administrators often have a short window in which to perform backup and restore, ON-Bar delivers the highest performance possible by taking full advantage of the inherent parallelism provided by DSA. Parallel backup and restore utilize the full processing power of tightly coupled and loosely coupled architectures by dividing and spreading the workload across all available CPUs and devices. In doing so, ON-Bar parallelizes the reading and writing of data to significantly speed up the backup and restore process.

To further increase performance, ON-Bar also offers point-in-time restore and incremental backup. Point-in-time restore allows the administrator to restore a database to a specific date and time, and incremental backup permits the administrator to back up only the data that was modified since the last backup. These combined capabilities enable ON-Bar to deliver outstanding performance and scalability that are unmatched by other database vendors.

High Availability

ON-Bar offers various features that administrators can use to perform backup and restore functions without forcing the database to be brought down. These features include on-line backup and restore, and partition-level backup and restore. Combined, these features significantly minimize both planned and unplanned downtime.

Today, many businesses require 24 hours a day, 7 days a week operation. Hence, administrative operations, such as database backups, must be performed without the database being brought down. ON-Bar supports on-line backup, which enables administrators to back up the entire database or portions of the database while the database continues to run. ON-Bar also supports on-line restore, which accomplishes the recovery of noncritical database objects while the database server is on-line. With on-line restore, users are provided continued access to the database while sections of the database are being recovered.

ON-Bar also supports partition-level backup and restore. Partitioning enables a table to be spread across multiple disks, making it appear as if it is a group of small tables. With table partitioning, backup and restore operations can be performed on one partition at a time while other portions of the table remain available to users.

Reliability

The purpose of maintaining a backup copy of the database is to guard against data loss. It is pointless to perform a backup operation if the copy of data cannot be used to successfully restore the database system. Therefore, reliability is probably the most important factor in the selection of a backup and restore utility.

ON-Bar provides a set of simple commands that administrators can use to reliably back up and restore data. These commands are easy to use and understand, and they eliminate any confusion associated with executing backup and restore operations. For example, the following command performs a backup of all dbspaces and blobspaces associated with the database instance:

```
onbar -b
```

The following command performs a physical restore of dbspace yyy:

```
onbar -r -p yyy
```

At the end of each operation, an entry is recorded within a message log to notify the administrator of the job status.

ON-Bar provides a set of catalog tables to keep track of various backup information—such as database instance and backup objects—as well as to ensure compatibility among the ON-Bar program components. ON-Bar is also equipped with an emergency boot file, which stores a summary of the catalogs, including information that pertains to critical dbspaces and logical logs. In the event of a failure, the emergency boot file can be used to restore all database objects, including those necessary to bring the database online.

Because of this function, the emergency boot file should be backed up along with other critical files, such as the ONCONFIG file, sqlhosts file, oncfg file, etc. For complete details on what needs to be backed up with each level-0 archive, refer to the documentation that is provided with ON-Bar.

To ensure that the most recent changes to the database are backed up, ON-Bar can be configured to run an automatic and continuous backup of the logical logs. As soon as a logical log file is filled, ON-Bar automatically performs a backup of the log and continues to back up the next log file, once filled. Therefore, in the event of a failure, customers can recover their databases with minimal data loss.

Manageability

ON-Bar is easy to install and comes preconfigured with a set of default parameters. To address special backup or restore needs, ON-Bar offers a set of configurable parameters. ON-Bar also provides various error-handling capabilities, such as the automatic retry of the backup operation (in case the initial attempt was unsuccessful).

ON-Bar provides administrators with multiple methods for invoking a backup and restore session. A session can be invoked through the command line or through various Informix administration graphical user interfaces (GUIs), such as the Informix Enterprise Command Center (IECC). ON-Bar can also be invoked through third-party storage managers. By providing customers with the option of selecting the interface that is most familiar to them, ON-Bar significantly enhances manageability and usability.

To ensure that backups are performed on a regular basis, various schedulers provided by operating system and system management environments can be used to schedule an ON-Bar backup operation. Backups can be scheduled to run with minimal or no operator intervention. Once the backup is completed, administrators can take advantage of the automatic tape labeling feature provided by various storage managers to properly store the backup media.

Flexibility

A wide range of third-party storage managers, available in the market today, address the increasing amounts of data that must be backed up and restored. These third-party storage managers provide support for sophisticated storage devices to increase performance, and they offer advanced functionality that enhances security, reduces storage space, and minimizes operator intervention.

However, to use these third-party storage managers to back up databases, customers must copy data from the database into operating system files and then use the storage management product to back up those files. This method consumes both time and memory, is complicated, and not easily automated.

ON-Bar solves this problem by conforming to an industry-standard application programming interface (API) that integrates with third-party storage managers. This API provides the database with direct access to the storage manager, so that backing up a database is no different from backing up an operating system file. With ON-Bar, users have a wide range of third-party storage managers to choose from, providing the flexibility of selecting the storage manager that best meets their enterprise backup needs.

For companies that do not require the performance and the

sophistication of a third-party storage manager, ON-Bar provides its own storage manager. The Informix storage manager enables users to back up a local database by using the native tape or disk drives provided by the hardware vendor.

ON-Bar Architecture

The ON-Bar backup and restore system (Figure 12-2) consists of three major components:

- The onbar program;
- The X/Open Backup Services API (XBSA); and
- A storage manager.

Note, Informix provides a storage manager with the ON-Bar backup and restore system, but customers can purchase a third-party storage manager and its associated XBSA interface, as described later.

Although Informix provides the three components within the ON-Bar backup and restore system, customers can purchase a third-party storage manager and its associated X/Open Backup Services

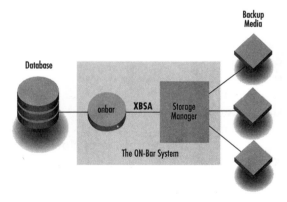

Figure 12-2: The ON-Bar backup and restore system.

API (XBSA) interface. Third-party storage managers are discussed in greater detail later in this chapter.

Two other components of ON-Bar should also be mentioned: the catalog tables and the emergency boot file.

The onbar Program

The onbar program executes backup and restore requests. When a request to execute a backup or restore is received, the onbar program initiates a session with both the Informix database server and the storage manager. For a backup, the onbar program retrieves dbspaces, blobspaces, and logical log files from the database server and passes them to the storage manager. For a restore, the onbar program requests dbspaces, blobspaces, and logical log files from the storage manager and passes them to the database server.

The onbar program can receive backup and restore requests from various sources, including a UNIX command line, a storage manager, or an integrated system management environment, such as the Informix Enterprise Command Center.

The X/Open Backup Services API

The onbar program uses an XBSA to exchange information with a storage manager. XBSA is an industry-standard API developed specifically for the exchange of backup and recovery information between a database and a storage manager. Other database vendors, such as Oracle, have built proprietary interfaces within their backup utility to integrate with different storage managers. This form of integration is not only nonconforming but also time consuming to implement.

By conforming to the XBSA specifications, the onbar program can work with a wide variety of storage managers that provide the XBSA interface. The storage manager can be the Informix storage manager, which comes bundled with the ON-Bar backup and restore system, or it can be a third-party product provided by storage management vendors (SMV). Adherence to the XBSA standards enables Informix customers to take advantage of the added functionality and performance of industry-leading storage managers to provide a fast, reliable, "plug and play" backup solution.

The Storage Manager

The storage manager is an application that manages the storage devices and media used for backup and restore requests. During a backup, the storage manager receives the database objects through its XBSA interface and writes the objects to the storage devices. In a restore, the storage manager retrieves the requested database objects and sends the objects through its XBSA interface to the onbar program.

The storage manager can be a third-party product such as one of those described later in this chapter (see page 251). There are many benefits to using a third-party storage manager. They include support for a variety of storage media, ranging from simple tape and disk, to autochanger devices such as stackers, robots, and jukeboxes. A third-party storage manager typically comes equipped with a scheduler, so that backup operations can be easily automated to reduce operator intervention.

Customers who do not require the high-end features can use the Informix storage manager (ISM) to back up data to simple disk and tape devices. Regardless of the business environment, ON-Bar gives customers the flexibility to choose the storage manager that best meets their needs.

ON-Bar Catalog Tables

The sysutils database is the Informix catalog database that tracks the activities of the OnLine database server (see Figure 12-3). A set of ON-Bar related tables within the sysutils database tracks the database server, the database objects, and the actions taken during the backup or restore operation. To ensure compatibility among component versions, a table is provided to track the versions among the onbar program, XBSA, and the storage manager.

Emergency Boot File

The catalog tables are accessed when an ON-Bar session is invoked and provide pertinent information about the history of the backup activities. However, when an off-line restore is required, the sysutils tables are not available since the system is offline. Therefore, an emergency boot file is provided as a substitute for the sysutils tables during an off-line restore.

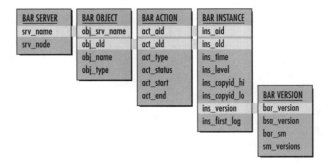

Figure 12-3: ON-Bar catalog tables.

The emergency boot file contains information about all the database objects in the database, including critical dbspaces such as the root dbspaces. During an off-line restore, the emergency boot file information is used by ON-Bar to request the correct backup objects from the storage manager in order to bring the database to an online mode. The emergency boot file can then be used to bring the remaining dbspaces on line.

How ON-Bar Works

The ON-Bar system separates the backup or restore procedure into two steps. The first step for backups involves extracting the data from the OnLine server. Next, the data is sent to the storage manager, which stores the data onto secondary storage media. For restores, this process is reversed: data is extracted from the storage media and restored to the OnLine server. The onbar program and the storage manager communicate through the XBSA interface.

When ON-Bar is invoked, it determines how many objects are involved. If there are multiple objects, an ON-Bar instance is created for each object. These instances are then spread across all the available processors in the system for parallel processing.

Each ON-Bar instance creates a new XBSA session that ON-Bar uses to exchange data with the storage manager. Data passed between the ON-Bar instance and the XBSA session is accomplished via shared memory.

In the case of a backup, the storage manager writes the data to the storage devices once the data is passed to it by the XBSA sessions. In the case of a restore, the storage manager retrieves the

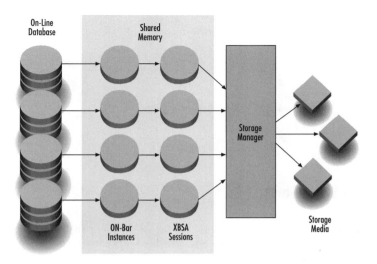

Figure 12-4: Parallel backup.

data from the storage devices and passes the data to the XBSA sessions. Some third-party storage managers offer features to intelligently distribute data across multiple devices to improve concurrency and space efficiency, and this data distribution can further increase the performance of backup and restore operations.

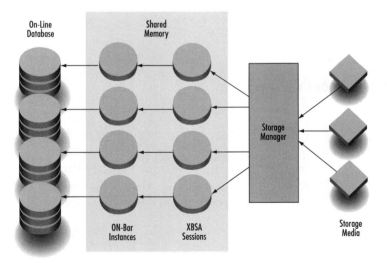

Figure 12-5: Parallel restore.

ON-Bar: Technical Overview

This section discusses the ON-Bar utility in more detail. Topics include:

- ON-Bar key features; and
- Invoking ON-Bar.

ON-Bar Key Features

With databases growing at a rapid pace, the key to any backup and restore utility is the ability to perform parallel backup and restore. As discussed in the previous section, ON-Bar delivers true parallel backup and restore capabilities by taking advantage of DSA's internal database parallelism.

In addition to parallel backup and restore, ON-Bar offers a broad range of features to address the full range of business requirements. These features include:

- On-line backup and restore;
- Partition-level backup and restore;
- Incremental backup; and
- Point-in-time recovery.

On-Line Backup and Restore

ON-Bar can backup and restore a database without requiring that the database be brought down. Executing an on-line backup simply requires an administrator to specify the database objects that need to be backed up and to execute the backup command. For example, the following command can be executed while the database is on-line:

```
onbar -b dbspace1 blobspace1
```

Database restore can be on line, off line, or mixed. On-line restore, sometimes called a warm restore, allows administrators to perform a restore while the database is on line. It is used to restore noncritical dbspaces and blobspaces. Off-line restore, also known as a cold restore, requires that the database is off line when it is being restored. An off-line restore is required when a whole system is to be restored or when a critical dbspace, such as the root dbspace, must be restored.

Mixed restore is an off-line restore followed by an on-line restore. It first restores critical dbspaces during an off-line restore so that the database can be brought on line. Once the database is on line, users can immediately log on to the database to access the portion of the database that has been restored to a physical and logical consistency. The remaining noncritical dbspaces and blobspaces can be restored while the database is on line.

Partition-Level Backup and Restore

Data partitioning allows large tables to be intelligently divided into smaller partitions and distributed across multiple disks, and it is one of the key ingredients that makes database parallelism possible. By breaking large tables down into finer granularity and spreading them across multiple disks, administrators can distribute and execute database operations across multiple CPUs and disks in parallel, hence significantly increasing performance and availability.

Database backup and restore are two operations that can be performed at the partition level. When a table is properly partitioned, multiple partitions can be backed up and restored in parallel to improve the speed of the operation. This approach was demonstrated in Figure 12-4.

Although ON-Bar supports on-line backup, an administrator may choose to perform a backup in off-line mode because it offers better performance. However, off-line backup, although faster, means that the database is unavailable for a brief period of time. In a 24 hours, seven-days-a-week environment, this unavailability may be unacceptable. Partition-level backup offers the best of both worlds, allowing a portion of the database to be taken off line for backup while leaving the remaining portion on line for transaction processing, hence delivering both high availability and performance.

Figure 12-6 illustrates how a partition of the table can be brought off line for backup while the rest of the partitions remain available to the users.

Similarly, a partition-level restore can significantly improve avail-

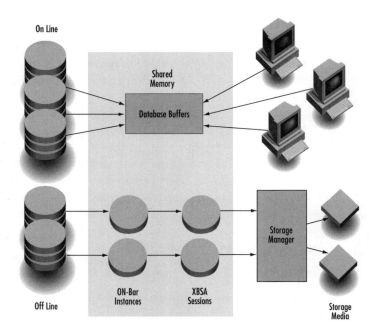

On Line

Shared
Memory

Database Buffers

Off Line

ON-Bar
Instances

XBSA
Sessions

Storage
Manager

Storage
Media

Figure 12-6: Enhancing availability through partition-level backup.

ability by enabling the administrator to restore a database at the smallest granularity possible. For example, suppose the database is partitioned across five disks, and disk #4 unexpectedly fails. In this example, it is not necessary for the administrator to restore the entire database. Only the data stored on disk #4 requires restoring. The remaining disks are available to the end users for processing.

A partition-level restore can also enhance the availability of a full-system restore. For example, suppose a server crash caused a corruption to the database such that it needed to be restored from the backup media. In such a case, the administrator would first need to recover all the critical dbspaces, such as the root dbspace, off line. After all critical dbspaces are restored, the database can be brought on line to recover the remaining tables. If the tables have been partitioned across multiple storage devices, they can be restored in parallel to speed up the recovery process. Once a partition is restored to a physical and logical consistency, the data in that partition is immediately available to the users for transaction processing while the remaining partitions undergo recovery.

Incremental Backup

Each database page contains a date/time stamp. This date/time stamp is updated each time a record on the page is modified. Using this date/time stamp, administrators can back up only the modified pages, instead of backing up an entire partition or table; this process is referred to as an incremental backup. On large tables with relatively few updates, incremental backups significantly reduce the time to perform the backup operation.

When a date is specified during a backup session, ON-Bar uses this parameter to check each page. If the page contains a date that is greater than the last backup date and time, then the page is written out to the storage medium. Otherwise, ON-Bar skips the page and moves on to process the next page. For example, Figure 12-7 shows that the last backup was performed on 11/14/96. When a backup is performed on 11/20/96, ON-Bar copies the pages with a date stamp greater than 11/14/96 (for example, 11/17/96 and 11/19/96) and skips pages with a date stamp less than or equal to 11/14/96 (for example, 11/09/96).

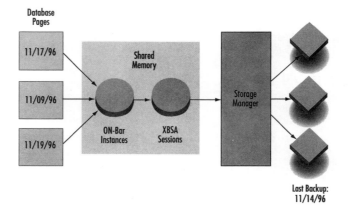

Figure 12-7: Incremental backup.

Point-In-Time Recovery

ON-Bar provides a feature that allows administrators to restore an entire OnLine installation to a specific point in time. This feature is called point-in-time (PIT) recovery.

PIT recovery is especially useful when an application logic error causes a corruption within the OnLine instance. Using PIT recovery, the administrator can bring the data back to a consistent state just before the time of the application error.

To invoke PIT recovery, the administrator specifies a date and time during the restore. ON-Bar uses this parameter to process records until it locates the first transaction-bounding record greater than the specified date and time. At that point, ON-Bar stops processing the records and initiates a fast recovery, which rolls back all the uncommitted records before the user-specified date and time.

For example, suppose the last physical backup was performed on 11/10/96 and that logical backups were performed daily since the physical backup. On 11/15/96, an application error corrupts the database instance. The administrator determines that the error causing the corruption may have occurred between 11/14/96 and 11/15/96, and decides to restore the database to 11/13/96 by issuing the following command:

```
onbar -r -w -t "13-Nov-1996 00:00:00"
```

The above command uses the physical backup storage media to restore the database to 11/10/96, then proceeds with the processing of the logical backup storage media to roll forward all committed transactions that occurred on or before 11/13/96.

Invoking ON-Bar

ON-Bar can be invoked through various different interfaces. The three most common interfaces include the following:

• Command-line interface;
• Informix Enterprise Command Center; and
• Third-party storage manager GUI.

Command-Line Interface

ON-Bar can be called directly from the operating system command line. ON-Bar offers a set of simple-to-use commands for backing up dbspaces and blobspaces, backing up logical logs, and restoring data. Table 12-1 several examples for invoking ON-Bar, using the command-line interface.

Command Line Example	Functionality
`onbar -b dbs_central_tbls dbs_lookup`	Invokes ON-Bar to back up dbspaces.
`onbar -l`	Invokes ON-Bar to back up all full logical log files.
`onbar -r dbspace`	Invokes ON-Bar to restore a dbspace.

Table 12-1: Examples of the use of ON-Bar from the command line.

Informix Enterprise Command Center

Informix provides a system administration environment called the Informix Enterprise Command Center (IECC) for managing and monitoring database servers. This GUI-based environment significantly eases the management of a distributed database environment by enabling administrators to manage dispersed databases from a central management console.

All Informix management utilities, including ON-Bar, have been integrated with IECC to enable distributed management. IECC discovers all the database servers, database objects, and administrative applications that have been installed and configured and displays them in the management console in the form of icons. With everything displayed on the management console, administrators can easily perform administrative tasks by selecting the database server, the database object, and the tool to use.

For example, to perform a backup of dbspace 1 on database server 5, the administrator simply specifies database server 5 from the management console. Once selected, IECC drills down on the server and identifies all the database objects configured for server 5 where the administrator can select dbspace 1. The administrator can then invoke the ON-Bar utility on database server 5 through the management console to perform a backup on dbspace 1.

The administrator can also choose to simply log on to server 5 and invoke the ON-Bar utility through its command-line interface. Regardless of how ON-Bar is invoked, the utility must already be installed and configured on the node where the operation is performed.

Third-Party Storage Manager GUI

ON-Bar can also be invoked through a third-party storage manager GUI. When a backup or restore session is executed from the storage manager GUI, the storage manager automatically invokes ON-Bar, and passes the parameters and the execution request to the onbar program. The process of calling the onbar program by the storage manager is completely transparent to the administrator who executes the request.

Figure 12-8 illustrates how a backup can be initiated with the Legato NetWorker GUI. Although different products have different

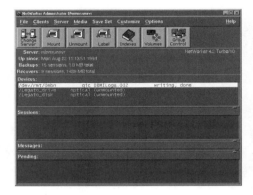

Figure 12-8*: Invoking ON-Bar through the Legato NetWorker GUI.*

GUIs, the underlying concept of executing an ON-Bar operation through GUIs is similar across all third-party storage managers.

Storage Managers

The storage manager can be the Informix storage manager, or it can be a third-party product provided by a storage management vendor.

Informix Storage Manager

For businesses that do not require the high-end features of a third-party storage manager, Informix provides a simple device manager called the Informix storage manager (ISM). Bundled with ON-Bar, ISM lets administrators back up and restore OnLine databases to simple devices, such as native tape or disk drives provided by system hardware vendors.

ISM can be used to accomplish the following tasks:

- Create, modify, and delete devices;
- Group devices into logical collections;
- Determine whether volumes, storage objects, and devices are locked or busy;
- Release locked storage object volumes, storage objects, and devices; and
- Verify volume names and labels.

To ensure reliability, ISM records all backup and restore requests and actions within an event log. The administrator can use this event log to obtain key information about the job that was performed, such as whether the operation completed successfully.

Third-Party Storage Managers

While ISM is an excellent solution for customers who back up their databases to simple storage devices, it does have some limitations. For example, it is restricted in the number of concurrent streams and devices supported. Given these restrictions, ISM is limited in its support of large, distributed database environments where sophisticated storage manager features, such as autochanger capability and support for a large number of concurrent streams, are critical.

Instead of enhancing ISM to provide all the features necessary for supporting large, distributed environments, Informix has chosen to conform to the industry-standard XBSA interface to enable easy integration with industry-leading storage managers. This strategy lets Informix concentrate on providing customers with the best database system possible, while giving customers the flexibility to choose among the best-of-breed storage managers for their storage management needs.

Currently, Informix is working with over 20 storage management vendors on the XBSA integration. This section provides a brief description of four storage managers that are already integrated with ON-Bar through XBSA. They include IBM ADSTAR Distributed Storage Manager, Hewlett-Packard OpenView OmniBack II, Legato NetWorker, and EMC Data Manager.

IBM ADSTAR Distributed Storage Manager

IBM ADSTAR Distributed Storage Manager (ADSM) is a comprehensive storage manager that not only provides support for data backup, restore, and archive but also addresses high-end needs, such as disaster recovery and hierarchical storage management. Key features of IBM ADSM include an intuitive, easy-to-use GUI that was designed to have the look-and-feel characteristics of the platform it runs on; client/server authentication to protect from unauthorized access; efficient use of storage media; and support for a broad range of devices.

IBM ADSM supports all IBM operating environments, including OS/2®, VM, AIX, VSE/ESA, OS/400™, and MVS. The non-IBM operating systems supported include HP-UX and Sun Solaris. The backup server must run IBM AIX or Sun Solaris. IBM also plans to support HP-UX as the backup server platform.

Hewlett-Packard (HP) OpenView OmniBack II

HP OpenView OmniBack II is a storage manager targeted for enterprisewide backup and restore in a multivendor distributed computing environment. It supports features including central backup and restore administration, automated backup and restore, distributed administrative task delegation, an easy-to-use GUI, a wide range of central and distributed backup device support, and support for all common types of data within UNIX and PC environments.

HP OpenView OmniBack II can be used to back up and restore data on a broad range of platforms, including all popular UNIX and PC operating environments. The backup server can be an HP or Windows NT server. The backup devices can be central or remote yet are controlled centrally from either platform.

For larger environments with terabytes of data, HP offers a hierarchical storage management (HSM) solution called HP OpenView OmniStorage™. OmniStorage and OmniBack II are integrated, allowing OmniBack II to back up the HSM files directly and efficiently.

Legato NetWorker

Legato NetWorker is an enterprise storage manager designed to support today's large, complex distributed computing environments. The base product can be configured for network backup, recovery, archival, and file migration for all data and applications stored across the enterprise. The backup server operating systems supported include Microsoft NT, Novell NetWare™, SunOS™, Sun® Solaris,

IBM AIX, HP-UX, and SCO® UNIX. Key features include exclusive distributed "smart" architecture for client parallelism, support for media robotics, automated resource management, and global menus that are consistent for local, centralized, or remote administration.

Legato delivers a variety of modular, advanced management options that can be easily integrated into NetWorker. These options include hierarchical storage management support, autochanger support, mainframe extension, and SNMP framework integration.

In addition, NetWorker can be enhanced with Legato's BusinessSuite™ for on-line database and application protection. For large data centers and data warehouses, Legato provides PowerEdition™ for very high-speed data protection exceeding 400 GB/hr.

EMC Data Manager

EMC Data Manager (EDM) is a hardware and software backup and recovery solution that is ideal for networked and distributed environments. Designed to promote performance and scalability, EDM can deliver an aggregate throughput of 70 GB per hour, supports storage capacity up to 10 TB, and is capable of supporting hundreds of clients and the largest databases. Other features of EDM include support for multiplatforms, including Sun, IBM, HP, Digital, Sequent, Pyramid, AT&T, NCR, SGI, and DG clients; an easy-to-use GUI to promote centralized management; and various high-availability features.

EDM also offers many features to promote unattended and automatic backups. It provides automatic volume management capabilities and complete integration with robotic library units. Additionally, EDM tightly integrates media management with backup rotation scheduling to ensure the efficient use of media.

Conclusion

The Informix ON-Bar backup and restore system delivers the high performance, high availability, manageability, reliability, and flexibility needed for data warehouse environments and other large scale databases.

Through the industry-standard XBSA interface, ON-Bar supports a wide range of best-of-breed storage managers. By conforming to an industry-standard solution, Informix gives customers the flexibility to choose the storage manager that best meets their storage management needs. Furthermore, a standards-based solution ensures that ON-Bar can be easily integrated into companies' enterprise backup and restore strategies.

About the Author

Daniel A. Wood is a principal engineer in the Resolution Team at Informix Software, Inc., Menlo Park, California.

A Manager's Guide to Informix Database Protection

by John Maxwell

Introduction

The size of Informix databases continues to grow at a phenomenal rate. Databases in the 10 to 100 GB range are typical and, according to the Gartner Group, the average database will grow by 1,000 percent between the years 1995 and 2000. The acceptance of data warehousing is also driving this growth because of the replication of data from central data stores.

Two major trends continue to influence the size of Informix databases: *downsizing* and *enterprise applications*. In the first case, Informix relational databases are used to downsize applications so that they support the business operations which were once exclusive to the mainframe. For example, online transaction processing (OLTP) applications are increasingly moved to high-availability Informix environments. Second, the acceptance of product suites—such as SAP™ R/3, Baan™, and PeopleSoft™—which exploit the high performance and cost competitiveness of open systems, also drive the growth of Informix databases.

Advances in relational database technology to support large Informix databases, however, have not been matched by corresponding improvements in the storage management tools that are essential to protect the databases. Informix has developed optimized on-line backup utilities. These utilities conform to the X/Open® Backup Services API (XBSA) specifications and thus integrate with third-party storage management tools for added backup and restore functionality to support large, mission-critical database environments.

The requirements associated with the backup of large Informix databases include the following:

- Completing backups and restores for large, growing databases in the allotted time;
- Making provisions for autochangers or built-in scheduling;
- Managing the manual effort required to write and maintain scripts and to track backups, backup media, and logical logs, which often takes a significant amount of time; and
- Streamlining the training and time required to learn multiple products, e.g., separate database and file system backup tools.

Currently, the most commonly used tools by Informix database administrators (DBA) are ON-Tape™ and ON-Archive™. Yet, ON-Tape's performance is limited to a single data stream. ON-Archive, on the other hand, offers parallelism but cannot utilize that parallelism with high-end tape devices. Due to the lack of jukebox/library support and built-in scheduling, neither product can provide "lights out" operation. Lastly, as databases grow in size and complexity, the task of protecting large amounts of data rapidly outpaces the performance of the tools.

As organizations deploy relational database applications on Informix for mission-critical business automation and enterprise applications, there is an ever-growing need for effective tools that can protect databases from accidental data loss and associated downtime. The Informix ON-Bar utility, when used in conjunction with Legato NetWorker® and the BusinesSuite™ Module for Informix®, provides fast, automated backup and restore for the protection of mission-critical Informix databases. This integrated solution protects corporate data while minimizing the impact of backup and restore procedures on users.

Database administrators require the following characteristics in tools for database backup protection:

Performance
- Support for multitasking, backup, and restore parallelism;

- Effective utilization of high-performance devices;
- Streaming of multiple data files to multiple tape drives;
- Support for high-speed devices, such as Ampex DST, IBM 3590, StorageTek Redwood™, and Sony DTF, for maximum performance in demanding environments;
- Support for incremental backups that back up only the pages that have been modified; and
- Support of local backups for maximum speed or "over the wire" backups to a dedicated backup server, for simplified disaster recovery.

Automation
- Support for autochangers, that is, the automatic labeling, loading, and tracking of tapes;
- Automatic determination of the data files, dbobjects, and logical logs to back up and restore;
- Automatic loading, storage, and rotation of tapes for every database host;
- User notification via email and log files;
- Graphical scheduling;
- Automated, continuous logical log backup; and
- Seamless integration of database backup with file system backup for centralized management.

Low Maintenance
- Automatic backup scripts, which do not require a high degree of Informix backup expertise to write and maintain;
- Self-updating backup scripts, which do not become obsolete with changes to the database structure;
- Centralized management and administration;
- Parameter files that are easy to write and maintain; and
- Automatic determination of the dbobjects and logical logs to save and/or retrieve.

Integrated Support
- Integration and support of file system backup; and
- Common tool and interface for UNIX and Windows NT systems, and support for other RDBMS products.

The previously listed characteristics can assist the Informix DBA in protecting data from accidental loss and erasure.

Requirements for Database Backup and Restore

The growth of relational database applications on client/server Informix systems will continue to increase dramatically, and this trend can add to the already heavy burden imposed on the DBA. Continued reliance on manual scripting techniques is unacceptable, especially for mission-critical applications, where even a small amount of unscheduled downtime is extremely costly to the organization. In fact, according to the International Data Corporation (IDC), the average cost of downtime for one hour is $76,000. To address the needs of the DBA for database backup and restore, a fundamental set of storage features is desired, as follows:

- High-performance operation to fit backups in the allotted backup window;
- Simplified backup and restore administration; and
- Increased robustness.

Solution Architecture

Ideally, the solution for relational database protection is composed of two optimized services:

1. A database-knowledgeable "front end" to manage the intricacies of placing the database in backup mode, saving the correct data files in the right order, and maintaining records of the data saved for a subsequent restore.
2. A "back end" to provide storage management services for the automation of scheduling, media and device handling, and reporting.

The architectural approach taken in developing Legato's backup and restore solution for Informix databases incorporates these two optimized services.

Legato NetWorker BusinesSuite Module for Informix is a high-capacity, easy-to-use network data storage management solution that provides backup and restore services via ON-Bar, and utilizes the X/Open Backup Services Application Programming Interface (XBSA API). BusinesSuite provides support for local or "over the wire" backup to a dedicated storage server, and tape management for autochangers. In addition, it achieves this protection from its unique client/server technology, which allows database backups to be sent to UNIX or Windows NT servers (see Figure 13-1).

The client/server architecture of NetWorker gives the DBA the flexibility to perform a backup locally—on the database server—for maxi-

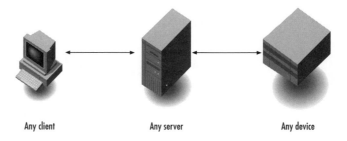

Any client   Any server   Any device

Figure 13-1 NetWorker BusinesSuite provides true client/server interoperability.

mum data transfer rates, or "over the wire" to a dedicated backup server for centralized file and database backup.

NetWorker also provides protection for critical Informix files, such as the emergency boot file and ONCONFIG file, to ensure that the environment is protected from any degree of disaster.

A Cooperative Solution

Legato Systems and Informix have teamed up to provide a reliable, high-performance backup and restore solution for Informix databases. Informix, the leader in relational databases, provides front-end services through the ON-Bar utility—a high-performance, "database aware" facility that drives the backup and restore process.

Legato, the leading provider of data protection solutions for UNIX, Windows NT, and NetWare environments, developed the NetWorker BusinesSuite Module for Informix as the connection between ON-Bar and NetWorker. ON-Bar, when used with the BusinesSuite Module and Legato NetWorker, provides fast, automated backup and restore protection for large mission-critical Informix databases (see Figure 13-2).

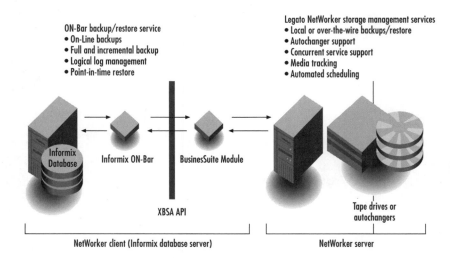

ON-Bar backup/restore service
• On-Line backups
• Full and incremental backup
• Logical log management
• Point-in-time restore

Legato NetWorker storage management services
• Local or over-the-wire backups/restore
• Autochanger support
• Concurrent service support
• Media tracking
• Automated scheduling

Informix Database   Informix ON-Bar   BusinesSuite Module

XBSA API

Tape drives or autochangers

NetWorker client (Informix database server)   NetWorker server

Figure 13-2 *Informix's ON-Bar, the BusinesSuite Module, and Legato NetWorker provide fast, automated, backup, and restore protection for large mission-critical Informix databases.*

Data Flow

ON-Bar streams data in parallel to NetWorker through the BusinesSuite Module for Informix (Figure 13-3).

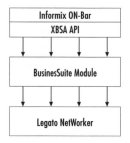

Informix ON-Bar
XBSA API

BusinesSuite Module

Legato NetWorker

Figure 13-3 *Informix database backup with the BusinesSuite Module and Legato NetWorker.*

Consistent, Reliable Data Protection

NetWorker works with ON-Bar to provide comprehensive protection for large Informix databases. ON-Bar provides a database-aware mechanism to back up and restore Informix dbobjects (dbspaces, blobspaces, and logical log files) while maintaining database security and referential integrity. NetWorker provides storage management services for ON-Bar, accepting data from the utility and storing data on tapes. The tapes are indexed and tracked to make restoration simple and fast. NetWorker also provides a mechanism for the automatic notification and centralized monitoring of database backups.

High-Performance Protection

ON-Bar and Legato NetWorker work together to provide optimal performance during backup and restore operations. The NetWorker/Informix environment achieves superior performance for backup and restore operations with its ability to stream data from multiple data files in parallel to each device. With parallelism, NetWorker enables the tape device to stream at maximum speed, thereby eliminating a common bottleneck that results from the starting and stopping of tape drives. ON-Bar extends this parallel

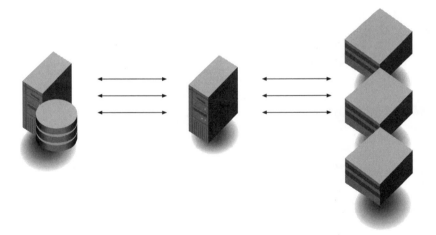

Figure 13-4 NetWorker backs up or restores multiple data files to one or multiple devices simultaneously.

performance by offering concurrent read/write access to data files spread across multiple disks spindles (Figure 13-4).

The parallelism built into the architecture of NetWorker, together with the ability to drive data storage devices at their optimal speed, ensures the fastest backup speeds possible. In addition, NetWorker's throughput scales efficiently as processor boards, disk spindles, and storage devices are added to the system. Fast, parallel streaming of data files also ensures rapid job completion for minimal disruption to users. The ON-Bar utility performs backups while the Informix database server is in on-line or quiescent mode.

Automated, Unattended Operations

The NetWorker Autochanger Software option provides fully automated, unattended "lights out" backup and restore by dramatically reducing media handling. NetWorker's media manager automatically labels and tracks valid tapes, eliminating the possibility of accidental erasure. Using *media pools*, the network or database administrator can segregate Informix data from other backups on a separate set of media or send large database backups to the fastest media devices available.

Simple, Enterprisewide Backup Administration

With NetWorker, a system administrator can schedule an Informix database backup from any node on the network. Java-based, Windows, and Motif® graphical user interfaces allow for easy, intuitive navigation of the NetWorker feature set. NetWorker simplifies backup and restore and reduces the administrative burden by automating and centralizing backup operations. In addition, NetWorker's client/server architecture provides a consolidated storage management solution for the heterogeneous networks of servers and desktop systems (Figure 13-5).

ON-Bar/NetWorker Operation Examples

Ad Hoc Database Backup Example

To execute an ad hoc backup, the DBA uses the ON-Bar command-line interface. The following examples are in a C-shell format.

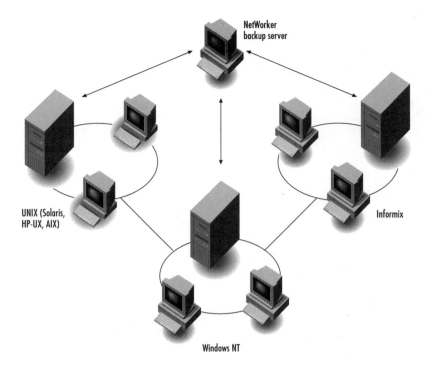

NetWorker
backup server

UNIX (Solaris,
HP-UX, AIX)

Informix

Windows NT

Figure 13-5 *NetWorker protects databases and file systems across the network.*

Note
To use ON-Bar commands for on-demand NetWorker backups, log on as "informix" or "root."

The commands shown in the subsequent code example accomplish the following tasks:

- Perform a Level-0 backup of `dbspace01` on an INFORMIX-Dynamic Server instance named "venus";
- Back up all logical log files associated with `dbspace01`;
- Close the current logical log; and
- Back up the closed logical log.

Code Example Using ON-Bar Commands

```
setenv NSR_SERVER jupiter
setenv NSR_DATA_VOLUME_POOL DBMIData
setenv NSR_LOG_VOLUME_POOL DBMILogs
setenv INFORMIXDIR /usr/informix
setenv INFORMIXSQLHOSTS $INFORMIXDIR/etc/sqlhosts
setenv ONCONFIG onconfig.std
onbar -b -L 0 dbspace01
onbar -l -c
```

During an on-demand NetWorker backup, the NetWorker server creates an entry for each file in the on-line client file index and records the location of each set of files (called a *save set*) in the on-line media database.

Scheduled Database Backup Example

For scheduled backups, NetWorker's graphical scheduling mechanism can be utilized to automatically execute ON-Bar at specified intervals. Figure 13-6 is an example of the screen in which schedules are defined.

Figure 13-6
NetWorker's graphical scheduling.

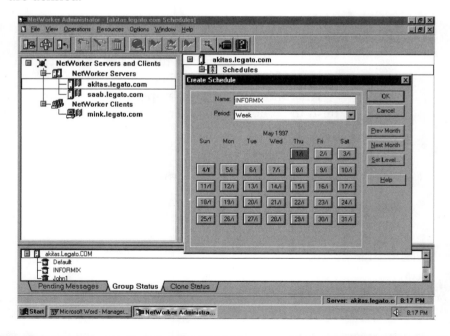

Database Restore Examples

ON-Bar commands can be used to restore the data backed up from a scheduled or on-demand NetWorker backup. The shared XBSA library translates the Informix names passed by ON-Bar into a NetWorker save set for retrieval from the NetWorker server's on-line client index and restoration to Informix.

Physical Restore Example

```
setenv NSR_SERVER jupiter
setenv INFORMIXDIR /usr/informix
setenv INFORMIXSQLHOSTS $INFORMIXDIR/etc/sqlhosts
setenv ONCONFIG onconfig.std
onbar -r -p dbspace01
```

Physical restores replace lost or corrupted dbobjects from NetWorker backup media. A physical restore can be performed as either a whole-system or selected dbspace restore.

Logical Restore Example

```
setenv NSR_SERVER jupiter
onbar -r -1
```

Logical restores recover the server transactions made since the last dbobject backup, followed by a rolling forward of the logical logs backed up for the dbobjects. If different backup sessions are involved, the log rolls forward the transactions completed since the backup time recorded for each restored dbobject.

Combined Restore Example

```
setenv NSR_SERVER jupiter
onbar -r dbspace01
```

Combined restores utilize a single command to perform a physical restore, which is immediately followed by a logical restore.

Point-in-Time Restore Example

```
setenv NSR_SERVER jupiter
onbar -r -t time -w -p
```

Point-in-time restores involve performing a whole-system, physical restore of Informix data from a whole-system backup to a specified time instead of the default, which is the time of the last Informix backup.

ON-Bar and NetWorker BusinesSuite determine automatically:

- The data files needed to restore the database to the specified time;
- The logical logs that are needed;
- The tapes on which the data will be located; and
- The proper tape to load or request.

In this way, ON-Bar and NetWorker BusinesSuite eliminate the overhead of determining where data is stored and what files are needed and allow the DBA to focus on recovering files as quickly as possible.

Summary

Legato Systems and Informix have teamed up to provide a robust and efficient system to protect Informix data in the corporate enterprise. The Legato-Informix solution brings automation, high performance, and centralized management to on-line Informix database backup.

About the Author

John Maxwell is a product marketing manager with Legato Systems who is responsible for high-performance database backup solutions. He has 15 years of experience in storage management.

About Legato Systems

Legato Systems, Inc., headquartered in Palo Alto, California, develops, markets, and supports enterprise storage management software products for heterogeneous client/server computing environments. Legato is a technology leader in the enterprise storage management and database backup software market because of the heterogeneity, scalability, performance, and ease of use of its software products.

The company's flagship software product, NetWorker, supports many storage management server platforms and accommodates a variety of clients, servers, and storage devices. NetWorker BusinesSuite offers fast, on-line backup for leading relational database management systems (RDBMS) and applications. Legato's long-term strategy is to create an integrated set of solutions centered on enterprise storage management that enhance and simplify computing as a whole. Legato Systems is located at 3210 Porter Drive, Palo Alto, California, 94304. For more information, contact Legato Systems via phone at 415 812 6000, fax at 415 812 6032, fax-on-demand at 415 812 6156, or the Web at http://www.legato.com.

Determining Available dbspaces

by Gary D. Cherneski

Introduction

Managing database instances that contain large amounts of disk drives can be an overwhelming task. Instances that contain two- or three-hundred disk drives are quickly becoming the norm. When implementing a large database at the physical level, the database administrator (DBA) generally maximizes the use of highly fragmented tables and indexes. However, the resulting number of dbspaces and chunks can easily reach unmanagable proportions.

Throughout the life of a database instance, tables and indexes will be dropped and re-created, although not always in their original chunks. Inevitably, this activity causes an interleaving of used and available disk space among the drives that are dedicated to the instance. Utilities, such as `onstat -d`, quickly become cumbersome as the number of chunks grows. The solution is provided by a script that reports the device name and its available free space, and lists the offset and maximum size of the chunk that can be created. The script, `get_avail_space`, accomplishes this task.

Script Description

This script queries the **sysmaster** database and accumulates information on all drives for that instance. Then, the script determines if any space is available in the offset sequence, and displays the device name and the offset and maximum size of that space.

Note

The following utility should run as user **Informix**. This utility has been tested on a Sun Microsystems SPARCcenter™ 2000 running Solaris™ 2.5.1 and Informix Dynamic Server, version 7.12.

Script That Determines Available dbspaces

```
########################################################################
######
#!/bin/ksh
#
# SCRIPT:       get_avail_space
# WRITTEN BY:   Gary D. Cherneski
# DATE:         23 August 1996
#

export INFORMIXDIR=${INFORMIXDIR}
export INFORMIXSERVER=${INFORMIXSERVER}
export ONCONFIG=${ONCONFIG}
export PATH=${PATH}
outfile=/tmp/freespace$$.out

print "\n\nObtaining freespace information for drives.\n\n"
dbaccess sysmaster -<<! >$outfile 2>/dev/null
set isolation to dirty read;
select b.fname, (b.offset*2) OFFSET, (b.chksize*2) CHKSIZE, ((b.offset + b.chk-
   size)*2) TOTAL
from sysdbspaces a, syschunks b
where a.dbsnum=b.dbsnum
order by 1,2 ;
!
```

```
# all drives are the same size
drive_size=655360

#Note: no white space after the pipe, backslash on the next line.
cat $outfile|\
nawk 'BEGIN { x=1 }
     {
     # The following will eliminate all lines that
     # begin with a newline (a blank line)
     if( $1 ~ /fname/ ){
         fname[x]=$2
     }
     if( $1 ~ /offset/ ){
         offset[x]=$2
     }
     if( $1 ~ /chksize/ ){
         chksize[x]=$2
     }
     if( $1 ~ /total/ ){
         total[x]=$2
         x++
     }
     }END{
         for( i=1; i<=x; i++){
             if( fname[i] == fname[i+1] ){
                 if( total[i] != offset[i+1] ){
                     # There is a gap between the previous total size
                     # and the next offset size
                     printf("DRIVE NAME = %-10s OFFSET = %-10d MAX SIZE = %-
   10d\n",fname[i], total[i],offset[i+1] - total[i])
                 }
             }
             else{
                 if( total[i] < '$drive_size' ){
                     printf("DRIVE NAME = %-10s OFFSET = %-10d MAX SIZE = %-
   10d\n",fname[i], total[i], '$drive_size' - total[i])
                 }
             }
         }
     }'|sort -k 5,6
print "\n\n"
rm $outfile
```

Sample Output

```
DRIVE NAME = /DRIVE/D270    OFFSET = 255000    MAX SIZE = 56000
DRIVE NAME = /DRIVE/D270    OFFSET = 586000    MAX SIZE = 69924
DRIVE NAME = /DRIVE/D271    OFFSET = 255000    MAX SIZE = 56000
DRIVE NAME = /DRIVE/D271    OFFSET = 586000    MAX SIZE = 69924
DRIVE NAME = /DRIVE/D272    OFFSET = 255000    MAX SIZE = 56000
DRIVE NAME = /DRIVE/D272    OFFSET = 586000    MAX SIZE = 69924
DRIVE NAME = /DRIVE/D273    OFFSET = 255000    MAX SIZE = 56000
DRIVE NAME = /DRIVE/D273    OFFSET = 596000    MAX SIZE = 59924
DRIVE NAME = /DRIVE/D274    OFFSET = 255000    MAX SIZE = 56000
DRIVE NAME = /DRIVE/D274    OFFSET = 594000    MAX SIZE = 61924
DRIVE NAME = /DRIVE/D275    OFFSET = 255000    MAX SIZE = 56000
DRIVE NAME = /DRIVE/D275    OFFSET = 586000    MAX SIZE = 69924
```

Conclusion

The provided script defines the `drive_size` as a constant; in other words, each drive that is dedicated to the instance is the same size. Some modification to the script will be necessary if this condition does not apply.

About the Author

Gary D. Cherneski is a senior database administrator at the Arrowhead Consulting Company in Englewood, Colorado. He is currently contracted to MCI in Colorado Springs, Colorado, to work on MCI's data warehouse. Gary is also a member of the board of directors for the Informix User Group of Colorado. Gary can be contacted via email at: garyc@rmi.net.

The Future of Data Warehousing

A Platform for the Universal Warehouse

by Malcolm Colton

Introduction

Data warehousing is engaged in deriving new information from collections of historical data. It attempts to answer such questions as "How are we doing? How did we get here? What can we do better?" Often, these warehoused data collections are very large and require special hardware and software for their management. Often, the data is summarized and restructured from the operational data stores, and complex algorithms must run against the data warehouse to derive the required information. Increasingly, corporations want to warehouse data that is intrinsically more complex than traditional alphanumeric data. An object-relational database management system (ORDBMS) like Informix Dynamic Server with the Universal Data Option[1] proves to be an ideal platform for warehousing data of any degree of complexity that is manipulated by very complex algorithms. This chapter discusses major data management issues in data warehousing and suggests how object-relational technology can be applied to solve the issues.

[1] For general information about object-relational technology, see *Object-Relational, The Next Great Wave*, by Michael Stonebreaker, Addison Wesley, 1996. For information about the Informix Dynamic Server with the Universal Data Option, see documentation on Informix's Web site at http://www.informix.com.

Basic DBMS Aspects of Data Warehousing

Building and maintaining a data warehouse is a complex exercise, and most aspects are beyond the scope of this chapter. This chapter focuses only on the issues related to the data warehouse's data store and how to build the applications that surround it. Within this context, several elements require attention in managing the data in a warehouse:

- Data structures;
- Algorithms;
- Data visualization;
- Data and system management; and
- Legacy integration.

Data Structures

There are three major data structure requirements for a data warehouse platform:

- Flexible and comprehensive data models;
- The flexibility to easily change the model; and
- A broad range of indexes to support a variety of queries.

Fundamental to asking questions of data is organizing the data in such a way that it supports the questions. A wide variety of knowledge and areas of interest dictate a wide range of possible data structures. Thus, for a data management platform to be useful for a wide variety of data warehousing tasks, it must be incredibly flexible in its ability to efficiently model data. Classical relational databases, which are limited in the kinds of data structures and the complexity of the algorithms they support, are unsuited to many data warehousing tasks. Examples include:

- Demographics;
- Time series;
- Geodetic data; and
- Images, video, sound, and other rich media.

A data warehouse platform must also be flexible, not only in modeling the structure of the data but also in providing index data structures that deliver high-speed shared access to the data. While proprietary, closed, special-purpose systems were used initially for data warehousing, companies are increasingly building their data warehouses on a relational database (an architecture often called relational on-line analytical processing, or ROLAP). Current relational database management systems (RDBMS) typically provide B-trees, hash, and bitmap indexes. As we will see, an ORDBMS is much more flexible in this area.

A business may grow by mergers and acquisitions, or it may divest itself of divisions or subsidiary companies, or it may simply change focus as market conditions shift beneath it. As a company transforms itself in response to changing market conditions, the intrinsic meaning of historical data changes, and data warehouses must change to reflect this new understanding. For example, the state of California recently suffered a number of drought years. Climate researchers wishing to examine historical records of drought turned to the photographic archives kept by the state. However, although the collection contained photographs of value in assessing the effect of drought in the past, the photos were often not categorized in a useful way because the photograph was not taken to show drought effects. A more useful search of the archive requires a restructuring based on the automatic recognition of photographs that relate to drought by the direct analysis of the images' content.

Current technology dictates that the data warehouse remain separate from the transactional data used to run the business since they require different optimizations. A transactional data store is usually highly normalized, meaning that data is stored once and only once in the simplest possible way. Great care is also taken to minimize the number of indexes to only those required to run the production applications. This simplification makes modification highly efficient but entails complex, expensive queries. The data in the warehouse, on the other hand, is often highly structured, summarized, and multiply indexed, rendering modification very expensive, but queries very efficient. One consequence of this division between operational and historical data is that it is much harder, or even impossible, to ask data warehouse questions of operational data, so analysis always trails operational data by some time interval that can be measured in days or even weeks. A more flexible platform holds out the tantalizing possibility that a single data store can be used for on-line transaction processing (OLTP), as well as data warehousing—provided that neither form of processing pushes the performance envelope too hard.

Algorithms

Data structures exist to support the analytical algorithms that extract meaning from the data. The real value of the warehouse comes from the analysis performed by the algorithms, so it is vital that the data management platform supports a flexible way to define algorithms. While, in principle, there are a number of possible locations to store and manage the data processing algorithms, the (DBMS) is a good choice for several reasons:

- It locates the algorithms in close proximity to the data, minimizing data movement;
- It provides a central point of access for the algorithms, enabling a single copy to be shared efficiently between multiple applications. This simplifies maintenance since the single copy can be modified once, and the new version is then instantly available to all applications; and
- The DBMS is a sophisticated platform that provides parallel operation and shared data management, and a number of other features simplify the task of creating high-performance systems.

An RDBMS provides only stored procedures written in the SQL language, which severely limits its functionality as a data warehouse platform. SQL is an incomplete programming language that lacks many of the constructs of a general-purpose programming language like C or C++. Furthermore, it is interpreted, and this makes it very slow as compared to a compiled language like C or C++.

As companies move into the world of complex, highly structured data—such as images, maps, and time series—SQL shows another of its rigidities. The SQL language of an RDBMS is based on the SQL-92 standard, which defines only a handful of alphanumeric datatypes. More complex data that does not fit into these datatypes is stored as a binary large object (BLOB). The SQL language has no constructs for manipulating the internal content of BLOBs and forces the application to export BLOBs to another application for processing. In the case of a data warehouse—where the data store is very large—this massive movement of data is impractical and severely limits the utility of an RDBMS to support warehouses of complex data. A more flexible platform can support the running of complex algorithms against simple alphanumeric data, as well as newer, complex data.

Visualization

Ultimately, the output of a data warehouse query must be analyzed by humans, who require some visualization of the data. This can be as simple as a spreadsheet or a printed report, or as complex as a virtual reality display. Much creativity often goes into delivering the information in an evocative way, which renders it easy for people to grasp patterns and connections in the data and leverages the pattern recognition "wetware" of the human brain. This is an area of intensive research, with much to be learned about how the human brain interprets visual information and the formatting of data so that it elicits the brain's attention.

Increasingly, the World Wide Web (the Web) is used as a delivery mechanism on corporate intranets. Therefore, a good data warehouse platform must provide excellent support for both the delivery of preplanned and ad hoc visualization of data across the Web.

Data and System Management

Managing any database system can constitute a significant fraction of the total cost of system ownership, so a data warehouse database, like all others, must be easy to manage using the vendor's tools and/or third-party tools. But the size and complexity of data warehouses make additional demands which require special treatment.

Database size has a dramatic influence on the backup and restore strategy. With a database in the tens of gigabytes range, it is still credible to routinely dump the database and restore it—or better, the failed portion of the database—in the event of a hardware failure. A database measured in terabytes is a different matter—it is no longer feasible to back up or restore the entire database, and other strategies must be used to ensure that the system can recover from hardware failures. For example, a system can use RAID technologies extensively, with the assumption that failures are rare enough to be tolerated and that the data will be rebuilt as required. Optimally, a data warehouse DBMS must rebuild fragments of indexes and tables, rather than require rebuilding the entire object.

For effective querying across such large data stores, the database must use hardware in parallel. Among other things, the data must be spread over multiple disks and drives in a way that maximizes the parallelism available. To enable this, the DBMS must support a number of flexible options for partitioning the data—whether by round-robin, primary key, hashing, or user-defined algorithms.

Integrating Operational and Legacy Data

While the warehouse itself is the primary source of data for its applications, many applications also need access to operational data or data lying in unwarehoused legacy systems. A typical case is a decision-support system that analyzes the historical data from a data warehouse, merges it with the operational data that has not yet migrated into the warehouse, and yields an up-to-the-minute view of the data. Such a comprehensive view of the data is often accomplished in stock trading support applications, where a historical analysis is combined with an analysis of the recent activity that is available from real-time data feeds.

There are two choices here: either the application or the DBMS can manage the data. Integrating data in the application makes use of the computing power of the client, rather than the server, which may be appropriate in many cases. However, it does complicate the client-side applications which, for a number of reasons, systems managers want to simplify as far as possible. On the other hand, data integration in the DBMS requires extending the DBMS to access the foreign data sources in an optimized way.

Data Warehousing in Practice

Scrubbing

Creating a data warehouse often forces a company to examine the definition of its terms in a vastly different way. Discrepancies are always found in the way that data of the same meaning is stored in different systems. What is the real meaning of *customer, discount, account,* or *account balance*? Sometimes, data of very different meanings is intermingled, and sometimes, data with the same meaning is stored differently, or stored multiple times. The process of resolving all these data disputes is called *data scrubbing*, and the scrubbing typically occurs as the data is exported from legacy systems into the warehouse. If the warehouse is periodically refreshed, then scrubbing is a repetitive task. Scrubbing can be performed in middleware, but the warehouse database itself is the repository of data warehouse semantics and seems the obvious platform for scrubbing.

Growth

There is rarely a good reason to remove data from a warehouse since by definition, it is often a historical repository. The result is inexorable growth. This growth presents storage questions to the system manager, as well as new problems regarding the warehouse DBMS. Once the data is very large, statistical sampling techniques become vital. If a question can be answered with 95-percent accuracy by reading only a fraction of the data, this clearly represents a significant savings in processing time. Visualization also becomes more important as the amount of data overwhelms a person's ability to comprehend it in a less compelling form.

Data Liquidity

Data warehouses are usually created from operational data which, because of the stringent demands of high-performance transactional systems, often adheres to a very different structure than is optimal for a warehouse. While OLTP data from a relational DBMS may be hypernormalized, data in older legacy systems may not even be in a *first normal form*. Hence, data must be transformed as it enters the data warehouse. This transformation often involves summarization, so it is important that the DBMS can incrementally compute aggregates and other summaries as data is progressively loaded.

Of course, the data warehouse DBMS must also adequately index the data to provide a rapid response to a variety of questions. For example, it is important to consider bitmap indexing, indexing on the output of functions applied against the data, and indexing of multidimensional and other complex data.

Data Marts

Subsets of the entire data warehouse are often extracted to form *data marts*—smaller data warehouses designed to be used by a particular department or to answer specific questions. Maintaining the currency of the data marts is one of the ongoing management tasks for the data warehouse manager. The algorithms used to determine what data belongs to a particular mart are often complex, and it is important that the data warehouse platform can accept complex algorithms to create the data mart extracts. The requirements of the data mart's data management platform are very similar to those of the warehouse itself, with the exception that the requirements for managing large amounts of data are somewhat less. Note, however, that one customer may create a 100 GB data mart from a terabyte data warehouse, where the entire data warehouse of another customer may occupy less than 100 GB: *mart* and *warehouse* are relative, not absolute, terms.

DSA Support for Data Warehousing

Informix database managers are built on the same foundation: Dynamic Scalable Architecture (DSA). This architecture provides a number of critical features that ensure robust scalable operation across large machines, user communities, and data sets. Some of its more important features are described as follows.

Multithreading

DSA provides a robust and highly efficient threading model that supports large numbers of concurrent database processes, thus minimizing the cost of context switching between the threads. DSA also provides maximum throughput for applications with very large numbers of users. Originally designed for the demands of large OLTP applications, this feature also enables a large community of knowledge workers to share the same data warehouse.

Asynchronous I/O and Shared Data Cache

Using the threading mechanism, DSA servers automatically retrieve data in parallel across multiple disks and channels. This optimizes the throughput for applications against large data stores. Of course, data retrieved from disk is held in the shared server cache and is available to other applications that need the same data. The server automatically adjusts the size of this cache according to demand.

Parallel Operations

Taking advantage of the threading mechanism, DSA is able to allocate tasks across a number of "virtual processors" so that it can divide a single insert, update, or delete across several CPUs at the same time on a symmetric multiprocessing (SMP) machine. DSA takes this further and can also allocate multiple threads to a sort or merge—significantly decreasing the response time for queries that involve sorting, summarization, or aggregation.

Similarly, DSA provides parallel operations for index creation, backup, and restore. Because of the very large size of many data warehouses, parallel operations are required in order to complete such operations in a reasonable time.

Informix Dynamic Server with the Universal Data Option for Data Warehousing

Built on Dynamic Scalable Architecture, Informix Dynamic Server with the Universal Data Option has all the features of DSA that make it a powerful data management platform. In addition, it offers a number of object-relational features that support data warehousing:

- The ability to store and manage complex structured data;
- The ability to execute algorithms of any degree of complexity in the server against simple or complex data;
- The ability to define indexes based on the output of complex functions;
- The ability to define multiple index types for the management of different data domains;

- The availability of plug-in datatype and function extensions from data experts; and
- A built-in gateway kit for the integration of foreign data stores.

Complex Datatypes

Since Informix Dynamic Server with the Universal Data Option is an object-relational DBMS, it can present an open interface to developers who wish to model complex data. This interface, which is consistent with the emerging direction of the SQL-3 standard, enables a developer to create new datatypes that are managed within the server with the same rich functionality as the more familiar alphanumeric datatypes defined by the earlier SQL-92 standard. Unlike the relational DBMS, which is forced to store complex structures as unstructured BLOBs, an ORDBMS can "see" inside the structure of a complex datatype and provide full relational functionality against it: manipulation and modification of subcomponents, content-based queries, comparison, and indexing.

There are a number of options for creating new datatypes within the Informix Dynamic Server with the Universal Data Option:

- Datatypes based on other datatypes, which inherit their structure and behavior; and
- Complex datatypes made up of other datatypes.

A new datatype is defined on top of Informix Dynamic Server (with the Universal Data Option) smart BLOB object, which provides the necessary underlying database functionality, including the incremental logging of changes to subcomponents. The server provides constructors for sets, multisets, and lists as part of the datatype definition. Every object within Informix Dynamic Server with the Universal Data Option can have a unique 64-bit object identifier (OID), and an OID can be used to create structures based on pointer references.

Because Informix Dynamic Server with the Universal Data Option supports inheritance, a developer can create a datatype definition based on an existing datatype. A wide variety of structural and behavioral information can be inherited. Inheritance is one of the major benefits of object-oriented modeling; designers find it very intuitive to define data models based on full or partial inheritance from superclasses.

Composite datatypes can be constructed from simpler pre-existing types as building blocks to create increasingly complex structures. This is one way to implement a *star schema*, in which allied data elements are linked to a central coordinating entity. For example, a number of customer activities may be linked into a "star" that is clustered around the basic customer record.

Once a datatype is defined, it can be used to create a table or a column within a table. Tables also support inheritance, so it is possible to create a table hierarchy that matches part of a data class hierarchy. Complex structured columns act normally in the SQL language, with their subcomponents defined using "extended dot" notation. For instance, a developer can create an address_t type that contains street_t and city_t types, and then create a column that holds a complex address:

```
create type address_t
  (street street_t,
   city           city_t);
create table customers
  (name    name_t,
   address address_t);
```

A developer can then access the city part of a customers row by using the following SQL:

```
select c.address.city
from customers c
where <some condition>
```

Or, the developer can choose to retrieve the whole structured address with the following simple SQL:

```
select address
from customers
where <some condition>
```

This example restructures normal alphanumeric data, and many data warehousing tasks can benefit from this functionality. Increasingly, however, customers intend to warehouse more complex data, such as images, videos, maps, documents, etc. The extensibility of Informix

Dynamic Server with the Universal Data Option makes this possible for the first time, because a developer can define the structure of these complex datatypes within Informix Dynamic Server with the Universal Data Option and provide full relational services against the complex data.

Casting

The Informix Dynamic Server with the Universal Data Option is a strongly typed system which ensures that different datatypes are not mingled in inappropriate ways. For example, product volume sales may be measured in liters, pounds, dozens, and square meters. It makes no sense to add such disparate units together, and Informix Dynamic Server with the Universal Data Option can prevent such errors.

Where different datatypes must be compared or converted, Informix Dynamic Server with the Universal Data Option provides the ability to define *casts*. Casts define the algorithms used to perform conversions. For example, a developer can create a cast that interconverts Italian lira and English pounds by looking up the current or historical conversion rate. Once a cast is defined, Informix Dynamic Server with the Universal Data Option can use it to automatically support queries that span multiple datatypes and performs conversion as required between types. Storing casts in the DBMS makes it possible to locate them in an easily managed central point, improves standardization by ensuring that all applications which use the database employ the same technique to perform the conversions, and reduces coding by providing easily reusable components.

Extending the Client

Of course, the DBMS is only part of the application environment. If the DBMS is to be extended to manage new and complex kinds of data, then so follows the client. In a classical client/server application, this extension presents serious problems as multiple applications installed on a large number of client machines can require upgrading each time that the server is extended. However, new client-side developments—driven largely by the emergence of the World Wide Web—offer ways out.

Client-side architecture is moving rapidly toward a component model, where an extensible platform accepts plug-ins of various kinds—even at runtime—to support new kinds of data. A well-known example is the Netscape browser, which accepts plug-ins and applets to manage and display different kinds of data. For example, with the aid of a Real Audio plug-in, a Netscape® browser can play Real Audio sound files through a PC's sound system. The browser also accepts *Java™ applets*, small applications written in Java, which execute under the control of the browser and extend the browser's capabilities.

Informix Dynamic Server with the Universal Data Option is an excellent repository for application components. Once such components are stored in the server, the DBMS can ensure that it returns to client applications not just the data they want but also the application extensions to display and manipulate the data. For example, a document query can return Microsoft® Word™ files, Adobe® Acrobat™ files, VRML scenes, and PowerPoint presentations. Informix Dynamic Server with the Universal Data Option can ensure that it returns the components that client applications need to manage diverse datatypes.

Complex Functions

Data structures are an important part of defining a warehouse data model. Equally important are the algorithms that are used to manipulate the data. A legacy relational DBMS limits server-side application code to stored procedures written in SQL—a slow, interpreted, clumsy, and incomplete language. Informix Dynamic Server with the Universal Data Option, on the other hand, enables developers to write data manipulation code in any high-level language that generates a shared library (a DLL in Windows NT™ or .so file in UNIX).

Using a general-purpose language has a number of advantages over SQL or a proprietary query language:

- It executes much faster than SQL because it is compiled rather than interpreted;
- The general-purpose language provides better programming facilities—both within the language and in the supporting development environment—than is available for SQL, making it easier to write complicated algorithms and ensure their correctness;
- Because such languages are so widely used, they are well standardized and a huge population of expert programmers is available.

Routines are dynamically linked into Informix Dynamic Server with the Universal Data Option as required at runtime, and they become part of the normal SQL syntax. A client application developer using Informix Dynamic Server with the Universal Data Option sees a DBMS filled with not just the required data but also the behavior needed to support an application. Such developers typically call server-based routines when building their applications instead of accessing the data directly. This *encapsulation* of the data by the routines insulates client application developers from implementation details and frees system developers to modify the underlying data structures without requiring the modification of client applications. Such encapsulation also enables a developer to create *self-describing* data structures that respond to application questions about their structure and the functions defined on them, rendering it much simpler to integrate such data into a variety of applications.

For example, a developer using the customers table previously created can create a function, called *proximity*, that computes customers' distances from the nearest retail store. Once this function is created, it can be used by an application developer to find customers located close to stores and to compare their buying behaviors with those who live farther away, as follows:

```
select c.name, c.address, s.store_id
from customers c, stores s
where proximity(c.address, s.address) < 20;
```

Locating significant pieces of application code in the server rather than in the client supports the increasingly important *thin client* model of application development. This model seeks to minimize the cost of maintaining (possibly very large numbers of) clients by locating functionality in a smaller number of more easily maintained locations.

Typically, the thin client model is implemented by relocating functionality to middleware, but an ORDBMS also allows the code to be relocated into the server. The server offers significant performance superiority over middleware as a data management platform, as follows:

• The algorithms are located adjacent to the data, thus minimizing data movement overhead—a major concern when working with the large stores of data warehouses. Co-locating algorithm and data is critically important if the routine is used to qualify rows because it removes the need to move enormous amounts of data to a middleware platform merely to determine if it should be retrieved.

- The cost of the invocation of a server-based routine is significantly less than that of a middleware routine—especially if the protocol used for the invocation is an expensive one like CORBA and if the routine is invoked on a row-by-row basis.
- The ORDBMS provides a sophisticated platform for these routines. Without the need to write code to support specific features, it provides highly efficient shared data access with the asynchronous retrieval of data from multiple disks and drives, automatic parallelization, and transaction support. In middleware, these issues must be managed by the application itself and require considerable complex code.
- Because the routines are typically only part of a query, locating them in the server enables the DBMS optimizer to select the optimal path to the data to satisfy the application query. The definition of a routine used by Informix Dynamic Server with the Universal Data Option includes the information given to the optimizer to help it accomplish this task. If the routines are in middleware, no optimizer has an overview of the entire system, and thus suboptimal query plans are all too possible. In large data warehouses, a poor query plan can mean that a query completes in days rather than seconds.

Note that this discussion is not meant to suggest that middleware is always a poor solution to an application problem. On the contrary, Informix Dynamic Server with the Universal Data Option supports a number of middleware protocols which enable it to both call distributed objects and be called by them. However, these protocols are best used for the function for which they were designed: interprocess communication. They are unsuitable and inefficient as a data management architecture.

User-Defined Aggregates

A special kind of user-defined routine is a user-defined *aggregate.* As the name suggests, aggregates are routines that summarize data. The SQL-92 standard defines a handful of standard aggregates like average, sum, maximum, and minimum. Data warehousing applications often require much more sophisticated summarizations, and

Informix Dynamic Server with the Universal Data Option provides features that enable developers to create aggregates that run over a result set or complete table to summarize information in a highly efficient way. A frequent requirement in data warehousing applications is to find the *top n* of some class: the top five selling products, the most valuable 100 customers, etc. *Top n* can be implemented as a user-defined aggregate.

A major advantage of aggregating in the DBMS rather than in the client application is that less data flows over the client/server network connection, dramatically increasing the speed of the query.

Appropriate Indexing

Due to the large volume of data stored in data warehouses, optimizations for speed of access are critical. A DBMS contains data structures, called *indexes*, that speed access to the data. Without the right index, the only strategy available to a DBMS optimizer is to scan an entire table looking for the right rows. A useful analogy is the well-known phone book, which is ordered alphabetically. By this ordering, it is possible to find a phone number quickly. Without the ordering, it would be necessary to read the book from the beginning until encountering the required name.

Existing RDBMS use B-Trees as their primary access method, while some also support hash and bit-map indexing. Unfortunately, there are many classes of data for which these indexing methods are quite unsuitable in principle, for example, documents and maps. The RDBMS has two problems in dealing with such data:

• It is forced to store complex data as BLOBs, which it is unable to index;
• It is unable to create the right kind of index to support the data.

Informix Dynamic Server with the Universal Data Option, on the other hand, is unlimited in its ability to create indexes on any kind of complex data, and developers can create new kinds of indexes that can plug into one of its open interfaces. These features enable Informix Dynamic Server with the Universal Data Option to effectively index a wide variety of datatypes.

Effective access to complex data requires two additional features of Informix Dynamic Server with the Universal Data Option: functional indexing and user-defined index operators.

Functional indexing enables the server to create an index on the output of a function applied to the data, rather than just on the raw data itself. For example, an index created on the bits of a collection of images has little utility. One created on the output of a function that extracts features from the image is much more useful, since it enables images to be accessed on the basis of their semantic content, for example, "find pictures that look like this one." The search for customers who are located some distance from stores, reproduced below, is best supported by an index created on the proximity function.

```
select c.name, c.address, s.store_id
from customers c, stores s
where proximity(c.address, s.address) < 20;
```

By using an index on the output of *proximity(customers.address, stores.address)*, Informix Dynamic Server with the Universal Data Option is able to efficiently answer queries like the previous one.

User-defined operators enable a system developer to define the order of entries in the index to Informix Dynamic Server with the Universal Data Option, in other words, to define the semantic meaning of *greater than*. An example is the sorting of Scottish names. In Scotland, MacTavish, M'Tavish, and McTavish are considered semantically equivalent and sort next to one another. Without user-defined operators, it is impossible to create a system that sorts Scottish names correctly and simultaneously sorts other alphabetical information correctly. Another example is that of comparing faces. Face recognition software can analyze photographs to extract key features of faces, which can then be used to create an index that supports queries against facial similarity (for example, in an authentication system). But the similarity operator is more complex than just a numerical comparison of the output from a feature extraction algorithm. Full support for face recognition also requires the definition of the ordering of this output: user-defined comparison operators.

Integrating the Legacy

A data warehouse rarely stands alone; instead, applications access data from the warehouse and other systems. Informix Dynamic Server with the Universal Data Option contains a "gateway kit" called the virtual table interface (VTI), which makes it easy for developers to create applications that perform an optimized integration of data from foreign systems of any kind, from relational to flat files, to data feeds.

To use the VTI, a developer creates an empty table that maps to the desired structure of the foreign data. Attached to the empty table are functions that define how to perform select, insert, update, and delete statements against the foreign data source. As far as an application developer is concerned, the table then acts like a normal table under Informix Dynamic Server with the Universal Data Option and can participate fully in any SQL data manipulation language (DML) statement. At runtime, Informix Dynamic Server with the Universal Data Option automatically executes the functions attached to the table and returns rows into the DML statement exactly as if the rows originated from a real table of data in Informix Dynamic Server with the Universal Data Option. Because function developers can instruct the optimizer about the cost of functions, the optimizer can intelligently place access to a virtual table within a complex DML statement, thus enabling the creation of an optimized gateway.

If the foreign data source is structured differently than the local data (less summarized, for example), the VTI functions can reformat the data and perform aggregation as required to prepare the data for loading into the universal warehouse. This is also a way to scrub data as it is imported, via reference to preexisting data within the data store of Informix Dynamic Server with the Universal Data Option. VTI can also be used in a batch import situation in which the universal warehouse is periodically refreshed with data that is imported, reformatted, and scrubbed from the operational systems.

DataBlade Module Solution Components

While Informix Dynamic Server with the Universal Data Option can be extended by any customer to support new datatypes, functions, indexing schemes, and data integration through the VTI, one of its most appealing features is that many extensions are available from third parties who specialize in the management of particular kinds of data. These turnkey extensions are called DataBlade® modules, and they provide ready-made application modules for complex data management.

A DataBlade module typically contains the new datatype definitions and functions needed to manipulate datatypes. In the case of new classes of data, they may also contain new indexing methods. Sometimes, they also contain table definitions and other database components. Multiple DataBlade modules can be used to solve a given data warehousing problem. DataBlade modules are open and allow a developer to:

- Create tables and columns that use the datatype definitions;
- Create new datatypes that inherit structure and behavior from the supplied definitions;
- Override its function definitions; and
- Use its indexing schemes to create new indexes.

Informix Dynamic Server with the Universal Data Option in Data Warehousing

An object-relational DBMS offers much new functionality that is tremendously useful in managing a data warehouse, which is either made up of simple data accessed with complex algorithms or of data whose structure is complex. The DBMS can act as an intelligent and optimized gateway to foreign data or as the repository for complex data, algorithms, and access methods. This section examines how an object-relational DBMS like Informix Dynamic Server with the Universal Data Option is an excellent data warehouse platform.

The Universal Server as a Data Repository

With other technology, creating a data warehouse is an exercise in compromise. The data model must be mapped down onto the relatively primitive data management facilities of the DBMS, and inevitably there is some semantic loss during this mapping process. In many cases, this loss is so severe as to make the warehouse effectively impractical. An ORDBMS, on the other hand, is practically unlimited in its ability to model complex data structures and algorithms, enabling it to directly manage the data model and significantly reduce information loss between the model as designed and its implementation. This direct implementation of the model also makes it easier to build client applications because the data and its behavior more closely mimic the structure and behavior of the modeled organization.

Performance

Because data warehouses are typically very large, with the largest warehouses comprising the biggest databases ever created, extremely high performance is a fundamental requirement. Even fractional differences in performance can mean the difference between a warehouse that is usable or unusable, as they translate into minutes or hours of difference in response times. An ORDBMS offers a number of performance advantages over other implementations:

• For data stored in the ORDBMS, no time is spent in extracting data into a middleware layer;
• Object-relational technology moves the algorithms to the data, rather than vice versa. This significantly reduces data movement overhead for large data stores;
• User-defined and functional indexing provide efficient access to even nontraditional data like maps, documents, and images; and
• Since the ORDBMS contains a query optimizer, complex queries—even those involving user-defined functions—are automatically executed in the most efficient way possible.

The first three of the above points may represent a performance advantage of more than 100 to 1 against a standard RDBMS. The fourth point, the optimizer, guarantees consistently efficient query plans.

Some Informix customers have implemented applications on RDBMS technology, found its performance to be unsatisfactory, and then reimplemented on Informix Dynamic Server with the Universal Data Option. They have realized considerable savings in code, sometimes discovering that an ORDBMS implementation takes less than half as much code as an RDBMS implementation of the same application. This reduction in code, of course, means a reduction in development and maintenance time and cost. It stems partly from better code reuse in an ORDBMS, partly from the easier and more natural implementation of complex algorithms in a general-purpose programming language, and partly from the availability of complex application components in the form of DataBlade modules.

DataBlade Modules for Data Warehousing

Some DataBlade modules which were useful in data warehousing at the time of writing are briefly described as follows. Note, however, that new DataBlade modules are becoming available almost daily. The Informix Web page at http://www.informix.com contains an up-to-date list of the DataBlade modules which are currently available.

Documents: Adobe, Excalibur, PLS, and Verity

The fastest emerging market for complex data warehouses is that of documents. Every corporation has a vast store of unmanaged documents that relate to its business. Examples include legal documents, design and manufacturing specifications, change orders, manuals, and order forms. Document management DataBlade modules offer the first chance to bring these document stores under digital control, providing the ability to rapidly perform a variety of text searches based on word stems, semantic networks (thesauri), or fuzzy matching.

Maps: Andyne, ESRI, Informix Geodetic™, and MapInfo™

Geospatial DataBlade modules enable companies to warehouse large collections of geographical data. Application examples include land-use planning, mining, pollution control, fleet management, analysis of demographic patterns, and CAD diagrams. Informix provides a DataBlade module to manage data even at the scale where the shape of the earth becomes significant, for example, mapping satellite imagery to the earth's surface. Other DataBlade modules provide the ability to transform a U.S. postal address into a latitude and longitude pair, and support spatial queries based on proximity. These DataBlade modules typically also include client components that simplify developing client viewers of the spatial data.

Statistics: Fame, StatSci, and TimeSeries

The analysis of large numeric warehouses almost always involves the statistical analysis of data. StatSci, a division of MathSoft, has created a general-purpose statistical library DataBlade module that implements over 100 statistical functions. Informix provides a TimeSeries DataBlade module that specializes in managing data whose time sequence is significant, such as stock price records or sales records. Fame, the leading time-series vendor on Wall Street, has extended this DataBlade module with its own algorithms to create a sophisticated library for managing and manipulating time-series data.

Data Scrubbing: Ecologic and Electronic Digital Documents

Several companies are developing DataBlade technology to assist in scrubbing a database. For example, this technology can be used in name and address scrubbing, and enables a company to easily remove duplicate names from its mailing list—even when names and addresses are phrased differently—or to discover orders among different companies for similar parts, thus enabling a consolidation of buying power.

Data Mining: Angoss and Neovista

Data mining tools examine data to discover new relationships between data elements. Because these data mining operations can run across large parts of the data warehouse, or even all of it, it is vital that the algorithms run very near to the data. Embedding data mining tools inside a DataBlade module ensures that data mining activities run as efficiently as possible.

Informix Dynamic Server with the Universal Data Option as Middleware

While it would be simpler if all warehouse data could reside in the Informix Dynamic Server with the Universal Data Option, this is an unrealistic assumption in the current world of multiple complex legacy systems, some of which are the core operational systems of the business. There are two ways of dealing with foreign data: import it into a central warehouse, possibly with periodical refreshes; or use middleware to connect the systems in real time. Informix Dynamic Server with the Universal Data Option offers important advantages in both scenarios.

As a data store, its advantages have been described. In addition, Informix Dynamic Server with the Universal Data Option shares system management facilities and bulk load facilities with its Informix sibling products built on the Dynamic Scalable Architecture.

Middleware provides a layer between the client and server that can transform data as it is retrieved from or updated to other data sources. Informix Dynamic Server with the Universal Data Option provides a platform for building middleware that is extensible. It enables the management of any kind of protocol to connect to any kind of data source and apply any kind of manipulation to its data while transforming it into an arbitrary new structure. All this is accomplished on a platform designed to scale over multiple disks, multiple CPUs, large memory, large data stores, and large numbers of users. It is secure, robust, and transactionally consistent, and it possesses sophisticated tools for backup and recovery.

Informix Dynamic Server with the Universal Data Option presents a standard open interface to client application developers. The applications interact with data, using SQL in a way that shields application developers from all the legacy complexity while still providing highly efficient access. Application developers write as if all the data were resident in Informix Dynamic Server with the Universal Data Option, a very simple and highly productive architecture.

Data Security

Much data warehouse information is very sensitive; it may be a company's best estimate of its past and current position, confidential medical information, or the collection of all of a company's contracts or design documentation. Securing access to this data is critical. The extensibility of Informix Dynamic Server with the Universal Data Option carries over into the realm of security, where it delivers not only the standard RDBMS facilities but also a programmable security interface.

Where the current RDBMS provides excellent basic security by restricting user access to data or stored procedures, it lacks the ability to easily implement more sophisticated methods or security at other points in the system. Routines of Informix Dynamic Server with the Universal Data Option can be attached to tables as triggers and execute at select, insert, update, or delete times. Because these routines are written in a general-purpose language, they can implement additional security functionality of any kind, including dialog with other systems.

Data warehouse security provides some interesting challenges. For example, it is common to treat aggregate data as more or less confidential than single-item data. For example, epidemiological studies of a pattern of a particular disease are less sensitive than the individual medical records from which they were derived. On the other hand, while a doctor may have access to his or her patients' medical records, that does not carry the right to see summaries that show the performance of the HMO. A warehouse has to be careful not to allow inappropriate aggregation: after all, a single item is an aggregate of size one. In some cases, it is important to block access to a particular piece of data. In extreme cases, "cover stories" may be returned to those with insufficient access to know the real story. Informix Dynamic Server with the Universal Data Option provides a platform on which to implement any security model.

In some areas, the level of sensitivity regarding information justifies the encryption of network traffic. The openness of the medium can play a part here as well: radio is a less secure medium than telephone. Because encryption and decryption can be performed in the ORDBMS itself rather than in another layer, the data is significantly less exposed to attack. For example, a DataBlade module that understands the SET security model enables Informix Dynamic Server with the Universal Data Option to act as a trusted participant in electronic commerce applications while completely shielding the data from unauthorized access.

Administration

Some studies suggest that system administration represents a significant fraction of the cost of DBMS ownership. Informix Dynamic Server with the Universal Data Option has tools that simplify the management of the system.

All the data within Informix Dynamic Server with the Universal Data Option is backed up and restored as a unit. It is always transactionally consistent. As with all DSA products, Informix Dynamic Server with the Universal Data Option can restore to a point in time, a single object, or a single disk. Informix Dynamic Server with the Universal Data Option has a high-speed backup mechanism and supports incremental backups, thus minimizing backup time. Its high-speed parallel restore reduces downtime after a system failure. It can participate in replicated systems that reduce the risk to data through redundancy and distribution.

The Informix Enterprise Command Center enables a system administrator to take charge of any number of distributed Informix servers from any point on the net. Such tools promote even "lights out" warehousing in a remote location. Informix Dynamic Server with the Universal Data

Option's open interfaces enable it to be managed by a number of SNMP-based, IIOP-compliant system management tools.

Web-Enabled Warehouse

The World Wide Web is an important delivery platform for applications that were once implemented using only classical client/server technology. Since the warehouse will be used for all kinds of research queries, it is important to note that it is easy to Web-publish ad hoc information from the warehouse, since otherwise the cost of maintenance proves very high. As well, it should be easy to create turn-key, Web-delivered reports.

The Informix Web DataBlade module and Web development environment are designed to deliver "query dialtone" to any Web-connected device, and they support the rapid and simple deployment of Informix Dynamic Server with the Universal Data Option's data onto the Web. The Web DataBlade Module supports the concept of "application pages," which contain parameterized database queries as well as the standard HTML page layout information. Parameters from the user's query screen are dropped into the queries which Informix Dynamic Server with the Universal Data Option executes, and it then formats the resulting data into HTML for display on the page. This "cyberpublishing" of the data simplifies the provision of general Web services to data warehouse information workers without incurring high maintenance costs. The Web DataBlade Module also supports the concept of device-dependent rendering and allows the server to create pages in the appropriate format and level of detail for a variety of devices. Using third-party DataBlade modules, developers can create applications that use the *push* model of information delivery; instead of waiting for users to browse their way to the required information, the application automatically delivers the information to users.

Because Informix Dynamic Server with the Universal Data Option provides programmable access to the data returned across the Web, all the security features mentioned in the *Data Security* section also apply to Web applications, including participation in secure electronic commerce.

Visualization: Brio, Business Objects, Cognos, and Formida

While Informix Dynamic Server with the Universal Data Option can deliver any kind of data or analytical product, the best use of the information requires that it be presented to its users in a visually compelling way. General-purpose data visualization tools are available in specific data areas, simplifying the delivery of information in a form that triggers the pattern-matching "wetware" of the human brain. Statistics and maps in two and three dimensions are well served with excellent tools. Increasingly, third-party tools, such as Brio™, Business Objects™, Cognos™, and Formida™, are appearing to simplify the creation of applications which deliver information in a visually compelling way.

Summary

Data warehousing is increasingly viewed as a vital part of conducting business. Without an examination and analysis of past events, a company is flying blind and risks failing to realize its maximum potential or losing its competitive edge. Current ROLAP solutions suffer from the severe compromises that must be made to model complexity in an essentially simple system. Informix Dynamic Server with the Universal Data Option, together with its rapidly expanding suite of DataBlade modules, is an exciting new alternative that overcomes some of the critical limitations of the standard relational engines to deliver the high-performance modeling and manipulation of complex data and complex algorithms.

About the Author

Malcolm Colton is a frequent contributor of articles to *Informix Tech Notes* and is a widely published author of articles related to object-relational technology.

Building Complex Decision-Support Models Using a Universal Warehouse

by Jacques Roy

Introduction

This chapter discusses the challenges of implementing a complex data warehouse and presents a solution using Informix Dynamic Server with the Universal Data Option. This information was originally presented at the Informix Worldwide User Conference on July 25, 1997, by Brian Miezejewski of the Sabre Group and Jacques Roy of Informix Software.

Database Background

In the early days, database technology was based on a hierarchical model. Application programs were closely tied to the physical representation and organization of the data. The introduction of the relational model was a significant improvement. The two major features introduced were the logical representation of data and a nonprocedural language. By relying on the logical representation of the data, application programs required few changes, if any, in the event of database changes. Specifically, physical changes made to the database to improve performance required no application changes.

The object-relational model builds on the strength of the relational model and improves on it. By allowing developers to add new datatypes to the database server as first-class types and to manage them as such, the object-relational model elevates the logical representation of the data to a business representation. This facilitates communication between the domain experts and the computer experts. It also renders the applications less susceptible to changes—the interface to the business datatypes can remain constant even if business rules change.

A type is considered first class if it is fully managed by the database server. In brief, if the database server recognizes a type like any other base type (integer, decimal, character, etc.), the type is then considered a first-class type. It does not require interventions outside the server to be manipulated and does not have additional restrictions, compared to the base types.

What Is a DataBlade Module?

The Informix Dynamic Server with the Universal Data Option features have been grouped under the term "DataBlade Modules technology." This term is widely used in written and verbal communication as the solution to a variety of business problems.

DataBlade Modules are a set of user-defined types and manipulation functions that are packaged together to solve specific business problems. The user-defined types may identify a new datatype based on an existing one, a complex type representing a collection of values, or a new representation that is better suited to the problem at hand.

The server uses the manipulation functions to incorporate and support the needed functionality. They can include arithmetic operations, comparison operations, conversion operations, and business-specific operations. These manipulation functions can be written in C, Java, or the stored procedure language (SPL). A set of functions can be implemented in SPL for proof-of-concept and later rewritten in C to improve performance.

DataBlade Modules give the user access to the technology of a domain expert. When a company has a specific in-house expertise, it can as easily develop its own datatypes and manipulation func-

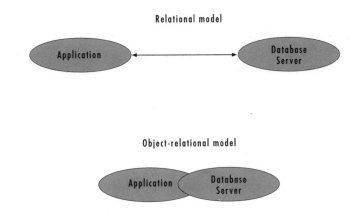

Figure 16-1 *The object-relational model provides for the integration of application business objects.*

tions, and package the expertise for internal use as a standard across databases and applications.

The end result of this technology is a better integration between an application and a database server. This leads to a more flexible design, which results in simplified application programming and better performance.

Features of Informix Dynamic Server with the Universal Data Option

In addition to the ability to extend the server to handle new datatypes, Informix Dynamic Server with the Universal Data Option includes, among other things, the following useful features:

Table/Type Inheritance and Polymorphism

Table/type inheritance and polymorphism provide a smooth implementation of an object design. Table inheritance enables the use of polymorphic functions that provide different functionality based on the table that is processed. It also provides the added benefit of data partitioning to complement the implementation provided by the Dynamic Scalable Architecture (DSA).

Functional Index

It is now possible to create an index based on the result of a function. An obvious candidate for this kind of index is a date field. This method eliminates the need to store a "quarter," or week number value when it can be derived from the date through a simple function.

R-Tree Index

This kind of index supports spatial and other multidimensional queries. For example, this index could be used to index age and income relationship.

Smart Large Objects

A smart large object can be read partially from any position within the data to reduce data movement. For example, operations on a time series access only the required data instead of reading the entire large object, as in a standard binary large object (BLOB) implementation.

Universal Data Warehouse: The Problem

The Sabre Group faced the challenge of creating a departmental decision support system (DSS) data warehouse for a commercial airline.

A typical data warehouse uses multiple data sources. The Sabre Group's warehouse is no exception. It uses about 415 different data sources; over 200 of these sources are used regularly. The format of the data is not homogeneous because less than 5 percent of the data is controlled by Sabre, and raises several issues, as follows:

- Heterogeneous formats—The data is provided in different representations with different formatting.
- Multiple aggregation levels—Some data represents monthly totals; other data is grouped by week or is represented at the transaction level.
- International languages—Some sources are of international origin. Differences may be in the language and identification of the data.
- Data quality—There is no quality control over incoming data. Some sources may contain duplicate information, conflicting information, and even test data. The information may be incomplete or inaccurate.

To add to this complexity, the format of currently used data sources may change over time and new data sources may be created. The original sources are well over 10 terabytes (TB) in size.

The airline industry faces some challenges that limit the efficiency of relational databases and force a reliance on custom applications. To illustrate the problem, consider the following examples:

- **Datetime**

  Relational databases provide a datetime base type, which assumes that all recorded activities occurred in one location. In the airline industry and in transportation in general, the location of the time needs to be considered because of time zone issues. If a flight leaves Dallas at 8:00 and arrives in Denver at 9:00, we cannot assume that the flight took one hour. In extreme situations, flights arrive before they left!

  In addition to the time zone issues, an airline must consider the daylight-saving time policy that applies at a specific location. Even in the United States, the daylight-saving time policy is not consistent. The variation spans from no daylight-saving time to different dates for the change, and in some cases, different policies are in effect at different locations within a state.

- **Flight matching**

  A specific flight leg may use different types of equipment on different days. The flight time may change for various reasons, yet it is still considered the same. Finally, the flight number may change and remain the same flight. This kind of "fuzzy" matching is virtually impossible to perform within a relational database.

First Try

Several years ago, The Sabre Group decided to attack this problem by using state-of-the-art technologies, including object-oriented methodologies. The development was accomplished using the SmallTalk programming language and accessing a relational database. The hardware was selected from "open system platforms" using commodity processors. A symmetric multiprocessing (SMP) machine was employed to maximize the parallelism of SQL query processing.

The resulting two-tiered system provides two major benefits. It maximizes the parallelism of queries for optimal performance and provides the user with a business view of the information. All of the

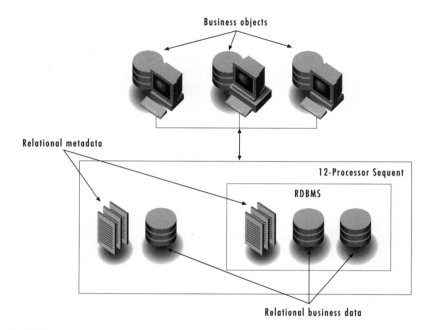

SmallTalk application
Sun UNIX and Windows NT clients

Business objects

Relational metadata

12-Processor Sequent

RDBMS

Relational business data

Figure 16-2 *The Sabre Group's system architecture.*

translation between the business model and the relational model is handled with business objects, which are included in the client application. The size of the database is approximately 120 gigabytes (GB).

The implementation of the original data warehouse uncovered several problems:

- **Slow object-mapping**
  The creation of the business objects involved much data movement. In many cases, the business rules could only be applied after the data was transported to the application. Furthermore, the business requests generated large, complex SQL queries.
- **Nonintegrated data**
  The data warehouse handled only specific data sets. Many more data sets required attention. Because this data warehouse was not integrated, the business experts spent a considerable amount of time studying the data source before processing to

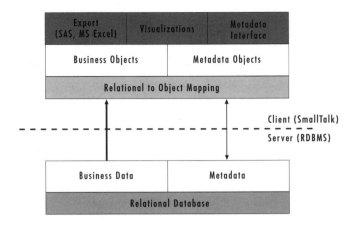

Figure 16-3 *The Sabre Group's application architecture.*

obtain useful results. There was the potential that simple errors could generate erroneous results, which could, in turn, result in disastrous business decisions.

- **Difficult to maintain**

  The addition of new application code or the modification of old code often required additional modifications to SQL statements and stored procedures.

- **Multiple technologies**

  The system was made up of SmallTalk code, SQL statements, stored procedure code, etc. This mix required a wide skill set, which was difficult to find when hiring new employees.

- **Client-based business objects**

  The business objects and, therefore, the business rules were tied to the client. They could only be reused in custom client applications. Because these custom applications must provide additional capabilities—such as report generation, printing, export facilities to other tools, etc.—the size of the application and development time were impacted, as was overall responsiveness to user requirements for new functionality.

Clearly, something needed to be done to handle the vast majority of the data that was still outside the warehouse. However, the business model proved to be a success. The users were able to navigate through the data in business terms, which made the data warehouse easier to use.

The Integrated Data Server

The integrated data server is the second generation of Sabre's decision-support system. It aims to provide a single point of contact with all of the different data sources. The goal is to create a multi-terabyte object-oriented data warehouse. Both the design and implementation are object oriented, from the business concepts to the data representation.

Several database technologies have been evaluated, including the leading object databases. After several months of evaluation, the object databases were rejected for lack of scalability, among other reasons. The object-relational technology shows the most promise. It provides the object-oriented concepts of hierarchy and polymorphic dispatch, allows the creation of new datatypes, and retains the SQL language and scalability. Sabre selected Informix Dynamic Server with the Universal Data Option because it is by far the most complete and mature implementation currently available on the market.

In the integrated data server, maximizing parallelism is crucial to providing the required response times. At the present time, the data warehouse is expected to grow to an estimated size of 3.5 TB. This raises an interesting issue that as the project is more successful,

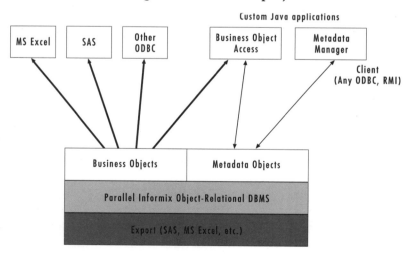

Figure 16-4 Integrated data server architecture.

the demand for it will grow. Demand could necessitate duplicating the data warehouse on separate machines to provide the required computing power to an increasing number of users.

This new implementation will include data warehouse and business process metadata. The metadata will provide the means to adapt to changes in the data sources, without requiring modifications to the applications.

The airline industry has specific needs that cannot be met with the standard SQL datatypes. For example, an SQL datetime type cannot be used directly without additional information. Time zones and daylight-saving time must be taken into consideration. Some regions do not use daylight-saving time. Among those that do, some have different rules that govern the application of changes. By creating a new business type, it is possible to encapsulate the appropriate behavior. The new business type then becomes a first-class type within the database server. Application programs can take advantage of the new functionality without the addition of new code. This benefit extends to common, off-the-shelf products like Excel™, SAS, etc. The server-side implementation also has the additional benefit of providing a consistent implementation of business types. This benefit extends also to the implementation of business rules. In this way, different applications will not provide different answers to the same questions.

Object-Oriented Design and Implementation

As mentioned earlier, the integrated data server makes use of the current object-oriented (OO) framework technology to render both the metadata object models and business object models extensible. The metadata models take advantage of the table inheritance feature of Informix Dynamic Server with the Universal Data Option. Extending a model can be as simple as creating a new table under a hierarchy and adding a few functions to implement the additional functionality.

To preserve the OO aspect of the implementation, all business types must be implemented as specific datatypes. This means they must be either distinct datatypes of existing types or implemented as opaque datatypes. The representation of an airport field must be of the "airport" type, not of the char(3) type. Similarly, revenue must have its own type, rather than the money SQL datatype.

The new business datatypes also incorporate the business rules, including rules on comparisons. For example, LG_PAX_CNT = LG_PAX_REV (passenger count versus passenger revenue) can be disallowed as part of the datatype definition. Comparison rules provide instant error detection of semantically incorrect statements, which protects against the return of a result that may not be recognized as erroneous. The business rules also include conversion rules, in which monthly revenue can be compared to daily revenue to provide a valid result.

Using Strong Typing

The programming world gained a powerful tool when strong typing was adopted in the ANSI C language. The strong typing provided by function prototyping generates warnings when a function call appears to be misused. Such warnings identify many potential problems in production code, leading to higher software quality.

The use of strong typing, in combination with precisely defined object operations, is essentially the same as teaching business rules to the Informix Dynamic Server with the Universal Data Option. The integrated data server creates user-defined types (UDT) for each business types, including:

- Identifiers: AIRPORT, AIRLINE, EQUIPMENT, etc.
- Counters: PASSENGERS, MILES_FLOWN, etc.
- Money: REVENUE, COST, etc.

The operations are then implemented between these business datatypes. The operations obey the business rules. The goal is to implement rules such as COST that can be subtracted from REVENUE, but not vice versa. Some rules may require explicit cast from one business datatype to another. Other rules may implement an implicit cast that allows for automatic conversion, for example, when manipulating monthly and weekly revenue.

Type-Based Integrity Check

Relational database systems provide a way to validate columns so that they follow the specified rules. This implementation works at the column level, not at the type level. This makes sense, considering that the relational model has a definite number of predefined datatypes. Integrity checking is already implemented in the database server for these datatypes—nothing more is required.

The implementation of integrity constraints in the business datatype eliminates the need to add the constraint in the database schema each time the type is required. If business requirements change, the integrity check needs to be modified in only one location, thus simplifying maintenance.

The integrity check is implemented in a support function of the business type. It can be implemented in the C language—a fast, compiled language that provides the performance required in modern data warehouse systems. The flexibility of compiled languages can be exploited to implement arbitrarily complex constraints with minimum overhead. Furthermore, small lookup tables can be cached in the server for faster processing.

What Makes the Integrated Data Server Universal?

The integrated data server stores and manipulates a universal set of datatypes. By this, we mean that all the business datatypes are represented, and some build on other business datatypes. With the definition and behavior centralized in the database, universal reuse of the functionality is available through any of the interfaces. This results in universally open access to all stored data via either custom applications or common off-the-shelf products that access the repository through a standard database interface like ODBC.

Conclusion

Informix Dynamic Server with the Universal Data Option provides new possibilities for data warehouses that must handle complex types such as a universal datetime or the difficult business rules that govern the matching of flights. Informix Dynamic Server with the Universal Data Option is a perfect match for data warehouse applications. It is built on a mature technology that provides high performance through the parallel execution of SQL queries. Its object-relational features can be exploited to adapt the database to the business environment instead of making the business model fit into a rigid framework. It also provides a smooth migration from object-oriented design to its implementation.

The implementation of business datatypes simplifies the formulation of queries by working at a higher level of abstraction. Applications that use these types are more stable since they operate at the business level. The use of a stable interface to the business objects shields application code from revisions in the business rules; thus, applications are more resilient to change, providing lower maintenance costs and a faster response to new user requirements. The server-based objects provide additional performance benefits through compiled functions and a reduction in the data movement between the database server and the application program.

Informix Dynamic Server with the Universal Data Option opens the door to new solutions for existing problems. It provides a set of capabilities that enables the use of more direct solutions and enables businesses to be better equipped to maximize their performance.

About Sabre Technology Solutions

Sabre Technology Solutions (STS) is a division of The Sabre Group. The Sabre Group is a leader in the electronic distribution of travel-related products and services, and is a leading provider of IT solutions for the travel and transportation industry. It is headquartered in the Dallas-Fort Worth, Texas area.

For more information, consult the Web site at:
http://www.sabre.com

About the Author

Jacques Roy is a member of the Advanced Technology Group at Informix Software, Inc., Denver, Colorado.

Index

C

Cache, 225-26
    read cache, 225
    write cache, 226
Cache hit, 225
Capital expenses, 22
Casting, 286
Centralized storage controller vs. independent disks, 224-25
Cherneski, Gary D., 272
Circular development life cycle (CLDS), 7-8
Classification and Regression Tree (CART), 135-36
Cleaning data, 129-30
Clustered symmetric multiprocessors, 171-72
Cognos, 299-300
Colton, Malcolm, 300
Complex query, 211-12
Computer Systems Advisors (CSA), 65
Concurrent engineering, and cycle time, 48
Conjugate gradient, 142
Control partitioning, 181
Conversion programs, writing, 95
Coon, Nancy Ann, 230
"Creeping budget" phenomenon, 21
CSA CASE tools, 65
Cut-through routing, 221

D

Data:
    information vs., 68-69
    normalization of, 9
Data analysis, 87
Data analyst skill set tip, 81-82
Data architecture, 70-71
Database administrator (DBA), 52, 154
    and data placement, 208-9
Database backup protection, See Informix database protection
Database backup/restore, See Backup/restore
Database design, 8-10
    normalization, 9
    star join structure, 9-10
Database load, 211

Databases, background of, 301-2
DataBlade Modules, 292-93
    data mining, 296
    for data warehousing, 294-96
    defined, 302-3
    documents, 295
    maps, 295
    scrubbing, 296
    statistics, 295-96
Data-bridging software tools, 31-32
Data buffer, SCSI target devices, 213-14
Data cleaning, 129-30
Data consolidation, 73, 74-92
    data analysis needed for, 84-86
        subject area analysis, 84-85
        synonyms/homonyms/analogs, 85-86
    data analyst skill set, tip for, 81-82
    domain analysis, performing, 77-79
    flattening out data into logical records, 75-77
        foreign keys, identifying, 82-83
    logical record, tip for, 77
    primary keys, determining, 79-81
    representative data, tip for, 79
    source data documentation:
        analyzing, 74-75
        tip for, 75
    steps in, 74-83
    synonyming, tip for, 83
Data conversion, 73, 92-94
    conversion programs, writing, 95
    exception processing, determining, 96
    testing, 95-96
Data-driver analysis, 90-92
    tip for, 92
Data fragmentation, 181
Data growth, 19-20
    and storage, 281
Data integration, 67-98
    business rules, understanding, 88-90
    data analysis, 87
    data architecture, 70-71
    data consolidation, 73, 74-86
    data conversion, 92-96
    data-driver analysis, 90-92
    data population, 94-95
    data sourcing, 72-74
    data transformation vs., 69
    metadata, 71-72

J

Java applets, 287
Joins, 83

K

Klauer, Patricia, 97
k-nearest-neighbor (kNN) technique, 133
Knowledge analysis, 41-43
    data source and quality analysis, 42
    knowledge requirements definition,
      41-42
    knowledge use analysis, 42-43
Knowledge deployment, 124-25
Knowledge discovery, 122, 124-25
Kraft, Jonathan, 120, 163

L

Landy, Alice, 146
Learning, creating environment for, 49
Leaves, defined, 136
Legacy data, 195-96, 280, 291-92
Legato NetWorker:
    backing up using, 250
    BusinesSuite Module for Informix,
      252-53, 256-59
    operation examples, 262-66
Legato Systems, 266, 267
Lift, defined, 144
Lift analysis, 144-45

M

McLuhan, Marshall, 193
Manage Data, Inc., 98
MapInfo DataBlade module, 295
Margin, 144-46
Massively parallel processors (MPP), 170,
    206, 208
Match models, 142-44
    optimizing, 143-44
Maxwell, John, 266
MCI case study, 226-29
Measures, in dimensional modeling, 102
Memory-based reasoning (MBR), 133,
    134, 142-43
MetaCube, 118-19
    Aggregator, 114

OLE object interface, 118
    ROLAP Option, 110
Metadata, 32, 33, 71-72, 90
Methodology, process vs., 38
Mietla, Dale, 49
Miezejewski, Brian, 301
Miller, Marvin, 50, 204
Mirroring, 223-24
Missing values, 129-30
Model data set, 143
Modified newton, 142
Multidimensional database manage-
    ment systems (MDBMS), 31-32
Multidimensional data warehouse, and
    aggregation, 108-12
Multiple learning tools, 133-34
Multithreading, 282

N

Neovista DataBlade module, 296
Network topology, 140
Network weights, 141
Neural networks, 133, 134, 139-42
    creating, 139-40
    hidden layer, 140
    input layer, 139
    network weights, 141
    optimizing, 142
    output layer, 139-40
    training, 140-44
    training algorithms, 142
NewTHINK, Inc., 50
Nicholson, Rob, 230
Nodes, classification trees, 136
Noise, 129
Normalization, 9
    disadvantage of, 118-19
    partial, 119

O

Obscure data, storage of, 20
OLAP data mart:
    designing on relational databases,
      99-120
    See also Aggregation; Dimensional
      modeling
ON-Archive, 256
ON-Bar utility, *See* Informix ON-Bar utility

One-time capital expenses, 22
Ongoing expenses, 22
Online analytical processing (OLAP) systems, 30, 149
    See also OLAP data mart
Online transaction processing (OLTP) systems, 30, 32, 79-80, 169, 210, 277
ON-Tape, 256
Operational data store:
    accessing, 195-97
    ad hoc queries, 196-97
    legacy data, 195-96
Operational data systems (ODS), 190-91
Operational systems, 68
ORDBMS (object-relational DBMS):
    performance, 294
    universal server as data repository, 293
Organizational environment, selection/management of, 23-24
Organization chart, 13-14
Organizing data, 131-32
Output layer, neural networks, 139-40

P

Parallel SCSI, 212-15
    weaknesses in, 215
Partial normalization, 119
Partition-level backup and restore, 245-46
PeopleSoft, 255
Pine Cone Systems, 15, 26
PLS DataBlade module, 295
Poe, Vidette, 97-98
Point-in-time (PIT) recovery, 247-48, 266
Prediction phase, model building, 134
Presummarization, 108-9
Primary keys, determining, 79
Procedure design, 45
Process:
    defined, 38
    iterative application of, 47-48
    methodology vs., 38
    using as a guide, 48
    See also Data warehouse process
Project startup, 40-41
Project success, keys to, 48-49
Project wrap-up, 46

Proper architecture, creation of, 24
Proprietary multidimensional databases, 101-2
Proximity, 288, 291
Pruned subtree, 136
Pruning classification trees, 136-37

Q

Query cost, measuring, 154-55

R

Read cache, 225
Real Audio plug-in, 287
Recovery, *See* Backup/restore
Redundant array of independent disks (RAID), 184, 212, 223-24
Redundant paths, 220
Relational database management systems (RDBMS), 31-32
Representative data tip, 79
Response field, 128
Response time:
    and bandwidth, 210
    elements of, 209-10
Response values, 128
Restore, *See* Backup/restore
Return on investment (ROI), 144, 145-46
Root node, classification trees, 136
Roy, Jacques, 312

S

Sabre Group case study, 304-9
    first-generation DSS, 305-7
    object-oriented design/implementation, 309-10
    second-generation DSS, 308-9
    type-based integrity check, 310-11
    typing, 310
Sabre Technology Solutions (STS), 312
Sampling, 149-63
    accuracy/confidence, 158-61
    and aggregation, 152-56
    effectiveness of, 156-58
    as scalability/maintenance windfall, 156-58
    trusting samples, 161-62
    See also Aggregation; Scalability